Beyond Boundaries

EXPLORATIONS IN ANTHROPOLOGY
A University College London Series

Series Editors: Barbara Bender, John Gledhill and Bruce Kapferer

Joan Bestard-Camps, *What's in a Relative? Household and Family in Formentera*

Henk Driessen, *On the Spanish-Moroccan Frontier: A Study in Ritual, Power and Ethnicity*

Alfred Gell, *The Anthropology of Time: Cultural Construction of Temporal Maps and Images*

Tim Ingold, David Riches and James Woodburn (eds), *Hunters and Gatherers*

Volume 1. *History, Evolution and Social Change*

Volume 2. *Property, Power and Ideology*

Bruce Kapferer, *A Celebration of Demons* (2nd edn)

Guy Lanoue, *Brothers: The Politics of Violence among the Sekani of Northern British Columbia*

Jadran Mimica, *Intimations of Infinity: The Mythopoeia of the Iqwaye Counting System and Number*

Barry Morris, *Domesticating Resistance: The Dhan-Gadi Aborigines and the Australian State*

Thomas C. Patterson, *The Inca Empire: The Formation and Disintegration of a Pre-Capitalist State*

Max and Eleanor Rimoldi, *Hahalis and the Labour of Love: A Social Movement on Buka Island*

Pnina Werbner, *The Migration Process: Capital, Gifts and Offerings among Pakistanis in Britain*

FORTHCOMING:

Terence Turner, *A Critique of Pure Culture*

Chris Tilley (ed.), *Interpretative Archaeology*

Barbara Bender (ed.), *Landscape: Politics and Perspectives*

Stephen Nugent, *Amazonian Caboclo Society*

Beyond Boundaries

Understanding, Translation and Anthropological Discourse

Edited by
Gísli Pálsson

BERG
Oxford / Providence

First published in 1993 by
Berg Publishers Limited
Editorial offices:
221 Waterman Street, Providence, RI 02906, USA
150 Cowley Road, Oxford, OX4 1JJ, UK

British Library Cataloguing in Publication Data
A catalogue record for this book is available from the British Library

Library of Congress Cataloging–in Publication Data
A catalog record for this book is available from the Library of Congress

ISBN 0 85496 813 X (cloth)
ISBN 0 85973 021 3 (paperback)

The cover illustration 'America', designed by Joannes Stradanus, is
reproduced by kind permission of Plantin–Moretus in Antwerp

Many generations ago Aba, the good spirit above, created many men, all Choctaw, who spoke the language of the Choctaw and understood one another. . . One day all came together and, looking upward, wondered what the clouds and the blue expanse above might be. They continued to wonder and talk among themselves and at last determined to endeavour to reach the sky. So they brought many rocks and began building a mound that was to have touched the heavens. That night, however, the wind blew strong from above and the rocks fell from the mound . . . . The men were not killed, but when daylight came and they made their way from beneath the rocks and began to speak to one another, all were astounded as well as alarmed – they spoke various languages and could not understand one another. Some continued henceforth to speak the oriental tongue, the language of the Choctaw, and from these sprung the Choctaw tribe. The others who could not understand this language, began to fight among themselves. Finally they separated.

An American Indian version of the Biblical story of the Tower of Babel
(S. Thompson, Tales of the North American Indians)

Contents

List of Plates and Figures

Plates

Figures

Preface

The problem of social understanding and cultural translation is not a novel one. Nowadays, however, it seems particularly haunting and engaging. Recent developments in social theory (the focusing, for example, on the fieldwork encounter and the 'construction' and writing of ethnographies) as well as international culture and politics (for instance, the end of the Cold War and the rapid, sometimes dramatic, reshaping of political boundaries) invite anthropologists to re-address the classic issue of anthropological understanding with novel, fundamental questions on the agenda. It was partly with these developments in mind that a large number of anthropologists got together in Reykjavík in June 1990. The aim of the organisers of the meeting (the Fourteenth Meeting of Nordic Anthropologists) was to convene a group of anthropologists, with different ethnographic backgrounds and representing different academic traditions and diverse schools of social thought, to discuss the theme of 'understanding and translation'. All the chapters in this book are revised versions of papers that were submitted to the Reykjavík meeting. However, one of the contributors, Shlomo Deshen, was unable to participate in the event itself. Different versions of his article appear in *The Jewish Quarterly* (1990) and *Human Organization* (1992, 2). Wikan's article is shorter than the original version. The complete version of her article appeared in the *American Ethnologist* (1992, 3). Thanks are due to the editors for granting the necessary permissions to reproduce material earlier published in their journals.

A number of people not represented in the volume deserve credit for helping to make the meeting both academically successful and thoroughly enjoyable. Jóhanna K. Eyjólfsdóttir and Sigríður Dúna Kristmundsdóttir, my colleagues at the University of Iceland, acted as co-organisers of the conference as well as discussants in some of the sessions. Rayna Rapp (New

School for Social Research) and Anna-Lena Siikala (University of Joensuu) contributed extensively as speakers. Anne Brydon (University of Winnipeg), Níels Einarsson (University of Uppsala), Knud Fisher-Möller (University of Copenhagen), Jón Haukur Ingimundarson (University of Arizona, Tucson) and Hjörleifur Rafn Jónsson (Cornell University) acted as speakers and chaired sessions. The Reykjavík meeting and the participation of the contributors to this volume would not have been possible without extensive further support. In particular, I would like to mention the Armenian Academy of Sciences, the British Council, the French Embassy in Iceland, the Iceland-United States Educational Commission, the University of Iceland, the University of Oslo, the Icelandic Ministry of Culture and Education, and Icelandair. Piers Vitebsky (Cambridge University) gave important advice at an early stage in the preparation. Several of my students – especially Arnar Árnason, Sveinn Eggertsson, Nína Helgadóttir, Agnar Helgason and Katrín Anna Lund – provided invaluable help in the running of the conference and the preparation of the manuscript. I thank them all. Finally, special thanks are due to Emma Blackburn (University of Iceland) who read most of the manuscript and commented extensively on language and style.

GÍSLI PÁLSSON
Reykjavík, March 1992

Chapter 1

Introduction: beyond boundaries

Gísli Pálsson

The textual life of *savants*

In this book, nine anthropologists discuss the issue of understanding and translation from different theoretical as well as ethnographic perspectives. For quite some time, anthropology has been regarded as an 'art of translation' (Crick 1976: 164), a textual exercise, facilitating understanding across boundaries of time and culture (Feleppa 1988). The problem of translation is said to be 'at the heart of the anthropological enterprise' (Tambiah 1990: 3), 'anthropology's most important theoretical problem' (Larsen 1987: 1). Indeed, if there is a root metaphor, which unites different ethnographic paradigms and different schools of anthropological thought, it is the metaphor of cultural translation. Given such a metaphor, the role of the anthropologist is to go behind the baffling chaos of cultural artifacts, to discover order in the foreign, and to transfer implicit meaning from one discourse to another. Anthropologists are presented as semiotic tour guides, escorting alien 'readers' in rough semiotic space.

Recently, the anthropological enterprise has taken another, more radical, textual turn. Malinowski opens one of his books with a sweeping statement about the facts of life among South Sea Islanders – sex, he says, 'dominates in fact almost every aspect of culture' (1929: xxiii) – and for many anthropological *savants* today, the facts of texts occupy a comparable status. Many anthropologists have questioned the objectivity of anthropological 'rhetorics' and the authority of the ethnographer, emphasising

1

that ethnographies are artifacts of and situated in particular discourses and historical contexts. Textual images are used to illuminate almost every aspect of social life – and not just the making of ethnographies (see Hanks 1989). Culture, as the saying goes, is text. Interpretation is seen to require 'textualisation' of experience – 'the process through which unwritten behavior, speech, beliefs, oral tradition, and ritual come to be marked as a corpus, a potentially meaningful ensamble separated out from an immediate discursive or performative situation' (Clifford 1988: 38). Anthropologists, it seems, have increasingly gone along with the traditional claim of the literary scholar that 'the text is the thing' (Limón and Young 1986).

No doubt, analyses of the rhetorical aspects of scholarly practice and the ways in which scientific discourses are historically constituted have both enriched theoretical discussions in the social sciences and heightened the literary and temporal awareness of their practitioners (see, for instance, Stocking 1983; Ellen 1984; Clifford and Marcus 1986; Geertz 1988; and Sanjek 1990 on anthropology; Atkinson 1990 on sociology; and McCloskey 1985 on economics). Some social theorists, however, have raised serious doubts about the undertaking of the textualist and the translator, the ways in which social science is currently being represented, taught and practised, arguing that the metaphor of the text and the translator inadequately represent the scholarly attempt to make sense of social life. In anthropology, at least, one can sense a growing disillusionment with the textual imagination (see Ulin 1991). Friedman, for instance, criticises the 'spectacularization' of anthropology, the 'overwhelming fascination with the text, with the act of translation, the appropriation of the real' (1987: 168). Perhaps the big questions on the theoretical agenda need to be rephrased or rethought. This volume as a whole reflects such concerns.

Anthropological practice, after all, is necessarily based on intensive contact with living persons, on ethnographic fieldwork. As Malinowski argued, in a somewhat patronising tone, keeping fieldnotes and writing ethnographies is a rather unfortunate necessity: 'An anthropologist . . . cannot banish his few patient readers for a couple of years to a South Sea atoll, and make them live the life for themselves; he has, alas, to write books about his savages and lecture about them!' (1929: xxvi).

What matters most, for recent critics of the textualist approach no less than the architects of modern fieldwork methods, including Malinowski, is to participate in local discourse and to learn about others' lives. As Gudeman and Rivera point out, fieldwork is 'a perpetual discussion . . . . Texts are frozen, they are conversation-stoppers that deny the continuous remaking of social life. . . . The anthropologist produces a text . . . but only as one part of several larger conversations; and the anthropologist must certainly have a "good ear" as well as a facile pen' (1990: 4). Several of the contributors to this book – Abrahamian, Edelman, Ingold, Pálsson, Sperber and Wikan – argue for a reappraisal of ethnographic fieldwork, insisting that anthropology return to its classic concern with the ability to listen to other people's accounts and the willingness to partake in natural discourse.

Other reasons as well make the theme of understanding and translation particularly relevant for modern practitioners of anthropology, and these have more to do with events in the so-called 'real' world than any developments in the academy or anthropology alone. For one thing, over recent years the human social and ecological habitat has seen spectacular developments. Each of us is necessarily engaged in a long, *global* conversation – a conversation, incidentally, that is threatened with powers far more destructive and decisive than texts and poetry. Modern humans, whether they like it or not, inhabit an endangered 'global village' in a very genuine sense. Two striking recent illustrations are provided by the news coverage (sometimes 'live' via satellites) of the Gulf War – its global, political and environmental implications – and the abortive military coup in the Soviet Union and the disintegration of the machinery of the communist state. What lessons can be learned from these developments for anthropology? The global ramification of modern life and cultural discourse and its implications for anthropological practice is an issue explored from various angles in some of the chapters in this book, notably those of Deshen, Hannerz and Stefánsson.

While as a group the authors do not share a particular theoretical approach – a given paradigm for problem-solving and interpretation – all of them deal with the issue of going beyond boundaries in one sense or another. Their chapters suggest at least two different understandings of 'going beyond':

first, in terms of the mediating experience contained in the
ethnographic encounter and the construction of ethnographies;
and second, in terms of going beyond the *metaphor* of the
boundary and the cultural translator in analysis, challenging the
assumptions of discontinuity and otherness with which
anthropologists usually begin when defining the approach and
subject-matter of their discipline. The tension between these two
senses of 'going beyond' is the centre around which the present
book is built.

Quite appropriately, given the general theme of the volume,
the contributors represent several different academic traditions
and communities – Armenia, Britain, Finland, France, Iceland,
Israel, Japan, Norway and Sweden. The aim of this Introduction
is to chart the relevant theoretical landscape, to locate the
approach and arguments of individual contributors in the
context of general anthropological discussion, and to identify
areas of agreement and disagreement. It begins with a
discussion of the category of the Other and the three worlds
scheme, their place in western discourse, and their implications
for anthropology. It then moves on to the notion of translation,
the parallels between linguistics and anthropology, and the
relative usefulness of the metaphor of translation in relation to
anthropological practice. Finally, it deals with the idea of a
culturally divided world and 'cultural dyslexia' (defined as a
failure to 'read' other cultures and come to terms with
difference) and alternative visions of both social life and its
understanding. I distinguish between three different modes of
ethnographic production; the colonialist, textualist and the
'living discourse' – a mode of communication that roughly
corresponds to what Habermas refers to as the 'ideal speech
situation' (see McCarthy 1978). Only the last one, I conclude,
emphasising democratic communion and the continuity of the
social world, represents a truly post-Orientalist ethnographic
order.

The quest for the Other

The category of the strange and remote, central to the
anthropological project in the past (see, for instance, Todorov
1988; Torgovnick 1990; Bongie 1991), is a matter of much debate

in both social theory and moral discourse, for it inevitably suggests fundamental assumptions about human nature and social life. Leach (1982: 58) asserts, echoing a remark by Foucault, that while the species *Homo sapiens* is a unity in a zoological sense, the notion of 'other' peoples or 'people not like us' is a universal one: 'Because of their cultural inhibitions all men everywhere behave *as if* they were members of many different species.' Leach attempts to show that humanitarian efforts informed by the United Nations Declaration of Human Rights, efforts that preach tolerance, individualism and human unity, are seriously misguided in that they contradict the very essence of human nature, the persistent tendency to separate 'us' from 'them'. Others might argue that the role of humanitarian efforts is precisely to challenge human nature *as constituted* by political and economic orders that operate on the assumption that people are members of many different species. Assertions for and against statements of this kind are often grounded in the ethnography of 'primitive' societies; as Gellner remarks, we tend to solicit the vote of 'Stone Age' people in debates about moral issues, as if they were the 'Constituent Assembly of Mankind' in continuous session (1988a: 23–4). If we were to seek the advice of such an assembly, it would hardly be conclusive, and certainly not unanimous.[1] One problem is that discussions of boundaries and the category of 'the foreign' tend to be heavily ideological and rhetorical in tone. Leach admits, in relation to his claims about human nature referred to above, that his aim is 'to provide moral justification for . . . non-egalitarian presuppositions' (1982: 56).

The distinction between 'them' and 'us' is no doubt recognised in most, if not all, languages. And much evidence suggests that making social distinctions is part of the human

---

1. Many accounts of hunter-gatherer societies do support Leach's claim; according to nineteenth-century travellers in north-west Alaska, for instance, Eskimos kept a constant watch for foreign trespassers into local territory: 'Strangers were assumed to have hostile intentions unless they could prove otherwise, and they had to do that very quickly or blood would flow' (Burch 1988: 99). The Eskimo term for themselves suggests that they saw only themselves as fully human. Often, however, strangers were seen as a sub-human threat primarily because they represented the advancing frontier of colonial powers. While the Batek of Malaysia have strong emotional ties to their area (*pesaka*), the area where they have grown up and feel 'at home', they do not seem to be particularly on guard against 'strangers', on the contrary; they 'are not territorial in any of the usual senses of the term' (Endicott and Endicott 1986: 140). The Batek, the Endicotts claim, do not even 'think of areas as having definite boundaries' (ibid.: 157). Hunter-gatherer societies, Bird-David (1988: 28) concludes, are characterised by an open system; the !Kung and the Hadza, for instance, seem to try to maintain a boundaryless universe.

endowment: young children seem to be predisposed to evoke a rudimentary categorisation of social kinds (Hirschfeld 1988). But to extend the modern, hegemonic notion of the Other into the distant past, the pre-history of 'primitive' bands, as Leach seems to do, is surely an over-simplification. The systematic, one-sided appropriation of otherness, the 'Orientalism' identified by Said (1978, 1989), was not a recognised, legitimate subject on the agenda of Stone Age assemblies; Orientalism, Said emphasises (1989: 211), is a mode of representation 'erected in the thick of an imperial conquest'.[2] Quite possibly, the advent of writing and literacy marked a critical shift with respect to accounts of the outlandish. At any rate, the authority and significance of such accounts were greatly enhanced by new means of recording and preserving them – when they became parts of state ideologies. In Europe during the Middle Ages, which some scholars refer to as 'an age of ink' (Averintsev, see Gurevich 1988: 227), the desire to experience both difference and the crossing of boundaries became institutionalised in the literary genre of the travel account. The medieval world-view contained the category of *Homo viator*, a person who ventures on some kind of pilgrimage into distant lands, for personal pleasure or to save his soul, who then returned with extraordinary stories of anomalous beings, erotic adventures and dangerous events (see Todorov 1984). The copper engraving *America* (see Plate 1.1), showing the Florentine discoverer Amerigo Vespucci in the Caribbean, nicely illustrates the medieval fascination with the savage and exotic. As pictured here, the male, civilised European, with his ship and other symbols of power, embarks on a mystery tour into nature, encountering naked women, cannibals and anomalous creatures. The gulf between the gentleman and the savage could hardly be greater. For the medieval mind, the boundary between 'them' and 'us' was a dividing line between culture and nature.

From the medieval era onwards, 'western' culture has remained preoccupied with a radical distinction between 'them' and 'us'. Such a distinction was not only underlined in the genre of the fabulous travel account. Often, particularly during the nineteenth century, it surfaced in semi-ethnographic novels

---

2. The Orientalist thesis is not without critics. Thus Figueira argues (1991: 5): 'The politics of Orientalism arbitrarily links a text with certain cultural practices; it "colonizes" a text from the past by means of present-age discourse. . . I question the virile compulsion to view the West's reception of the East solely in terms of possession, power, and control.'

Plate 1.1. 'America': Vespucci among the Caribbeans Copper engraving, designed in Antwerp by Joannes Stradanus 1523–1605). Amerigo Vespucci undertook four trips to the New World (from 1497 to 1503). Courtesy Plantin-Moretus, Antwerp

which freely mixed descriptions of historical realities with imaginary events, in order to give a 'real' taste of the exotic. Fact and fiction went hand in hand for the purpose of exaggerating differences. Herman Melville's autobiographical novel *Typee*, which describes the encounter between civilisation and New Guinea savagery, is one example. In it, a French admiral who enters the scene to take possession of the place ('Tior') is confronted by the local patriarch-sovereign who holds a battle-spear in his hands: 'The next moment they stood side by side, these *two extremes in the social scale* – the polished, splendid Frenchman . . . exhibited upon his person all the paraphernalia of his naval rank . . . while the simple islander, with the exception of a slight cincture about his loins, appeared in all the nakedness of nature. *At what immeasurable distance, thought I, are these two beings removed from each other*' (Melville 1846: 35, emphasis added).

Anthropology, almost by definition, involves a journey (mentally, at least) into strange and distant lands, an attempt to understand the unique and bizarre – in short, going beyond the boundaries of time and society. For a discipline that specialises in scrutinising the Other, the category of the 'primitive' has been a particularly useful device. As Kuper (1988) shows in his analysis of the term's genesis and history, the idea of the primitive has always remained on board even while anthropological theorising has undergone radical changes and many concepts and theories have been discarded (see also Ingold, this volume). Not only has the idea of primitive society served a variety of ideological purposes, providing, for example, a mirror image of modern society, it was 'good to think' in that it generated some excellent scholarly discussions.

The anthropological usefulness of the primitive/modern dichotomy, however, has often been questioned, almost right from the start (see, for instance, Lowie 1924). And since the 1960s, it has been hotly debated. With decolonisation, functional anthropology (the 'child of colonialism' as some people had it) was subject to intense criticism because of its preoccupation with isolated, timeless tribal societies; Worsley, in an article suggestively entitled 'The end of anthropology?', questioned whether anthropology, given its dualist vocabulary, had any future at all (see Asad 1973: 9). Anthropology, some of the critics argued, was a discipline fatefully shaped by the forces of the past. Decolonisation meant there was no longer an anthropological object, an Other to be perused by detached and distant observers; there was no longer a fundamental division between the West and the rest. In short, anthropology had become obsolete. More recently, Kuper has advanced an equally critical argument: not only is the category of the primitive a historical construct, an idea reflecting the times and fashions of those who use it, the idea of primitive society is a fabrication which should be removed forever from the agenda of anthropology (Kuper 1988: 8).

The arguments of anthropology's critics in the 1960s, which envisaged the end of the discipline with the dissolution of the Other, were often discussed in rather simplistic and conspiratorial terms, but they nevertheless spoke of real concerns. Was not anthropology bound to wither away with the disappearance of the 'primitive' and the power relations that formerly sustained it? However, the events of the following years were to prove the critics wrong. While the pattern and timing varied somewhat from one country to another, generally anthropology became a highly fashionable academic subject and its practitioners entered an expanding market. On the other hand, the new relationship between Europe and its former colonies significantly altered the practice of anthropology, introducing new emphases of change and inter-social relationships, of development, and anthropology within western societies.

One world or many?

To explain adequately how anthropology flourished despite the apparent dissolution of its subject matter would, no doubt, require detailed and complex analyses of the professionalisation of the social sciences, new systems of funding, and academic expansion in the anthropological metropoles – analyses which would take us far beyond the scope of the present volume. One important factor, however, was the fact that 'the primitive', far from being discarded from the conceptual baggage of anthropology, was subsumed under a less simplistic and seemingly more neutral scheme – the division of all societies of the globe into three worlds. The Cold War, and its ideological offspring modernisation theory, added a new binary distinction to social scientific discourse whereby the 'developed', modern world, the world of technological sophistication, was subdivided into 'free' and 'socialist' parts – the First World and the Second, respectively. The residual category of the underdeveloped world – euphemistically renamed the 'Third World' – within a somewhat modified division of social scientific labour remained the speciality of anthropologists, since it was a world governed by tradition, religion and irrationality (see Pletsch 1981). The First World, in contrast, was the subject of sociologists and economists, since it was a world of utilitarianism and rational thinking, unaffected by religious and ideological constraints (some societies within the First World – those that belonged to the 'Fourth World' – continued, however, to be regarded as the subject of anthropologists). Not surprisingly, in former, particularly African, colonies, anthropologists became *personae non gratae*. Those who taught anthropology at African universities were sometimes forced to call their subject 'sociology'. British anthropologists, however, who tended to think of their subject as 'comparative sociology', easily identified with such a label.

To some extent, the notion of the Third World is merely a new, technical term for an older underlying concept of the Other. The idea that societies are separated by permanent boundaries – and yet rather elusive ones (for the exact lines of division have always been a matter of debate) – is still very much with us, even if under a new guise. While we tend to take the three worlds scheme for granted, in fact it begs many questions. Pletsch (1981) suggests that, like other 'primitive systems of classification', the three worlds scheme has its own *raison d'être*. He emphasises the significance of the Cold War context, arguing that, from the point of view of 'us' who inhabit the First World, the Second is more modern and less exotic than the Third, yet its very modernity, combined with its threatening ideology, makes it particularly dangerous: 'the socialist world is . . . the dangerous and inscrutable enemy that motivated the very invention of the three worlds concept . . . And *vis-à-vis* the first world, it is the "other" in the most profound sense' (Pletsch 1981: 576). The three worlds scheme has assumed considerable authority in social scientific discourse, in part due to the Cold War.

In the early years of the Cold War, western academics rediscovered the Greek concept of the 'ecumene' (*Oikoumenè*), a concept discussed here by Hannerz. For the Greeks, the ecumene encompassed the known and inhabited world beyond which lay the foreign world of darkness and barbarism. Twentieth-century geographers and anthropologists tend to use the concept of ecumene as a synonym for 'culture'. Kristof, for example, defines ecumene as 'communities of thought and culture' (1959: 282), and sees the boundaries between ecumene as relative: 'it may be sometimes meaningful to speak of the ecumene of the human race as a whole, but it may, at other times, be equally meaningful to differentiate between the ecumene of the Pygmies, of the Eskimos, of the Chinese civilisation, of the Islamic faith, etc.' (ibid.: 277f). And for Kroeber, ecumene consists of a 'specific, preponderant, interwoven mass of culture' (1945: 19). Sometimes, however, the concept of the ecumene was restricted to the ideological boundary between the 'free' world and the 'socialist'. Kristof points out that his use of the ecumene concept is similar to what Cold War political science refers to as 'cultural blocs', the East and the West. These blocs are 'worlds apart' – in other words, different ecumene separated by ideological boundaries.

The Second World, despite its otherness, it seems, was too modern for western anthropologists. Academic anthropology is still largely concerned with the *Third* World, although the anthropological study of the West enjoys increasing popularity. Outside universities, development work is the major market for anthropological expertise. The concept of 'interface', recently introduced by students of Third World rural development, echoes the discontinuity implicit in the three-worlds scheme, the plural notion of the ecumene, and their predecessor the concept of 'primitives'. In Long's usage, the concept of interface depicts 'areas of structural discontinuity inherent in social life generally but especially salient in "intervention" situations' (1989: 221). Interfaces, he suggests, characterise situations 'wherein the interactions between actors become oriented around the problem of devising ways of "bridging", accommodating to, or struggling against each others' different social and cognitive worlds' (ibid.: 232). But while the concept of 'interface' assumes that humans live in separate worlds, it also represents an attempt to understand cultural continuity, the flow and exchange *across* boundaries – the building of 'bridges'. Hannerz suggests that if anthropologists want to contribute to an understanding of the modern world, they should first of all study the bridgemakers (journalists, tourists, etc.) – look 'sideways', as he puts it, rather than across the boundaries between cultures.

Barth points out (1969: 11) that anthropological reasoning tends to assume wrongly that boundaries are unproblematical. Anthropologists, he suggests, tend to think of boundaries between social groups as permanent, 'natural' demarcations and to project some concept of ethnicity onto the realities they describe. Leach has developed a similar argument, pointing out that while in some places in the Kachin Hills Area social groups are clearly segregated, in other places they are 'jumbled up' (Leach 1954: 60). Some Kachins are highly conservative about language, but others 'seem almost as willing to change their language as a man might change a suit of clothes' (ibid.: 49). Indeed, the salience of concepts of ethnicity and boundaries may derive more from agrarian discourse, from state ideologies and nationalist rhetorics, than the realities of non-state societies – that is, from 'us' rather than 'them'.

Some of the contributors to the present volume advance the radical suggestion that anthropologists adopt the strategy of *assuming continuity* and then ask questions about the conditions of its suppression, about rupture and estrangement – trying to understand why the bridges 'break down', to continue the metaphor, rather than why they are constructed. Those who challenge the prevalent assumption of discontinuity may be informed by very different considerations. Some authors, Ingold and Wikan in particular, emphasise the inevitable experiential continuity of the human world irrespective of time and place. For them, there is nothing particularly 'modern' (or 'post-modern', if you like) about the phenomenon or state of continuity. Others, Hannerz in particular, emphasise recent changes, arguing that modern means of communication – including transport systems, space technology, and computers – have turned the life-world of humans into a rapidly contracting cultural universe. Significantly, international lawyers now speak of some areas – areas which belong to all humans (including the high seas) – as 'global commons'.

Hannerz suggests that innovations in communication have made the world a truly 'global ecumene', 'an area of persistent social and cultural flow', in that nowadays cultural artifacts move faster than ever before and over greater distances – both with people (tourists, migrants and professional travellers of all kinds) and mass-produced things and images embodying meaning. Modern 'information society' seems saturated with cross-cultural details. Popular culture is no longer preoccupied with assimilating the otherness of the contemporary human world, for this is a world where apparently nothing remains to be discovered. At least the exotic increasingly appears as just as understandable, or *mis*understandable, domain as that of our familiar home. In the absence of a convincing 'real' other, modern storytellers and mythmakers resort more and more to the strategy of 'importing' strangers. The ideological project of 'exoticism' manages to recover alternative space, an 'elsewhere' (Bongie 1991: 4), from outer space, or, alternatively, former times. Stefánsson's account (this volume) of Japanese translations of Icelandic sagas, in both text and comics, underlines the extensive travels of cultural elements in the global ecumene. The search by modern, Japanese comic-book artists for the Other in the mythology of distant lands shows little respect, Stefánsson suggests, for the distinction between the past and the future; for Japanese readers the saga-comics, based on medieval accounts, are 'science fiction'.

Cultural elements are not only exchanged in the modern world at a faster rate than ever before. Increasingly, political issues which formerly might have been regarded as purely 'local' in nature, at best multinational, assume global, international significance (see, for instance, Featherstone 1990). Abrahamian and Deshen (both in this volume) discuss two such issues – the recent nationalist uprising in Armenia and the Arab–Jewish debate in Israel, respectively. More importantly, the Cold War seems to have come to an end, rather suddenly and unexpectedly. The superpowers have signed a series of agreements on disarmament, and the authoritarian regimes of the Eastern bloc have disintegrated one after another, so rapidly that it seems necessary to assume some kind of ideological domino effect. The Berlin Wall has been demolished and turned into souvenirs, and the 'Iron Curtain' is rapidly disappearing into folklore and history.

If one assumes that the development of the three worlds scheme and the present social scientific division of labour were the results – partly, at least – of the Cold War, then anthropology is likely to change in the post-Cold War era. The rethinking of the western, Orientalist notion of the Other (which began some time before the end of the Cold War) is bound to accelerate (see Thomas 1991). Anthropologists and historians often emphasise that essentialist notions of the Other must be discarded (see, for instance, Sharabi 1990 and Prakash 1990 on the Arab world and India, respectively).

Relations of ethnographic production

Related to the notion of discontinuous worlds and the Other is the popular anthropological idea of ethnographic production as cultural translation. To what extent is it a useful one, we may ask; what kinds of problems are associated with it and what explains its authority in anthropological discourse? We may well begin by considering the nature of translation proper – of the reproduction of a text (a 'source') in a different language (a 'target').

While anthropologists often go to great lengths to examine the cultural translations of their colleagues, criticising their analyses and questioning their ethnographic authority, they rarely study translation proper, except perhaps in the self-reflective style of L. Bohannan (1966). Stefánsson's article is exceptional in the sense that it is an account *of* translators, of the ways in which Japanese scholars and comic book artists reproduce the sagas of medieval Icelanders and Norsemen. He has interviewed professional translators in order to clarify why they undertook their task and how they see the process of translation. Despite its distance in both time and space, the saga-world seems to have a particular appeal for modern Japanese readers, for they readily identify with the heroic deeds and morality of the 'Vikings'. Generally, the literary translators approach their sources with respect and empathy, in a language that, as one of them put it, 'permits the artistic work to rise again like a phoenix reborn to a new life in a different culture'. On the other hand, Stefánsson shows that the comic book artists do not feel constrained by the need to preserve the integrity of the original texts. In fact, they freely modify the characteristics of the saga-idols, to ensure their 'successful' translation. At times, they clearly impose Japanese cultural elements onto the Viking world to make it more comprehensible to readers. The artists are translators in a dual sense, engaging in both interlingual and intersemiotic translation, for besides attempting to cross the boundary of time and society, they move from text to image – from one mode to another, much like phonographic translators do with the graphic sign and the vocal to provide oscilloscopic images of sounds. Written translations, it is often pointed out, have played an important role in the shaping of the world. In an age of icons and images, visual 'translations' may be increasingly important in the same way.

Stefánsson's account draws attention to the fact that translation is never innocent but necessarily infused with attitude; decisions about whether or not to translate, what texts to select and what kind of receptor language to use are not as straightforward as one might think. Translation has a long history in the West (it is said to have begun with the translation of the Hebrew Old Testament into Greek) and attitudes to translation have not always been the same. In some cases, the Koran for example, a holy text has been carefully guarded against translation by the faithful. Another case in point is provided by eighteenth-century German nationalists, who argued that to preserve the German national character it was important to prevent contamination from other, alien languages. In *Fragmente* (1767), the philosopher Herder suggested that a language would greatly benefit from guarding 'itself from all translations' (in Steiner 1976: 78). In this case, the idea is not to protect a holy text from being translated, as with the Koran, but rather to avoid the corrupting influence of translations on the *medium* of translation, irrespective of what is being translated. In both cases, however, a boundary is being erected between insiders and outsiders by means of language.

In the opposite instance, where translation is encouraged or at least practised, the attitude also varies from context to context. One important factor is the relation of power between source and receptor, as Lefevere and Bassnett emphasise (1990: 11):

> although idealistically translation may be perceived as a perfect marriage between two different (con)texts, bringing together two entities for better or worse in mutual harmony, in practice translation takes place on a vertical axis rather than a horizontal one. In other words, either the translator regards the task at hand as rising to the

level of the source text and its author or . . . the translator regards the
target culture as greater and effectively colonizes the source text.

A translated text, then, indicates the relative submissiveness
or superiority of the translator and the authority of the receptor
culture *vis-à-vis* the source – much like a litmus paper changes
colour according to degree of acidity. For anthropologists, such
an observation strikes a familiar note.

Gender is another source of differences in approaches to
translation, as feminist scholars have stressed in recent years.
Some leading students of translation talk about the relationships
between translator and author not only in terms of a predator-
prey relationship – in Steiner's words (1976: 298), the translator
'invades, extracts, and brings home' – they also tend to employ a
violent sexual language; translation is an 'act of appropriative
penetration' (ibid.). The content of the source-text is represented
as a passive, female prey to be appropriated by a male
translator. This is the language of the one-way street, of the
'brutal rape' (Neild 1989: 239). Chamberlain (1988) discovers
similar notions – a 'patriarchal' code – behind the metaphors of
'chastity' and 'faithfulness', which translators often use when
talking about their works, legitimating their authority and
originality. The patriarchal, marital code, it seems, manages to
survive even the most radical, deconstructive onslaughts. Thus,
Derrida speaks of the 'translation contract', defined as 'hymen or
marriage contract with the promise to produce a child whose
seed will give rise to history and growth' (1985: 191). It is
tempting to read an equivalent message about virginity,
penetration and reproduction in Stradanus's representation of
Vespucci's travel to the New World (see Figure 1.1).

Assuming that cultural 'translation' takes place on *both* the
vertical and horizontal axis discussed by Lefevere and Bassnett
(1990), one may speak of different relations of ethnographic
production. How ethnographers – as visitors or guests – meet
their hosts (and how they are met by them), how they manage
their lives among them, and how they report what they
experience varies from case to case. In some cases,
ethnographers 'colonise' the reality they are studying in terms of
a universalist discourse, asserting the superiority of their own
society in relation to that of the 'natives'. This is the 'brutal rape'
referred to above – in other words, the 'classic', Orientalist

ethnography produced during the heyday of western
colonialism (Asad 1973). In some other cases, ethnographers
'submit' themselves to their hosts by relativising their world,
idealising and romanticising them. Such an approach –
exemplified by the works of many of the 'textualists' and 'post-
modernists' – largely developed in response to the fervent
critique of the links between anthropology and imperialism,
particularly during the Vietnam War; anthropology had to be
'reinvented' (see, for example, Jackson 1989: 183 and Friedman
1987). As we shall see later, however, in some respects
textualism is just as much a one-way street as the colonialist
discourse of the past.

   Several of the contributors to this volume argue for an
alternative approach to ethnography. The different concepts
adopted by different authors – the notions of 'spinal knowledge'
(Edelman), 'communion of experience' (Ingold), 'getting one's
sea legs' (Pálsson), 'interpretation' (Sperber) and the power of
'resonance' (Wikan) – address different aspects of the
ethnographic model of the empathic conversation. Again, there
are obvious parallels in literary discourse. Neild (1989) and
Chamberlain (1988) suggest a feminised translation metaphor,
which underlines the reciprocal or hermeneutic nature of the
enterprise (see also Robinson 1991: 49). Thus, Neild emphasises,
if the process of translation is to be described as a love affair, an
adequate theory of translation must recognise the role of
'empathy' and 'seduction'; the author 'reaches out' to the
translator, altering his or her consciousness just as the translator
alters the text (1989: 239). The language of seduction, however,
may well be accommodated within the metaphor of the predator
and prey mentioned above. The translators' language of
seduction, in fact, is strikingly reminiscent of the language
employed by some groups of hunter-gatherer-fishers (see
Pálsson, this volume). Just as the hunter may 'fall for' a potential
prey, the translator may be 'seduced' by a text. And just as an
animal may refuse to be killed, a text may refuse to be translated.

The metaphor of translation

The defining of anthropologists as professional, cultural
translators has appeared in anthropological discourse in various

contexts and under different guises, depending on theoretical and historical concerns. For American anthropologists, the metaphor of cultural translation has been a particularly compelling one. Not only has the concept of 'culture' been of central importance to them, linguistic models and metaphors have generally been regarded as highly relevant and useful for analyses of cultural phenomena. The cultural determinism inspired by Boas and the linguistic determinism of Sapir and Whorf, therefore, have much in common. Sapir and Whorf, as Feleppa notes (1988: 56), regarded the 'linguist's translation problem (and the ethnographer's problem generally) as one of "calibrating" radically different conceptual schemes of reference'. Similar ideas are evident in French structuralist anthropology. Lévi-Strauss (1963) applies the phonetic method, borrowed from the rigorous linguistics of Jakobson, to analyses of ethnographic details, including kinship systems. For him, radically different cultural systems are transformations of one another.

More surprisingly perhaps – given the difference in theoretical developments, in particular the primary concern with the social rather than the cultural – British anthropologists have also found the notion of cultural translation appealing. Significantly, a collection of essays published in honour of Evans-Pritchard was entitled *The Translation of Culture* (Beidelman 1971). It opens with a quote from Evans-Pritchard's *Theories of Primitive Religion*, which suggests that the 'semantic difficulties in translation' are the 'major problem' with which anthropologists are confronted. Asad points out (1986) that while the idea of cultural translation may not have been unanimously accepted by all the founders of the British school of social anthropology, it was nevertheless an important one. Asad's claim, however, that Malinowski never thought of his work in terms of the translation of cultures is not altogether correct. In his early essay on 'The problem of meaning in primitive languages', Malinowski refers time and again to issues of translation.[3] While the essay is largely concerned with the problems of translating primitive languages, at times

---

3. Malinowski points out, with reference to his Trobriand ethnography, that native conceptions are often foreign to European vocabulary and that direct translation is therefore impossible: 'Such words can only be translated into English, not by giving their imaginary equivalent . . . but by explaining the meaning of each of them through an exact Ethnographic account of the sociology, culture and tradition of that native community' (1923: 456). 'The ethnographer', Malinowski goes on, 'has to convey . . . [the] deep yet subtle difference of language and of the mental attitude which lies behind it, and is expressed through it' (ibid.: 457).

Malinowski seems to draw some general lessons for ethnographic practice. He claims, for example, that 'the learning of a foreign culture is like the learning of a foreign tongue: at first mere assimilation and crude translation, at the end a complete detachment from the original medium and a mastery of the new one' (1929: xxv). 'Exactly as I have to write in English, and translate native terms into English', Malinowski adds, 'so also I have, in order to make them real and comprehensible, to translate Melanesian conditions into our own' (ibid.: xxv–xxvi). Malinowski, then, was not immune to the linguistic metaphor of translation, even though he advanced a theory of language both very different from those of Boasian anthropologists and structural linguists and highly relevant for a discursive theory of ethnographic fieldwork – the notion of language as being a mode of action rather than a normative instrument of expression.

No doubt there are many reasons for the popularity of the idea of translation in anthropology. As Hannerz argues, the metaphor of translation was useful to explain to non–anthropologists what the discipline was all about – i.e. when attempting to translate *anthropology* to the public. There is more to the story, however, for translation was also useful at home, within anthropology. Given the close and prolonged relationship with linguistics, the imagery of grammar and the text was always implicit. Inspired by the success of structural linguistics, Kroeber asked 'What is the cultural equivalent of the phoneme?' (1952: 124). Cultures (or languages) might be different, anthropologists reasoned, but they were tangible facts – in other words, systematic or 'grammatical' phenomena, which lent themselves to objective description and analysis. The role of the ethnographer was to discover the rules that governed the system and to translate them into anthropological 'language'. One of the reasons, then, that anthropologists often talk about their project in terms of cultural translation is that they think of culture as something with the properties of language. Anthropologists, Bloch reminds us (1991), tend to think of culture as 'language like'.[4] The rise of positivism was another

---

4. It may be argued, however, that what is 'language like' very much depends on the theory one adopts. Consider, for instance, the enormous differences between Chomsky's concept of language as a 'mental organ' (1980: 39) and Wittgenstein's notion of the 'language game' (see Harris 1988). Obviously, the implication of the metaphoric association of culture with language hinges on what one means by 'language like'.

but related development that stimulated the use of the metaphor of translation. Keeping in mind the promises of machine translation and autonomous linguistics, ethnographers felt confident that discovering general 'laws' behind cultural diversity, transforming 'emics' into 'etics', was a relatively simple and straightforward task. To do 'ethnoscience', for instance, it was not necessary to bother with social theory at all, only to pay attention to minute details (see Keesing 1987b).

There were always *some* problems, however. Literary scholars and professional translators have often been concerned with the 'right' image of their source, and the 'faithfulness' and 'equivalence' of the target (see, for example, Hatim and Mason 1990); such concerns are reflected in the Italian proverb '*traduttore, traditore*' – 'translator, traitor' (see Gutt 1991: 170). And similarly, anthropologists have been troubled by questions of ethnographic 'accuracy'; witness the well-known debates of Redfield and Lewis on Tepoztlan and Mead and Freeman on Samoa. While positivist scholars were convinced that translation was none the less possible, and that such debates were methodological rather than theoretical, others drew attention to the theoretical and ideological differences that separated various schools of anthropologists. Much has been written, for example, on the mutual 'antagonism' of North American anthropologists and British social anthropologists (see Watson 1984). Ortner's claim (1984: 126–7) that 'we do not . . . hear stirring arguments any more' and that anthropologists 'no longer call each other names' certainly seems an overstatement. Redfield and Lewis, and Mead and Freeman, after all belonged to more or less the same academic community even though they may have spoken different 'dialects', but what if two very different 'languages' were involved? Can we really expect two anthropologists who represent separate academic communities – as different as, say, an Anglo-Saxon community and a Soviet one (two communities separated for decades due to the Cold War) – to be able to communicate intelligently about their projects? Abrahamian's article unavoidably raises such a question. His use of the concepts of the 'carnival' and the 'archaic' – both important concepts in Soviet historical anthropology – in the context of the ethno-politics of the present, probably sounds strange to many anthropologists in the Anglo-Saxon world. 'To fly from London to Moscow, from anthropological discussions at one end to similar discussions at the other', Gellner points out, 'is to shift from one climate and atmosphere to another' (1988b: 3).

But if national anthropologies are mutually unintelligible or, at least, difficult to translate, we may ask, is there much left of anthropolgy's interpretive and comparative enterprise? This, however, is to stretch the differences between academic communities beyond the reasonable. Despite his claim about differences in 'atmosphere', Gellner in fact manages to transcend the cognitive boundary between the Soviet anthropologist and the British with a convincing observation that is worth citing at some length:

> Of course, the days of deliberate ahistoricism among British anthropologists are long past. . . . But one *still* has the impression that each society trails its own past behind it, as a comet trails its tail. The tail is studied as *this comet's* tail, its interest is a function of the interest of the comet, not the other way around. Above all, these shining, even brilliant, tails do not meld and fuse into some world history; such an aspiration is barely thinkable. They tend to live their own lives, and on the whole they remain insulated from each other in time and space.
>
> It is here that the contrast with the instinctive thought-style of the Soviet anthropologist is most marked. One might say that for the Soviet scholar the interest of a comet, generally speaking, is a function of its tail, and that all such tails fuse, at least in principle, in an all-embracing history of mankind. The idea of an 'ethnographic present' . . . with its tacit bias towards a stability assumption, is barely thinkable in Russia. (Gellner 1988b: 2–3)

If one assumes that anthropologists are experts at cultural translation and interpretation – to think the 'barely thinkable', to paraphrase Gellner – must one not conclude that anthropology has a significant role to play in the contemporary world? While anthropologists are usually eager to point out the importance of their insights and expertise in the academic context, they are often reluctant to use their skills in the outside world. There are many reasons for such an attitude and some of them are easily understandable (see, for instance, Turton 1988). The work of some anthropologists who have attempted to apply their knowledge to the promotion of inter-cultural understanding (particularly in the area of business and tourism) tends to be rather shallow and simplistic, relying as it does on short field trips and superficial ethnographic knowledge. Hannerz emphasises that the work of what he calls the 'culture-shock prevention industry' are generally poor, more akin to the early works of missionaries than to serious anthropology.[5] And giving in to demands for political engagement and action–research, the innocent demand of the 1970s for 'relevance', could eventually lead to theoretical stagnation and sterility.

Yet placing oneself in the role of the detached 'observer' and treating other cultures as mere museum pieces for academic and theoretical consumption is both irresponsible and unrealistic, given the fact that observations are inevitably situated in a particular historical and political context. As Said emphasises, 'there is no vantage *outside* the actuality of relationships between cultures, between unequal imperial and non-imperial powers, between different Others, a vantage that might allow one the epistemological privilege of somehow judging, evaluating and interpreting free of the encumbering interests, emotions, and engagements of the ongoing relationships themselves' (1989: 216–17). Similarly, Hart (1990) contends that anthropologists must be more conscious about both their role in the past and their social responsibility in the future, 'swimming into the human current'. Deshen wonders why, in a century troubled by violence and bloodshed on an unprecedented scale, anthropologists have largely avoided addressing the urgent issues of their times, issues of peace and war. While some recent introductory textbooks do mention such issues and the number of anthropological publications on warfare has grown rapidly from the 1960s onwards (see Ferguson and Farragher 1988), generally anthropologists have occupied a muted position in the political discourse of the twentieth century. This mutedness, Deshen suggests, echoing the critique of Habermas (1989) of neoconservatism, poses intriguing questions for future historians of anthropological knowledge and practice. The thrust of his article, however, concerns the modern Israeli debate on Arab-Jewish relations and the Middle Eastern conflict. This is a highly polarised discourse, so much so that one can speak of two

5. The differences between the approaches of missionaries and anthropologists have, however, not always been that clear. Interestingly, when the publication of the journal *Practical Anthropology* ceased in 1972, a new journal *Missiology: An International Review* was established, continuing the editorial policy of the former (see Mandelbaum 1989: 49). Hanson (1979) has much to say about the parallels between the predicaments of the missionary and the anthropologist. For an interesting anthropological study of missionary work, see Hvalkof and Aaby (1981).

separate, incommensurable discourses, each of which represents the other as if it belonged to a hitherto untouched people. Deshen analyses the political and historical forces which have fuelled them – the 'hawkish' position of orthodox, right-wing hardliners, on the one hand, and the 'dovish' position of secular, left-wing liberals on the other. His aim is to practise advocacy in a domestic context, to formulate a new mode of discourse that could break the deadlock of Israeli politics, reaching people who most need to be addressed, the orthodox. That, in a way, is 'radical' translation at home.

Cultural dyslexia

If we take the textual metaphor seriously, presenting culture as text, anthropology becomes a study of reading. For psychologists, the successful reading of a written text, a highly complex mental operation, is a research topic in its own right. The *failure* to read, or the state of 'dyslexia', broadly defined as reading maldevelopment in normal people not resulting from a defect of the senses, is an issue that also has bothered psychologists. Positivist anthropology, as we have seen, has emphasised the successes of cultural reading, as has the model of autonomous linguistics; whatever their 'surface' differences, languages (or cultures) are similar in structure and, therefore, translatable. Recently, however, a mixed group of anthropologists who identify themselves with a series of labels – including 'interpretive', 'reflexive' and 'post-modern' – have drawn attention to the difficulties and failures of translation more than to the successes – focusing on what may be called 'cultural dyslexia', the inability to read the alien, cultural worlds of other people.[6] At a time when some of the walls of the real world, which effectively separated people in the past, are crumbling, notably the Iron Curtain, some modern social theorists lead one to believe that cultural barriers are insurmountable and that people live in fundamentally different worlds. They remain sceptical of the translator's enterprise,

6. The labels of the 'interpretive', 'reflexive' and 'post-modern', it is often pointed out, are fairly elusive ones and it is difficult, therefore, to generalise about those who use them to refer to their own practice. The notion of the 'post-modern' has been particularly hard to define, as the extensive literature on the subject demonstrates; see, for instance, *Postmodernism* (special issue of *Theory, Culture and Society* 1988, 5 (2–3)).

emphasising, like Quine (1960), the inevitable difficulties of radical translation.

Several of the contributors to the present volume adopt a critical stance with respect to the idea of impossibility of ethnographic translation. Wikan's approach, partially inspired by her Balinese informants, emphasises the 'power of resonance', an emotive-cognitive capacity that allows ethnographers to understand other people, to go 'beyond words'. The ability to make sense empathically of ethnographic experience, even in the absence of working knowledge of the local language, Wikan suggests, derives from fundamental similarities in human experience. The Balinese 'reached out' to her as a fellow human. On its own the reference to intuition, gut-reactions and emotional experience – whether it be Wikan's notion of 'resonance', Edelman's notion of 'spinal knowledge', or Pálsson's idea of 'finding one's sea legs' – may not satisfy the public demands of the scientific community. After all, some may argue, ethnographers have to be able to reason about emotions, to demonstrate to their colleagues, by means of words and arguments, that they have 'really' understood. Such an argument, however, reflects a highly western notion of understanding and communication, which deprivileges somatic signals *vis-à-vis* the intellect, a notion that has increasingly come under attack, and by students of texts and translation as well as anthropologists (see, for instance, Robinson 1991).

Whereas Wikan is concerned with societies usually regarded as rather different from that of her own, Abrahamian is working at home – with a 'text that is "written" in the mother tongue', as he puts it – and so are Edelman and Pálsson. Abrahamian discusses the problems of doing fieldwork in Armenia during the stormy political events of 1988 and 1989. For him these events are like an ancient 'festival', although this description is not to minimise their seriousness. Just as the festival negates the logic of 'ordinary' life by accommodating it within itself, 'ordinary' life negates the logic of the festival by accommodating playfulness and the carnivalesque. This kind of analysis derives its strength from a vigorous Soviet scholarship on the subversiveness of medieval popular culture (see Gurevich 1988). Abrahamian suggests there are structural similarities between ethnography and shamanistic dealings with the sacred world; both involve a 'journey' to another world, a somewhat privileged, prophetic reading of a 'proto-code' of one kind or another. But while Abrahamian emphasises the successes of the reading, he wonders whether the anthropologist is doing a real 'translation' at all, since doing fieldwork, or participating in protests and festivals, involves a Bakhtinian dialogue – a communication between different 'voices', all of which are shaped by mutual interaction (on the cultural theory of Bakhtin, see Hirschkop and Shepherd 1989).

Pálsson also refers to his fieldwork in Iceland as a journey – a fishing trip. For him, however, the journey does not so much involve a privileged, solitary trip to places unknown to others – the 'other' world of the 'shaman' in Abrahamian's model. Rather, the metaphor of the journey draws attention to the similarities in emotional as well as social experience of doing fieldwork and fishing in rough seas – in the progression, in one case, from the margin of the discursive community towards the centre, and, in the other, from nausea and seasickness to alertness and well-being. Edelman similarly questions the privileged access of the native anthropologist to the deeper structures of social life, emphasising that the problem is not so much to overcome 'home blindness'. But, like Abrahamian and Pálsson, she stresses the importance of dialogue and the intuitive knowledge gained through participation. Edelman's work involves anthropology at home in a double sense: not only does she speak the same language as her informants, the shunters (or 'switchmen') of a Swedish railway yard, prior to her fieldwork she herself worked as a shunter. Her aim is to articulate her implicit knowledge of shunting, the skills and the 'flow' of the job, and to convey her insight to the scholarly community.

Despite the differences in both the arguments and topics of their contributions, Abrahamian, Edelman, Ingold, Pálsson, Sperber and Wikan all attempt to go beyond positivist notions of the anthropologist as an 'observer', the kind of objectivism that characterises the social theories of Saussure and Durkheim. Saussure comments (1959[1916]: 13), in relation to the problem of translation, that when we hear people speaking a strange language, 'we perceive the sounds but remain outside the social fact because we do not understand them'. This follows from the distinction between the individual and social in his theory. According to Saussure, language (*langue*) is a system of inherent relationships, best understood as an autonomous entity outside the individual. But such a radical distinction between the outside and inside, the individual and social, fundamentally misconstrues the nature of human life, for it assumes an observer *removed* from society. One cannot remain outside the social fact, no matter how great the cultural 'distance' or the thickness of the language 'barrier'. Abrahamian's article, which comes closest to the textualist approach of all the contributions in this volume, emphasises that even if one assumes a distinction between inside and outside, the anthropologist must be inside and outside at the same time. The plight of the ethnographer, Abrahamian argues, is more like that of the hermeneutic interpreter.

If people (including anthropologists) are 'translating' all the time and apparently with success, must there not be more or less successful translations, more or less authentic reproductions of the source 'text' in the receptor language? And, if this is the case, what criteria should be applied for deciding what constitutes an authentic, successful translation? Similar questions and issues have been raised in many other fields of scholarship – including philosophy, literary theory and translation studies. Sperber's article emphasises the intuitive and personal nature of anthropological interpretation and the lack of explicit methodology. To make their analyses of cultural representations meaningful for their readers, Sperber points out, anthropologists grant themselves a certain degree of freedom. In doing so, they often depart from the details provided by their informants, introducing a new jargon, and employing their own metaphors. Often, therefore, 'faithfulness' – or resemblance in content – is exchanged for relevance: a gain in the latter means loss in the former. This does not mean, however, Sperber argues, that all interpretations are equally successful, only that the criteria used to distinguish faithful reproductions of representations from unfaithful ones are partly subjective. Absolute faithfulness may be an elusive goal for ethnography, but this is not to say that there are no *mis*representations and that one cannot distinguish wisdom from folly. Sperber identifies four types of anthropological accounts: interpretive generalisations, structuralist explanations, functionalist rationales and epidemiological models. He advocates epidemiological models – roughly defined as models which attempt to explain why some cultural representations are more 'contagious' than others – on the grounds that they render more reliable, for theoretical purposes, our native capacity to comprehend what others say and think.

Wikan suggests that anthropologists tend to impose a sense of peculiarity on the mundane and the familiar, moving from the bazaar to the bizarre. Much of what has been written about the people she has studied, she argues, seems to come out of 'another world'. Despite their anthropological reputation for being 'brilliantly exotic', to her the Balinese seemed plain and ordinary. Keesing has similarly criticised his fellow anthropologists for their excessively exotic readings of cultural texts, for producing interpretations that are 'simply wrong, constructed out of misunderstandings and mistranslations' (1989: 459). This kind of ethnography – the anthropological equivalent to what literary scholars call 'translationese', translation that sounds like a translation – is not a novel phenomenon. In the last century, Henry Maine attacked social theorists for their biased ethnographic approach. They 'uniformly ceased to observe and began guessing', he said, when dealing with the customs of '"archaic"' society, while they 'carefully observed the institutions of their own age and civilization' (1861: 70). Some modern cultural critics, however, cease to observe at all, whether at home or abroad (I emphasise 'some' because others are not all that extreme). In maximising the strangeness and alienation of their own world, the cultural critics invent Other in the familiar (Spiro 1990: 57). Orientalist scholarship, then, is practised at home on the assumption that humans generally, even close neighbours apparently speaking the same language, are far removed from each other in cultural terms – at 'immeasureable distance', as Melville would say. For many cultural critics, the contrast between 'observing' and 'guessing', emphasised by Maine, is not an important one, for if cultural texts invite several and equally plausible readings the issue of faithfulness and authenticity is beside the point.

It may be argued, on the other hand, that despite their apparent liberalism, allowing for many readings of cultural texts, interpretive anthropologists in fact practise an authoritarian approach, eliminating alternative interpretations of their ethnographic material (see Pálsson, this volume). Oddly enough, those who advocate interpretive anthropology – even those who claim to subscribe to a 'reflexive' approach, emphasising the interaction between informant and ethnographer – sometimes take a rather defensive stance when challenged by others (Sangren 1988). Perhaps, such a defensiveness is primarily a response to the conditions of constructing ethnographies in the modern global ecumene. Nowadays, texts and translations move from one continent to another in only a matter of days or hours, even minutes. The innocence of the exotic and the faraway is forever lost as our informants, whether we like it or not, read what we write and challenge our conclusions, almost from the moment we publish them. When confronted by the natives, it may be tempting to resort to ethnographic substantivism, assuming there are as many interpretations as there are interpreters, taking refuge in the protective environment of the ivory tower.

We may find it convenient, for certain purposes, to refer loosely to anthropological practice as one of 'mediating' between cultures, as an 'art of translation'. Thus, Hannerz speaks of ethnography as one kind of cultural management at points of relative discontinuity, and Abrahamian similarly suggests that the anthropologist often proceeds 'like a linguist trying to decipher an unknown text'. This is fine, but only up to a point. It is one thing to refer broadly to the anthropological enterprise, our attempt to make sense of ethnographic realities, as one of translation and quite another to describe culture as a text. Metaphors operate much like the railway system discussed by Edelman, for as we speak metaphorically we confine our thoughts to a particular 'track'. And as we change our root metaphors, we 'shunt' or 'switch' our thoughts from one line to another. The application of the textual metaphor in anthropology, as we shall see, is a tricky one, but before we discard the metaphor and dissociate anthropology from 'translation studies', we may well remind ourselves that there are many ways of translating. In fact, some of the works of those who study translation proper may be more 'anthropological' than textualist ethnographies. Thus, Robinson has forcefully argued for the importance of moving from text to life: 'Translation theorists, like their colleagues in the other so-called human sciences, like to talk about texts, intertextualities, structures of correspondence, and the like – all hypostatized abstractions. But the reality of translation and all human communication is *people*' (1991: 21). It is rather ironic to hear social scientists speak of a general 'linguistic turn' (Atkinson 1990: 6), moving from life to text, at a time when students of translation, most of whom are linguists and literary scholars, increasingly refer to a 'cultural' turn (Lefevere and Bassnett 1990: 4), moving from word and text as translation units to discourse and social context.

Understanding social life

The issue of 'mediation' or 'translation' logically suggests some degree of misunderstanding; if people fully understand each other, there is no need for translation. There exists a rich literature attempting to explain why the *in*ability to assume the role of others varies from one context to another. For instance, social thinkers from the Enlightenment onwards, including Montesquieu and Simmel, have debated the effects of competition, commerce and capitalism on attitudes towards 'strangers' (see Haskell 1985). Some have argued that commerce is detrimental to role-taking abilities and humanitarian sensibility, erecting boundaries between people. Others, however, have emphasised its interactive and moral virtues. Competition, Simmel argued, 'achieves what usually only love can do' in that it 'sharpens the businessman's sensitivity to the tendencies of the public, even to the point of clairvoyance' (cited in Hirschman 1982: 1652). Anthropologists have addressed such issues in an ethnographic context, attempting to understand the reasons for and maintenance of standing misunderstanding. Durrenberger (1975), for example, provides an account of recurring 'dramas of misunderstanding' in Thai-Lisu interactions in northern Thailand. The Lisu are egalitarian while the Thai are hierarchical. The two groups, therefore, have different ideas of contract and obligation which partly explains their mutual misunderstanding and mistrust. Discourse analysts have similarly examined the reasons why different groups in the '*same*' society repeatedly fail to understand each other. For Tannen (1990), male-female communication in North America is cross-cultural communication. She has argued that even though boys and girls grow up together in the most intimate relationships within the most fundamental social unit, the family, they often develop different styles of conversation. Tannen largely attributes the communicative differences between men and women to differences in social relations, much like Durrenberger does with respect to ethnic differences in northern Thailand: men have a hierarchical style, emphasising difference and ranking, like the Thai; women, like the Lisu, are egalitarian, emphasising connection and communion. As a result, men and women frequently misunderstand each other.

Clearly, one factor important for the maintenance of misunderstanding is the relative power of the groups involved, the 'terms of trade'. As a Sacramento Valley native once explained to a visitor: 'Everything in the world talks, just as we are now, the trees, the rocks, everything. But we cannot understand them, just as the white people do not understand Indians' (cited in McEvoy 1986: 31). Massive misunderstanding, then, is an aspect of discourse, rooted in particular historical circumstances and relations of power, in the political economy of cultural dyslexia. As Deshen reminds us in his discussion of the Israeli debate on Arab-Jewish relations, when two groups are alienated from each other, when there is no communion between them, misunderstanding occurs - a dialogue of the deaf.

But do not, we may wonder, Amerigo Vespucci and the native women referred to above (see Figure 1.1) somehow manage to communicate, despite the 'enormous' gulf between them? Or, for that matter, 'doves' and 'hawks' in Israel, husbands and wives in North America, or the Thai and Lisu? The weary philosophical debate on the possibility of a private language partly focuses on whether two people, speaking languages that apparently have nothing in common, will be able to understand each other and set up a working language literally from scratch. Wittgenstein's contribution to the debate emphasised that two people involved in a common task, say a builder and an assistant, will inevitably come to an 'agreement in definitions'. The 'language' they use is, of course, the same as that of Vespucci and the native: 'The common behaviour of mankind is the system of reference by means of which we interpret an unknown language' (Wittgenstein, cited in Harris 1988: 108). In a similar vein, Ingold, Sperber and Wikan stress our ordinary ability to understand other people. Western observers of encounters between European and non-European peoples were often surprised by 'how easily the language of expression and gesture could overcome cultural barriers' (Bitterli 1986: 28). And, Stefánsson reminds us, the Japanese have managed for centuries to apprehend even the most alien worlds through their successful borrowings of cultural items from abroad. Cultural theory generally assumes, on the other hand, that as a model of social life, the tower of Babel is a more adequate one than the Wittgensteinian notion of the 'common behaviour of mankind' for it postulates that people necessarily erect elusive, mental structures ('culture') over their heads. Carroll (1987: 4) discusses the misunderstandings that occur between the French and Americans as due to the different 'cultural texts' through which they perceive their worlds. If one assumes that people inevitably have problems with comprehending others, such difficulties are likely to *increase* with greater interdependence. Thus Fagan (1984: 14) argues: 'Few people find it easy to accept those who are different from them, whether the difference be that of color, creed, or simply way of thinking. This inability of humankind to comprehend others hightens the tensions in our industrial and nuclear world.' Given a textual approach to social life, the difficulties due to misunderstanding will not be reduced in the global ecumene.

The concepts of culture and boundaries – implicit in most discussions of social understanding – have been the subject of much theoretical debate. Asad (1987: 604) argues that anthropologists must challenge Eurocentric history by analysing how pre-capitalist societies made their own history and that the 'concept of culture is crucial in such an enterprise'. He is careful, however, to dissociate his own concept from both the traditional notion of culture as a bounded, homogeneous entity and the Marxist notion of the superstructural and ideological; for him, culture has more to do with social practice than a state of mind, as he speaks of 'cultural discourses that constitute objective social conditions and thus define forms of behaviour appropriate to them' (ibid.: 605). Others adopt a more critical stance with respect to the culture concept, at least in the plural. Leach criticises his colleagues for postulating cultural differences where none exists: 'When you encounter an anthropologist who writes about cultures in the plural . . . watch out!' (Leach 1982: 43). Wikan's article echoes such a position, suggesting that anthropology should dispense with the notion of cultural boundaries and language barriers. Drummond has raised similar doubts, pointing out that the process of 'communicating across cultures' is more complex and difficult than is commonly assumed. For him the problem lies with the notion that 'there are distinct, bounded cultures out there, little worlds waiting for their fieldworker to step off the boat and proceed to elucidate' (Drummond 1987: 219), not with the concept of culture itself. He advocates the culture concept of anthropological semiotics, stressing the priority of sign production: 'Groups or societies don't generate culture; culture brings forth societies' (ibid.: 220). It may be argued, however, that the emphasis on the priority of culture and sign production necessarily suggests a programmatic and oppressive concept of social life as a normative world devoid of creative agency. And this is precisely the problem with the metaphor of the cultural translator and the text alluded to in the previous section.

The notion that there are many cultures and not just one, it has sometimes been argued, invites alienation and disillusionment. As Ricoeur (1965: 278) pointed out: 'Suddenly it becomes possible that there are just *others*, that we ourselves are an "other" among others. All meaning and every goal having disappeared, it becomes possible to wander through civilizations as if through vestiges and ruins. The whole of mankind becomes a kind of imaginary museum.' From this point of view, the act of translation is an 'aimless voyage' (ibid.). Ingold (this volume) draws attention to the privileged but awkward status of the anthropological voyager in such a cultural universe. He suggests that not only does the idea of cultural translation establish dicontinuities, *artificially* presenting the world as something already divided, culture tends to be regarded as an autonomous entity independent of the people who represent it, as an external force exerting its influence upon the mind of the individual. Not only are people alienated from each other, they must be forever alienated from their own constructs. The metaphor of the text, Ingold argues, involves a fetishism of culture, of transforming the use-value of everyday life into the exchange value of exotic commodities for sale on the international academic market. And despite its somewhat attractive language of relativism, Ingold goes on, such an alienating discourse logically places the 'observer', in a position of absolute superiority: the 'natives' are depicted as being imprisoned by culture, while the anthropologist is presented as culture-free. The translator, to continue the linguistic metaphor, is not a polyglot but a person without language. The linguistic model that radically separates language and speech, structure and agency, Bourdieu (1990a: 33) similarly points out, 'amounts to placing the linguist . . . in the position of a Leibnizian God *in actu* the objective meaning of practices'. Indeed, to present anthropologists as cultureless experts in cultural reading and regard the rest of humanity as cultured dyslexics, is indicative of ethnographic immunity, an attitude of arrogance. Ingold suggests that anthropologists need to rethink their discipline, to develop a new discourse that reclaims the continuity of the social world, and that such a discourse has no place for the concept of culture. That is quite a challenging argument, given the weight of the culture concept in anthropological thought.

If anthropology rejects the tyranny of the text, the idea of cultural boundaries and the metaphor of bridging, what happens to the anthropological enterprise? The problem of where to locate boundaries has always bothered anthropologists. This is, in part, the so-called 'Galton's problem' often referred to in relation to comparative databases. We can never be sure that the ethnographic cases in our samples are genuinely independent or distinct cases to allow for meaningful 'cross-cultural' comparison.[7] How, then, do we elect the members of Gellner's Assembly of Mankind, referred to earlier, and on what basis? Do the members vote independently, to speak metaphorically, according to their own judgement, or do they simply reiterate the statements of their neighbours? A post-Orientalist scholarship – a scholarship that rejects a cultural, essentialist interpretation of the Other and the idea of the cultural mosaic – does not necessarily dismiss differences and anthropological comparison. Pletsch points out that the Other is always defined in terms of its difference from the observer, and that only if we can remember this will we have 'the epistemological basis for a differentiated understanding of the globe's societies' (1981: 590). While each society is situated in a particular context, to claim that there are as many kinds of

---

7. Some of the characteristics of 'immediate-return' systems in hunter-gatherer societies, for example, may derive more from their relations with *other* societies than any internal constraints, from the fact that they have been encapsulated by neighbouring groups (Woodburn 1988).

societies as there are contexts is to exaggerate. Rather than elaborate on the unique and the idiosyncratic, Pálsson argues, anthropological analysis should strive to establish both the contrasts and the parallels in the ethnography and to look for explanations for such contrasts and parallels. Icelandic discourse on 'nature', he suggests, must be understood in terms of social life and history. Notions of agency, production and gender – redefined from time to time as people attend to different aspects of social life – are based not on a cultural logic but a fundamentally social one.

As we move from text to life, we are bound to rephrase the old question of how people communicate across cultural boundaries and ask instead: how do we learn to understand the social world to which we belong? In other words, how do people become socially competent? Interestingly, students of literary translations have addressed similar questions, emphasising the need for a 'people-centred' theory, which discusses translation 'in terms not of structural equivalence but of *what translators and readers do* – how people interact in the many different activities surrounding translation' (Robinson 1991: 135). Edelman underlines in her account of the social world of shunting that in order to become a competent, 'safe' shunter (acquiring the skills involved in the proper handling of times and trains, in estimating speed, avoiding accidents, etc.) the beginner has to be carried by the world of shunters and the daily experience of work. If a textualist approach to social life leads to what Volosinov called 'passive understanding', 'the kind of understanding . . . that excludes active response in advance and on principle' (1973[1929]: 73), a social approach means engaging in practical activities. Ingold argues that learning means not simply absorbing or assimilating a normative structure or a stock of knowledge, learning to 'construct', but rather to be caught in an ever-flowing stream of practical acts, verbal and non-verbal. We become competent social beings, he suggests, by becoming attentive and responsive to our relations with others which is a matter of 'enskilment', not enculturation.

Much recent research on the development of social cognition supports the view that learning is a matter of practical involvement. Social understanding and moral development are no longer regarded as simply a matter of one-way accumulation of facts and social norms (what developmental theorists sometimes refer to as a 'bag of virtues') in a narrow context of instruction. Theorists of the 'social cognitive' approach in psychology emphasise that development occurs as a result of the active participation of the child in the flux of everyday life, and researchers focus on cognition during actual interaction rather than in a laboratory (see Damon 1981: 155). The child first develops social cognition as a member of a family. As Dunn argues, 'children are motivated to understand the social rules and relationships of their cultural world *because they need to get things done in their family relationships*' (1988: 189; emphasis in the original). Such understanding is quite complex, even at an early age. Some children, it seems, are capable of sharing a perspective at eighteen months, and before long most children are able to understand familial relations – relations of authority, hierarchy, age and gender – and reason intelligently about their social world. But, as Ingold points out, if children can do this, 'why cannot fieldworkers?' The evidence on children's social cognition contrasts sharply, of course, with the culturalists' thesis, mentioned above, about grown-ups being incurable dyslexics both at home and abroad.[8]

To speak of the enskilment of the fieldworker as growing up, emphasising the affinity of the ethnographer and the child, is illuminating, and in more than one sense. Not only does the construction of ethnographies by definition entail social learning, communication and the development of social understanding, as Habermas persists, are necessarily affected by the form of life involved. For Habermas, rational consensus and authentic understanding are the products of what he calls the 'ideal speech situation', a symmetrical discourse that allows for general participation relatively free from constraint. Idealistic as this may sound, it provides a model for a new ethnographic order, a post-Orientalist anthropology that emphasises life rather than text and reciprocal communicative interaction rather than domination. In a world of decolonisation and continuity – the modern, global ecumene – the post-Orientalist approach to ethnography is far more realistic than its predecessors, the modes of the colonialist and the textualist.

8. Some non-developmentalist psychologists, however, similarly emphasise the evidence for people's shortcomings in dealing with the cognitive demands of their life: 'the adult is viewed as a creature whose most impressive intellectual triumphs are matched by equally impressive failures' (see Flavell and Ross 1981: 310).

Living discourse

Summarising some of the arguments developed above, we may distinguish three modes of anthropological representation, each of which is characterised by particular relations of ethnographic production (see Figure 1.2). One approach, that of the colonisers or Orientalists, typically employs the vocabulary of universalism and superiority. The fractured discourse of such power-laden encounters is nicely analysed in Scott's work (1990) on domination, public accounts and 'hidden transcripts'. Another approach emphasises relativism and submissiveness, underlining the difficulties of reading the 'texts' of other cultures – the state of cultural dyslexia. While at first glance the reduction of all difference to culture and text suggests a reversal of the relations of ethnographic production characteristic of the colonial mode (the apparent replacing of dominance with submission), on closer inspection the colonialist and the textualist turn out to have much in common. In the latter's view, the modern savage is a victim of culture, a museum piece for the privileged scrutiny of anthropologists. Stretching the limits of a discourse already saturated with labels, we may say that just as colonialism was replaced with neo-colonialism, with new relations of dependency, Orientalism was replaced with neo-Orientalist ethnography. Both approaches – Orientalism and neo-Orientalism, colonising people and relativising their world – assume asymmetric power relations.

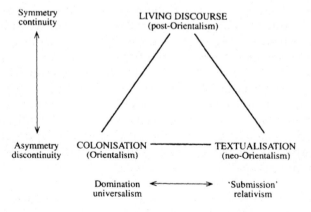

Figure 1.2. Three modes of making ethnographies

Given the inadequacies of the textualist mode and the neo-Orientalist ethnographic order, it is important to search for alternatives. One emerging approach may be called the mode of the 'living discourse'. In this case, anthropologists immerse themselves in a democratic ethnographic dialogue with the people they visit, forming an intimate rapport or communion and representing the experience as a moment in the stream of life, not as sundered pieces of text. While to some extent the contracts that come to prevail in such encounters are shaped by established relations of power, neither fieldworkers nor their hosts are the victims of culture and history, a political economy totally beyond their control. Together they negotiate both a form of life and a mode of representation.

The notion of the living discourse has much in common with the notion of the 'ideal speech situation' mentioned above. For Habermas, the latter represents 'the necessary but general conditions for the communicative practice of everyday life and for a procedure of discursive will-formation that would put participants *themselves* in a position to realize concrete possibilities for a better and less threatened life, on *their own* initiative and in accordance with *their own* needs and insights' (1989: 69; emphasis in the original). A good example of the ethnographic mode of the living discourse is represented in a work of Gudeman and Rivera on Colombia, significantly a joint venture of a foreign and native anthropologist, a work that underlines the need for 'expanding and democratizing the community of modellers' (1990: 190). Another example is provided by an account by Gewertz and Errington on the Chambri of Papua New Guinea. Althought Chambri lives may be regarded as texts, they argue (1991: 18–19), 'we must not be so preoccupied with textual concerns focusing on representation as to forget that they also have lives, lives affected in important ways by our Western power and interest.' This is post-Orientalist scholarship, an egalitarian discourse that presents anthropologists and their hosts as the inhabitants of a single world.

While the triad of colonisation, textualisation and living discourse is a rather simplistic formulation, such a scheme promotes appreciation of the role of power and asymmetry in fieldwork and anthropological practice generally. How we bring life into text depends upon our relations with our hosts. Ethnographies are not only informative with respect to the societies they reportedly describe; they often provide much information on ethnographers as well, on their 'receptor' society, and their relationships to the 'source'.

As we have seen, the anthropological notions of the cultural translator and the discontinuous world, implicit in the comparative enterprise, have been both persistent and powerful. Recent developments in social theory, however, suggest that we rethink the issue of translation, of going beyond boundaries. Wolf argues that ethnographers have always been 'in a world of sociocultural billiard balls, coursing on a global billiard table' (1982: 17). The characteristics of the modern world system – the exponential increase in cultural flow and the sudden breakdown of 'insurmountable' cultural and political 'walls', in particular the end of the Cold War – also suggest that anthropologists revise their image of the discontinuous world, breaking up the boundaries of their cherished tribes and villages. The issue of national and cultural boundaries within the global context has been extensively studied in some fields of scholarship, especially political science; one commentator describes the field of international relations as 'a succession of transient fads' (Young 1986: 104). Anthropology may have some fads of its own, but they have little to do with global interactions. With some notable exceptions (including Talal Asad and Eric Wolf), anthropologists have avoided the international context, faithful as they tend to be to all kinds of microcosms.

The futuristic image of the global village need not, however, be a particularly realistic one. We should not underestimate the human capacity for reinforcing existing barriers, inventing new ones, or reinventing those of the past; after all, over the last years we have witnessed recurring 'territorial' conflicts, not least in Eastern Europe and the Middle East. And, no doubt, Saddam Hussein and the Gulf War have brought about a sudden revival of folk Orientalism, in the Orient as well as the West. Nor should one conclude that the global village is necessarily a 'better' world than its predecessor. The erosion of boundaries, some people argue, simply means more boring sameness, greater exploitation and an increasing gap between North and South in terms of standards of living. As Kuper (1988: 240) points out, the modern image of the global village may be just as much a transformation of our image of our own society as the earlier image of primitive society. But while we may well keep Kuper's sober remark in mind, we can hardly escape the conclusion that, given the extensive changes that have taken place in the world system over the last years, the prevailing anthropological preoccupation with cultural discontinuities, with what Hannerz calls the root-metaphor of the global mosaic, is somewhat obsolete. If the travellers and ethnographers that recorded comparative data many decades (even centuries) ago were coursing on a global ethnographic 'billiard table', then the comparative anthropologist of the post-Cold War era, the age of cultural flow and continuity, is surely on slippery ground.

The idea that anthropology – or any academic discipline for that matter – is shaped by the social context in which it is practised, is not a novel one. Marx, Kuhn and Foucault and many others have outlined an 'epidemiology' of social theory, to paraphrase Sperber, pointing out that scientific paradigms and conventional standards of scholarship are inevitably rooted in history. Given the historicity of anthropology and its quest for knowledge, every major transformation in the social world is likely to lead to a reconsideration of the discipline. With decolonisation in the 1960s, anthropology was subject to intense criticism. Anthropology, however, did not wither away, contrary to the predictions of some of its critics; rather it was reborn and re-established on new terms, supported by greater institutional backing than ever before and enjoying increasing popularity. Nowadays, anthropologists have good reason to rethink their subject once again. Anthropology has commonly been thought of as an art of translation, a medium for communicating *between* different worlds, across boundaries, but if the human world is *both* experientially continuous and increasingly holistic and uniform then, certainly, the anthropological enterprise is bound to be redefined.

The papers that follow address the issue of going beyond boundaries from different ethnographic vantage-points and different theoretical perspectives. In general, however, they emphasise the need for an anthropological practice suited to the realities of the modern world. Collectively, they call for a new concept of anthropology – a new ethnographic order, to continue the metaphor of dependency theorists referred to above; an anthropology which dispenses with, or radically redefines, some of its key concepts – the Other, participant 'observation', discontinuities and cultural translation – and yet an anthropology that retains its classical concern with fieldwork, social understanding, and the multiple forms of social life, attempting to elucidate what it means to be human.

Acknowledgements

A short version of this Introduction was presented to a panel on 'Understanding anthropologists' understanding' at the meeting of the American Anthropological Association in Chicago in November 1991. I thank the audience for their comments, in particular Bruce Mannheim (University of Michigan) who acted as chairperson and discussant. I also wish to thank Anne Brydon (University of Winnipeg), E. Paul Durrenberger (University of Iowa) and Guðný Guðbjörndóttir (University of Iceland) for their extensive and thoughtful suggestions regarding some of the ideas developed here. Needless to say, the responsibility for any errors made here must rest with me.

Chapter 2

Mediations in the global ecumene

Ulf Hannerz

Once upon a time, back in the colonial era, in a new Nigerian town named Kafanchan, the British authorities decided to make the local administration of justice more sensitive to what they thought of as the customary law of the people in the town.[1] Now in Kafanchan this was easier said than done. The town was located within the territory of a small, weak Muslim emirate, on the outskirts of that large region of the West African savanna lands which had been under Hausa and Fulani domination, and so it was under the jurisdiction of a court which was older than the town itself and which administered Islamic law. The British, being committed here as in much of the Empire to a principle of indirect rule, certainly had to take the authority of this court into account. But this was a town built on a railway junction, drawing its population from just about every part of that large and internally very diverse colony which they had put together and named Nigeria. And many of these townspeople, especially those who had come up from the southern coastal areas, and who tended to regard themselves as the helpmates of the white colonisers in bringing the light of civilisation to heathen, backward lands, would not accept being subjected to a Muslim court, part of a local regime for which they had little or no respect. Thus the customary law of the land was not necessarily the customary law of the people on it. So the British instituted what they termed a Mixed Court, to be presided over by the

1. The Mixed Court in Kafanchan is discussed at somewhat greater length in Hannerz (1985).

local Muslim judge, the Alkali, but to be otherwise composed of representatives of the various immigrant ethnic groups, 'tribal members' who would hold their positions as experts on their respective traditions of customary law, and who would advise on these traditions as they became relevant to particular cases.

As I read the colonial records, this Mixed Court did not work too well. Actually, many of the immigrant ethnic groups settled most internal disputes out of court, so that the Mixed Court was usually left with the most difficult cases, often with litigants from different groups. The District Officer also complained to his superior of an 'enormous number of different kinds of native law and custom' to take into account. Yet this could only be a part of the truth. Surely, much of whatever might have been fairly clear-cut as judicial principles at home, in some distant rural area, did not apply so readily under the quite particular circumstances of life in a new urban community. Any law that would be practicable in Kafanchan would have to be to a degree non-native, uncustomary.

Uncertainty was thus just about maximised. The ethnic representatives seemed to allow themselves a great deal of leeway in interpreting traditions innovatively, and engaged in intrigues and factionalism among themselves. The Alkali, the Muslim judge, was simply scandalised by the easygoing legal manners and the procedural ignorance of his new colleagues. When for his part, in one case involving townspeople from the large Ibo group, the District Officer tried to make use of the government anthropologist C. K. Meek's *Law and Authority in a Nigerian Tribe*, an early standard work on the Ibo, the representatives of the group rejected its version of things. Responding to the District Officer's reports of his difficulties, his superior, the Resident of the province, noted that the 'tribal members' must understand that they were in court as 'assessors, not barristers to represent litigants of their own tribes'.

Recently, I was reminded of the Kafanchan Mixed Court, as it was in colonial days, when a controversy developed in Sweden over a case involving an immigrant from a Muslim country who had severely brutalised his wife. How would a court in his home country have dealt with him? Should it matter at all to the Swedish court that he was of a 'different cultural background', that his conduct in Sweden might be affected by other understandings of authority within the family, another sexual code of honour? And was it not a fact that allowing such considerations to enter into this particular case, or a case of this nature, was merely yet another indication of gender inequality? How would one decide in which instances, and in what ways, cultural differences should be taken into account in court? Whose reporting on cultural background facts could be accepted as authoritative? How acceptable is the implication of taking cultural differences into account that people would in fact not be equal before the law? Indeed it seemed that some of the problems faced by the Mixed Court in Kafanchan had, a half-century later, caught up with Sweden as well, and been joined by others.

These problems result, obviously, from the fact that culture travels – and in our time it travels quickly over great distances.[2] Culture travels, for one thing, when people travel; carrying some ideas with them, even if these ideas must be applied to new circumstances. Half a century ago, the Ibo who came up to Kafanchan by way of the new railway were the first or second generation to venture out in larger numbers from the Ibo homelands. These days, members of later generations of Ibo can come together to celebrate their New Yam festival in New York.[3] But culture is also on the move with artifacts, to some degree also carrying an abundance of meanings, again over great distances as industrialism and international trade combine. And as a somewhat special case of mobility by way of artifacts, there are the media which also help culture to make its way effectively through space. Kafanchan in the late twentieth century has television antennae over its corrugated zinc roofs.

In his 1945 Huxley Memorial Lecture to the Royal Anthropological Institute, Alfred Kroeber seized on the ancient Greek notion of the 'ecumene' (*Oikoumené*), the total inhabited world, to designate 'an interwoven set of happenings and products which are significant equally for the culture historian and the theoretical anthropologist' (Kroeber 1945: 9). The

2. The present-day mobility of culture forms the background of the World System of Culture project in the Department of Social Anthropology, Stockholm University, within the framework of which the presentation here has been developed; support from the Swedish Research Council for the Humanities and Social Sciences (HSFR) is gratefully acknowledged. For other work within the project see e.g. Hannerz (1987, 1988, 1989a and b, 1990) and Molund (1988).
3. See the brief account of the metropolitan New York segment of the Ibo diaspora by Mbabuike (1989).

ecumene of the ancient Greeks, of course, stretched only from Gibraltar towards India and a dimly perceived China. What we now face is a more literally *global* ecumene, as an area of persistent social interaction and cultural flow.[4] When it signals its complicating presence in the colonial Mixed Court in Kafanchan – which was after all not just an affair among different groups of Nigerians, but between them and the British as well – or in the Swedish system of justice, this is because law is one field where culture intersects with the power of territorially-based political regimes, and where de-territorialised, travelling culture consequently becomes more than usually problematic. But the global ecumene as a master organising idea raises a much wider range of questions of culture than this, issues which are indeed, as Kroeber had it, equally significant for a culture historian (in this case a culture historian of the present) and for the theoretical anthropologist – if these need actually be separate vocations.

Images of translation

It is sometimes suggested that anthropologists should bring their insights and expertise in translation to the task of making a viable cultural order. We may be tempted to engage in pleasant daydreaming here about a heroic and virtuous role for the anthropologist as a master interpreter, negotiator and adviser within the division of cultural labour. While at times daydreams may turn out to be constructive visions and they may be good as escapes, I think we may also do well to engage in some more realistic appraisal of where anthropologists fit into the global ecumene and to what degree we must reconstruct our understandings of culture.

The idea of anthropology as cultural translation is then itself one which can serve as food for thought. I suspect it began almost as an off-the-cuff metaphor, a rough approximation of what especially ethnography is about, useful not least in telling non-anthropologists about it; it is worth reminding ourselves

4. For a recent use of the ecumene concept in anthropology, see Kopytoff (1987). I find the notion of the global ecumene attractive both because it connects to an anthropological tradition in culture history and because it does not have to carry the full load of assumptions which may have come to be associated with the concept of 'world system'.

here that the pieces by which Evans-Pritchard (1951: 61) and his Oxford colleague Lienhardt (1954: 97) did much to put the idea into circulation, both originated as talks on the BBC. That is, they were already translating anthropology. Since then, the notion has been more widely adopted, but also debated. For there are ambiguities around it, relating to the idea of translation itself as a linguistic practice, as well as to the comparability of anthropology to this practice.

Perhaps we have two main ideas of the translator's role, when we think of translation in its ordinary sense. In one of them, a language is taken to be a rather standardised phenomenon, in two ways; each speaker of any one language uses it in much the same way, and any two languages relate to the world of meanings in much the same way. Here the translator should be like the ideal civil servant: conscientious, impartial, abiding by universal rules. We do not expect him to be original or creative, only reliable and preferably quick. We are perhaps most likely to find such translators inserted into the working life of international organisations, where, of course, the languages being translated tend already to have been standardised according to some common norm; there is seldom any funny business about pelicans being half-brothers here.

The other kind of translator is a lone wolf rather than an organisation man, somebody engaged in a labour of love. Translators in this category are acutely aware that they are translating, not so much a language as an idiolect, the very special way that one individual uses and even makes up meanings and means of expression. To this kind of translator we may be more willing to grant originality, even sometimes to the extent of claiming, perhaps with mixed feelings about the morality of it, that the translation is superior to the original. We also allow him more time; no simultaneity here but years, perhaps decades, of efforts between original and completed translation. Here, too, the translation is an end-result, to be responded to in aesthetic and intellectual terms both as a reflection of the original and as a work in its own right. The work of the bureaucratic translator, on the other hand, is instrumental. It facilitates further action and interaction.

There is, no doubt, rather more in the second kind of translator's work that we sympathise with as anthropologists: the loneliness, the puzzling over the original, the sense of engaging in a craft very different from routine administration or industry. But then again we must realise that ethnography is really something else entirely. As ethnographers we report on some number of interconnected people, rather than on the single author; we take note of a great many kinds of meaningful overt forms, some intentionally communicative towards somebody, and others not; we translate no doubt, but also do a lot of explication and contextualisation in our own voices, since not only overt forms but also the meanings themselves are in large part alien; and finally we compress the meanings once given all these varied overt shapes, plus our own explications and other comments, into the single form, the single communicative device, of a text. We may gloss over a great deal by referring to all this as the work of translation.

But I should not be too pedantic here. What has no doubt contributed to the appeal of the translation metaphor is the imagery of translation as something a bit out of the ordinary, a linguistic practice occurring at the margins of language communities where everyday life goes on monolingually. In much the same way, anthropology in its classic version has been unusual as a type of cultural management taking place at points of strikingly sharp discontinuity. Indeed Evans-Pritchard's Azande – and the possessive manner in which we have often talked about our fields and the people in them is of course significant here – have been a favoured example as anthropologists and philosophers have debated for some decades whether understanding other cultures is at all possible, and what might be the bridgeheads for such understandings (see especially Winch 1958; Wilson 1970; Hollis and Lukes 1982). Rather more down to earth, Clifford Geertz (1977: 788) has suggested that 'anthropologists have a number of advantages when addressing the general public, one of them being that hardly anyone in their audience has much in the way of independent knowledge of the supposed facts being retailed.'

The global mosaic and beyond

Historically at least, such assumptions of monopoly, and even the suspicion that cultures may be untranslatable, seem to have some affinity with a certain anthropological view of the world.

On the whole, it may fairly be said, our macro-anthropology, since we left diffusionism behind, was long one of a global mosaic rather than a global ecumene (a view which also in itself obviated the need for a more developed macro-anthropology). According to this view, often left implicit – and still lingering, one may suspect, here and there under the surface of consciously enunciated theory – cultures are practically separate worlds. Between them there is not much in the way of communication. The flow of meaning occurs mostly within them, in communities of shared consciousness and means of expression. It is inside such communities of shared understandings that anthropologists have preferred to situate themselves. And they make it seem as if they alone know the exit.

The imagery of the global mosaic, however, was no doubt always a misleading one, and this is only becoming more glaringly obvious in our times. In all fairness, I should say that Geertz, further on in the essay quoted above, made it quite clear that he did not believe that he alone knew about Bali. And he concludes a more recent work (1988: 147) by suggesting the necessity of enlarging 'the possibility of intelligible discourse between people quite different from one another in interest, outlook, wealth, and power, and yet contained in a world where, tumbled as they are into endless connection, it is increasingly difficult to get out of each other's way.' This seems close enough to the idea of the anthropologist as translator; and for once, we sense an area of agreement between Geertz and the late Edmund Leach (1973: 772), who wrote in that *Times Literary Supplement* edition on 'The state of anthropology' that 'social anthropologists are engaged in establishing a methodology for the translation of cultural language' and that 'in a shrunken world of communication satellites and supersonic airliners this is an important and worthwhile task, but unromantic.'

We may agree, too. But the truth is that in the global ecumene, with satellites, supersonic airliners and all, a great many other people seem to feel that the task of cultural translation is just too important to be left to the anthropologists. Already back in the Mixed Court in colonial Kafanchan, the tribal members found themselves in some competition over ethnographic authority with Meek, the text-producing government anthropologist. And by now, for sure, those days are gone when it may have seemed as if traffic between cultures

were in the hands of two occupational groups –
anthropologists, as it were, doing fairly general-purpose
translations in one direction, and missionaries (their presence
mostly concealed in the ethnographies) largely special-purpose
translations in the other. Understanding between cultures has
become, for many people, an issue that is recurrently faced as
one goes about one's everyday life. And it is faced in a great
many ways: routine or innovative, piecemeal or large-scale,
institutionalised or improvised, unsuccessful or at times
possibly successful, if sometimes only in the shape of working
misunderstandings.

One necessary ingredient in making anthropology contribute
realistically to an understanding of the contemporary world,
consequently, might be to look not only in front of us, first, at
whatever we take to be an 'other' culture, and then over the
shoulder, at an audience at home, but also sideways, at the
various other people also situated at the interfaces between
cultures and engaged in making the global ecumene. There are
journalists and film-makers there, tourists and tour guides,
social workers, jurists, business consultants. Some people
become involved only occasionally and rather peripherally.
Others have found a sufficient number of curious or concerned
people on one or both sides of some discontinuity to provide a
niche for a more orderly practice of cultural brokerage in the
strict sense. If we have already sensed that the single although
complicated concept of translation is not quite sufficient to cover
what anthropologists do, we should not try to extend it to all
these other kinds of cultural traffic as well. Perhaps we can think
instead of some term of less particular connotations to refer to
that entire family of varieties of cultural management in which
people engage as they find themselves somewhat
problematically positioned at points of relative discontinuity in
the distribution of meaning or meaningful form, but without
sharp discontinuity of interaction. The term I will use here is
mediation; of which ethnography is thus one kind, and
translation in the ordinary sense another.[5]

5. What I have in mind here, I should emphasise, is cultural mediation, not mediation
in social conflicts.

Uncertain units

Anthropologists, this goes to say, have been specialists in one kind of mediation, their own; but as long as they have stuck to the assumptions of the global mosaic, they have tended to marginalise issues of mediation as these occur in the ongoing life of their fields of study, and also to marginalise those fields of study in which mediations even take on a central part. True, now and then in the history of this discipline, there has been a period of some coalescence of interest around such conceptions as acculturation (Redfield, Linton and Herskovits 1936), or the relationship between great and little traditions (Redfield 1956), or plural societies (Smith 1965), or cultural brokerage at the local level (Wolf 1956; Geertz 1960). But they have usually not remained for long at the centre of the discipline, if they ever arrived there.

What I want to do here, apart from suggesting in a general way that it is time to take on the questions of mediation again, with a stronger commitment than before and with whatever new skills and insights we may have acquired since those earlier times, is to point, on the one hand, to a couple of matters in the social organisation of cultural discontinuity and mediation, and, on the other hand, to what are the implications of different modes of cultural expression for continuity and discontinuity within the global ecumene. In each instance, as it turns out, it is useful to keep in mind the idea of translation – if only to show its ambiguity.

The first of these matters is that of units. The imagery of cultural translation suggests to us that cultures are phenomena of the same nature as languages. And I think on the whole, given the persistent biases of anthropological thought towards assumptions of a global mosaic, a world of neat cultural packages, the idea here is that of language as something standardised, in the first sense as ascribed to the first kind of translator portrayed above. Language, that is to say, would be understood here as a sociocentrically defined phenomenon; it belongs to some bounded collectivity in which speakers are by and large exchangeable. Culture would then be conceptualised, explicitly but at least as often implicitly, along the same lines. As a person opens his or her mouth and speaks, in principle, you can tell what language it is, and what it is not. As a person thinks and acts, consequently, you should be able to say what culture he or she 'belongs to'.

However, this does not work; not in the global ecumene. Let me remind you, by way of exemplification, of Salman Rushdie and his novel *The Satanic Verses*. Probably the Rushdie affair was the first really global literary event; the kind of incident one can use to tease out some of the main tendencies in the contemporary cultural organisation of the world.[6] But I do not want to go into the Rushdie affair as such here, although I will refer to it again. Here I am concerned with the book itself. The very particular mixture of dream world and reality in *The Satanic Verses* can be seen in large part as a confessional statement on the part of a boy from Bombay, from a Muslim family, who has become a Londoner, an apostate and a cosmopolitan. Perhaps the concoction is altogether enjoyable only to someone who knows something of Islam without being a believer, somebody who finds his way around Bombay at least in outline, who has some insight into Indian popular culture, and who also knows something about the life of immigrants in London in the Thatcher era. And of course, this someone also has to be quite knowledgeable about, and interested in, all the formal possibilities of a literary work. I do not think it is easy to delineate that social network in which this writer is included along with his willing and competent readers, that network in which communication flows readily without disruption.

Culture here evidently becomes rather more like the language with which our second translator works; an idiolect, a personal perspective, where it is uncertain what one person shares with the next. But in fact any linguistic imagery, at least of the commonsense type employed by non-linguists, may be insufficient here; it tends to hide what may be great variation at the level of personal orders of meaning, and in some modes of expression, behind a preoccupation with the intrinsic tendency towards relative uniformity within one particular mode of communication. People can become quite idiosyncratically placed at different crossroads of personal experience and cultural flow. And when we insist on going beyond the personal perspective to cultures as again somehow collective, carried within some set of social relationships, we must realise that the units are increasingly to be understood as organisations of

---

6.   For comments on the Rushdie affair in its global context, see e.g. Akhtar (1989), Jussawalla (1989), van der Veer (1989), Fischer and Abedi (1990) and Ruthven (1990).

diversity, of varying extension in space, rather arbitrarily distinguished, overlapping. They are networks of perspectives, and perspectives towards other perspectives; where some of the differences between perspectives are differences of horizon. Under such conditions, old assumptions about what is 'within' a culture or 'between' cultures may in the long run not be very useful; ultimately, the global ecumene is the unit, with its single, large, cultural inventory.

Mediation interests

As discontinuities are normalised, now and again, our relationships with one another turn out to be relationships with an Other; or if I feel reasonably sure that I satisfactorily understand someone else, I may be equally convinced that I will have to intervene to help that someone understand somebody else again, whose perspective and characteristic forms of expression I am somewhat familiar with. As mediations, or at least the need for mediations, are just about everywhere, everybody may have to be a mediator from time to time.

Some people, however, are more mediators than others. They engage systematically with different kinds of discontinuities, and do so for different purposes, with different interests in mind. The tribal members of the Kafanchan Mixed Court, for example, turned out to be of one kind here, and not the one the colonial government had intended; as the Resident of the province had it, they were more barristers for members of their ethnic groups than assessors, drawing impartially on their expertise on tribal cultures. Mediation, that is, as they defined their task, entailed accounting for modes of action within the frame of another culture than that which was the court standard, in terms beneficial to those individuals whose conduct was questioned. As another kind of people, using other cultures as a resource within the global ecumene, we have those who at one time or other during the twentieth century have seen more or less their own Utopias realised somewhere else, and who speak of the cultures in question, consequently, to further their own political interests at home. Such Utopias may be South American Indian tribes for western anarchists, or the United States for post-Maoist Chinese. Lincoln Steffens, the American muckraker, went to the Soviet Union in the early 1920s and exclaimed as he came home, 'I have seen the future, and it works!' This, some seventy years later, may strike us as a bit premature.

No more examples of such variations. The point is simply that most of the people we see as we look at who else is doing cultural mediation work do so not just for the intrinsic pleasures of it, or because they are engaged in a pursuit of pure knowledge. They operate in particular political, economic or legal contexts, with particular long-term or short-term objectives. The distribution of culture and its discontinuities is not independent of the distribution of power and material assets. Asad (1986) has drawn attention to one aspect of this in his critique of British social anthropologists for their disregard, in depicting anthropology as cultural translation, of the real inequalities between languages in the world.

Anthropology is really in a rather unusual position here. I argued before that of the two types of translators, we are likely to identify more strongly with the individualising craftsman, whose endeavours result in something to be enjoyed for its own sake, on intellectual and aesthetic grounds. This is much like our own products. No doubt it is in part because we are thus so often preoccupied with understanding and appreciation as such, rather than with using knowledge instrumentally, that we are somewhat liable to that bias which some critics, internal as well as external, call culturalism. The curious thing about our ethnographies, of course, is that we write them in very large part for our own peers, in a metalanguage fairly inaccessible to others, as if translations of fiction or poetry were mostly to be read by other translators. If anthropology is to move further toward playing a part in shaping, not merely reporting on, the cultural order, then certainly one question must be asked: translation – or mediation – for whom?

For purposes of contrast, one other style of cultural mediation may be mentioned, the practitioners of which have obviously grown enormously in number only in the last couple of decades.[7] I think of it as the culture-shock prevention industry: institutionalised forms for preparing people to cope with other cultures than their own. 'Cross-cultural' training programmes are set up to teach basic rules

7. Mr Tommy Dahlén of the Department of Social Anthropology, Stockholm University, has embarked on a study of this complex of mediation practice.

of etiquette and inculcate sensitivity. There are overtones of sheer appreciation of otherness here, but more than that the objective is efficiency, practicality. For Westerners in recent years, as the concern with cultural mediation follows business, the strongest interest is in Japan and the Arab World.

There is also a burgeoning do-it-yourself literature in the field. A book entitled *Managing Cultural Differences: High-performance strategies for today's global manager* (Harris and Moran 1987), a popular reference in business courses at many universities, is one example. What strikes me about it, apart from problems of quality which I will not go into here, is how different writing about culture for business people is from writing about culture for anthropologists. This book draws consistently on a vocabulary of 'impact', 'performance', 'coping', 'dynamic', 'synergy' and 'cultural handicaps'. Cultural understanding, and plans for practical action based on such understanding, again and again take the form of tables, lists and flow charts.

What the culture-shock prevention industry actually accomplishes is not so easily evaluated. One may have one's doubts about the quality of insight that can be reached through course work for a couple of days or weeks, or through a frequently unsubtle handbook genre. Perhaps practitioners in this industry will soon have replaced missionaries as that other group of professional cultural mediators about which anthropologists will have the fewest kind words to say. What I want to make note of in this context, however, is that here, possibly, we find the nearest counterpart in cultural mediation of that first kind of translator, the quick and practical organisation man who is there to facilitate other people's work, and who has a tool kit of practical rules to apply to largely repetitive situations. Perhaps the government anthropologist in colonial times was expected to perform a similar part; that, however, apparently rarely if ever worked out.

The travels of modes of expression

The last issue I want to identify is how different modes of human expression fit into the global ecumene; what continuities or discontinuities they entail and what particular questions of mediation are involved.

A very prominent writer on language, translation and culture in recent decades, George Steiner (1979: 34), has noted how he has 'watched topologists, knowing no syllable of each other's language, working effectively together at a blackboard in the silent speech common to their craft'. Mathematicians, that is to say, at least as long as they are doing mathematics, do not have the same translation needs as those who express themselves in ordinary language; they do not confront the same discontinuities. And the point is more general: the different symbolic capacities of human beings may relate differently to cultural difference, and the idea of translation, being so closely linked to the particular communicative qualities of language, may be quite unevenly useful as a metaphor when it comes to continuities and discontinuities in other symbolic modes. Nobody sets out to take a piece of, say, typically Azande music and translate it into typically Icelandic music, carrying the same meaning so that Azande and Icelanders are thereby made to understand one another.

Back in the 1960s, that rather strange literature professor out of the Canadian prairies, McLuhan, set out to fashion himself as a super-anthropologist of the global ecumene; or as he saw it, 'the global village', based on the space-binding potentialities of the new electronic media. Of ordinary academic anthropologists, McLuhan (in Stearn 1967: 272–4) was rather contemptuous. They were Gutenberg men, imprisoned in the assumptions of a literate culture.

If the criticism were valid, it should hurt; and at the time, there was probably something to it. It is only in more recent years that anthropologists have become more self-conscious of the problems inherent in their turning living cultures into text; and the very image of ethnography as translation, and the ready adoption of it, might perhaps a little malevolently be taken as an indication of our old biases here.[8]

Now I am not proposing here that we should start doing our mediations in music or mathematics or sculpture or gesture instead. Some anthropologists may turn themselves into photographers and film-makers, but most of us will no doubt remain wordsmiths, although perhaps more aware of the implications of this commitment. What I am more directly

8.   As examples of the increasing awareness on the part of anthropologists that their commitment to the written mode can be in some way problematic, see e.g. Geertz (1973: 19), in a footnote; Goody (1977: 52ff); Fabian (1983: 71ff); and Clifford (1986: 115ff).

concerned with, however, is the relationship between different symbolic modes and the ever-shifting global diversity of culture. We know well enough where the barriers of incomprehension are in the linguistic mode. We have seen that in mathematics they are not the same. Not least the culture-shock prevention industry, inspired initially by the occasional anthropologist such as Edward Hall, has made us more aware of cultural differences in those gestures and body movements which once we may have thought of as raw human nature. One of my more curious field experiences in Kafanchan was at a meeting of the women's association of the Kaje people, where a visiting American home economics teacher lectured to farm wives and petty traders on 'body language', with their responses shifting between perplexity and gales of laughter.

In the last twenty years or so anthropologists have become more interested in the particular qualities of symbolic modes, although this interest has mostly been developed in the context of local studies. I would suggest that it may well be recontextualised within the global ecumene where, as McLuhan pointed out, the cultural technologies, the media, have been changing the rules of the game with respect to the use of symbolic modes. What used to be confined within communities or regions can now reach everywhere. And those symbolic modes which used to monopolise more far-flung communication networks now face new competitors. Think of creolised varieties of Third World music becoming world music. Or think of the success of Indian and Hong Kong films far outside what we would conventionally think of as their culture areas. Again, our assumptions about the boundedness and organic unity of cultures is thrown into some doubt by such instances of massive diffusion. Do some symbolic forms travel better than others, given the technological means to do so? Do representations in different symbolic modes, to borrow the vocabulary of Sperber (1985a; and this volume), involve quite different epidemiologies? Can they do without translations, without mediators, allow more immediacy? Or if mediation is called for, what is it, if we cannot always accurately call it translation?[9]

9. The late Sol Worth (1981: 72) has touched on such problems in his discussion of film anthropology, asking how cinematic understandings are distributed. Do 'film language' communities have anything to do with language communities; do they relate to the distribution of cognitive styles? In more general terms, I believe anthropologists might well aim at building a more coherent systematic body of knowledge concerning the different human modes of symbolisation. The formulations by Gross (1973) and Gardner (1983, 1984) may offer points of departure.

There are many question marks to confront here; and then things become more complicated still, as we take into account the different indigenous theories concerning the qualities of symbolic modes, and the discontinuities between them. Remember the Muslim judge in Kafanchan and his outrage at the cavalier treatment of written law by the tribal members of the Mixed Court. Or consider, although not quite in the same vein, the Rushdie affair. Ruthven (1990: 131ff), a British commentator on Muslim reactions to *The Satanic Verses*, has proposed that a difference of assumptions concerning the written word was centrally involved here. Those great many Muslims who certainly never read Rushdie's book, but who heard the rumours of it and were incensed, Ruthven argues, were people with an understanding of the power of words, and not least sacred words, rooted in oral cultures. To take materials from their world, treat it with the playfulness, mockery and intellectual distance characteristic of post-modernist print culture, and then turn it back to them, is a matter of playing with cultural dynamite. Yet one more way of being a cultural mediator, evidently, is to be a provocateur.[10]

To conclude: perhaps a spectre is haunting the world as the twentieth century is coming to a close, a spectre of cultural expansionism from centre to periphery resulting in large-scale loss of meanings and meaningful forms. Some might indeed see this not as a threat but as a promise. Cultural diversity has disadvantages as well as advantages. But the idea of the global ecumene is not in itself a scenario of homogenisation. Even those who recognise the power of the centre over the periphery draw different conclusions as to its implications for culture, and from this we may conclude that there are contradictory tendencies (see Hannerz 1989b). So far at least, and for the foreseeable future, the shift from the global mosaic to the global ecumene as a root metaphor for anthropology is a matter of drawing our attention to the fact that discontinuities have become increasingly relative, and that consequently, mediations are going on almost everywhere (see Stefánsson, this volume). They are, in fact, forever taking on new shapes, as new culture, and

---

10. This is not to say that Ruthven's argument here would be a sufficient analysis of the Rushdie affair; it may be contestable in itself, and the controversy has a great many local and other refractions in various communities, audiences and interest groups which would require other interpretations.

new differences, are continuously generated in this tumultuous world. Some of these mediations may be more like our own, others are quite different. To understand them and tell others about them, we as anthropologists may be mediating the mediations. We cannot just take our expertise for granted here, but neither should we withdraw into the hinterlands, or into history, or assume that overall frameworks for understanding the world can only come from elsewhere, outside our own discipline. We may have to keep rethinking our anthropology in order to keep up with the world; but doing so we may play some small part in a sufficiently coherent, and thus viable, cultural order.

Chapter 3

Doves, hawks and anthropology: the Israeli debate on Middle Eastern settlement proposals

Shlomo Deshen

In recent decades, social and cultural anthropology has proved to be of value in many fields of social practice. The achievements of applied anthropology are particularly salient in medical training and practice, in agricultural and community development, and in education. But in many other fields the application of anthropology has hardly begun. Astonishingly, this is so in the area of business and industrial administration, where after very promising beginnings with Edward Hall's work (see, for instance, Hall and White 1960), little has happened.

Even more remarkable is the near sterility of anthropology in the practice of international and inter-cultural relations, a field that lies close to the essence of a discipline that claims to be focused on culture (cf. Hannerz and Ingold, both in this volume). In a century that has been troubled on an unprecedented scale with hot and cold wars, nuclear and near-nuclear wars, Holocaust and genocides, anthropology has addressed itself little to urgent issues, which have led to immeasurable bloodshed. Specialists in the study of knowledge and the professions may concern themselves with under-standing this feature of twentieth-century anthropology, but for all anthropologists, the irrelevance, for all practical purposes, of the discipline to peace and war, the major anguish of humanity, should at least be a source of malaise.

The year 1989 was thrilling and uplifting to people in many parts of the world directly involved in the confrontation of the West and Communism. Even where a renaissance was aborted, in China, the ugly events of June 1989 there have at least raised hopes for another revolutionary attempt, which might yet succeed. There are even rumbles in Africa. But many other parts of the world seem to have remained untouched by 1989. Protagonists of the Jewish-Arab conflict, for instance, have maintained essentially unchanged stances.

My aim in this article is to contribute to an exploration of the potential of anthropological insight in the field of international relations, war and peace. Mercifully the Cold War has ended – without the benefit of efforts on the part of anthropological practitioners. But where, as in the Middle East, people gaze wistfully upon epoch-making and favourable events, which have not yet impinged on them significantly, there remains a role for applied anthropology.

The current confrontations between Jewish Israelis and Arab Palestinians, as well as many Arab and Muslim states, embed the resolutions of prior internal confrontations of moderates and extremists, 'doves and hawks', of the various adversaries. These separate internal political discourses of Jews and Arabs are crucially important in determining the outcome of the confrontations between the adversaries. I seek here to shed light on the kind of debate that Israelis maintain among themselves, leading on to a practical recommendation, which will flow from the analysis. This recommendation might prove constructive in the quest for a settlement of the tragedy. A comparable analysis of the internal Arab discourse, with a parallel concluding recommendation in terms of a settlement, would be desirable. But that is both beyond my competence and the scope of this article (for pertinent analyses, see Abraham 1983; Harkabi 1988; Steinberg 1988, 1989).

The political and historical context

Uncovering the nature of the Israeli debate on an Arab-Jewish settlement requires summarising some of the salient features of

Israeli politics and society.[1] One of the most remarkable of these
is the affinity of hawkish views and orthodox religious practice.
Judging by their overall performance in Israeli government
coalition-building ever since 1977, orthodox people and their
political representatives are evidently comfortable with
positions that tend towards the extreme right wing. The
movement for establishing Jewish settlements in territories
beyond the 1967 borders, the Gush Emunim movement, is very
popular among young orthodox people. Moreover, extreme
positions such as those of the underground cell of the early
1980s, 'The Faithful of the Temple Mount' group, not to mention
the parliamentary extreme right-wing parties, have an aura of
fascination. Although most orthodox people stop short of
actually joining these movements, they do constitute viable
alternatives that people do not reject out of hand. Even the
group of Meir Kahana, which voices aggressive racism, and once
managed to get elected to the Knesset before it was outlawed, is
a serious proposition that is considered and deliberated by
young people in particular.

This feature of the Israeli socio-political scene is a matter of
crucial significance in the overall context of the Middle Eastern
conflict, and in the debates concerning its resolution. My reason
for this evaluation is the following: the hawkish position in
Israel is fuelled from three distinct intellectual sources. One is
that of religious orthodoxy (particularly as currently interpreted
by followers of the school of Rabbi Z. Y. Kook, d. 1982); another
is that of secular right-wing étatism (stemming originally from
the ideology of Ze'ev Jabotinsky, d. 1940, and the Revisionist
Party). This second school of thought was maintained by old-
time associates of former Prime Minister Begin in the
underground movements of pre-Independence times, and by a
small number of writers (such as Y. Z. Greenberg, d. 1981, and
Yisrael Eldad). The third source is that of pragmatic politicians
and soldiers, such as Moshe Arens, Yuval Ne'eman and Ariel
Sharon, for whom considerations of secular *realpolitik*, free of

1. Different version of this article appeared in *The Jewish Quarterly* (1990) and in *Human Organization* (1992). The analysis presented here is based on a synthesis of copious materials. Short of attempting to offer all the references, I mention some basic publications: Lustick (1988) provides a useful bibliographic introduction; Liebman and Don-Yehiya (1984) give a basic overview from a political science perspective; Krausz (1985) and Kimmerling (1989) contain collections of fine sociological studies; Deshen (1982) provides an anthropologically-oriented overview that leads to the present analysis.

sentimental religious or moral trappings, are operative in preferring hawkish alternatives.

Of the three sources, the second is moribund, and for all practical purposes is no more active. The reason for this is that secular rightist ideologies lack attraction among rank-and-file Israelis, and particularly so among younger people. The ideologists of old Revisionist stripe have departed the scene and have not been replaced. (Of them all there remains primarily Eldad, who is still a vigorous and attractive speaker, but has no political following.) As a result of this, orthodoxy, in the guise of the Rabbi Kook school, is the main ideological bolster of the hawkish position. No other force competes with it in supplying spiritual vitality and depth to the position of the pragmatists, which in itself is ideologically sterile. The orthodox thus fill a crucial position in the Israeli right wing, and consequently in the overall Israeli political spectrum. This importance is distinct from the pivotal position of the orthodox in coalition arithmetics; even if the religious parties were to falter at the polls their ideological importance, as the essential powerhouse of the right wing, would remain unchanged.

The present position of orthodoxy in the Israeli political spectrum is startling when viewed in the context of the not very distant past. When Zionism emerged in Central and Eastern Europe about a century ago, leading rabbis were anything but enthusiastic about it. Despite the activities of a small number of nineteenth- and early twentieth-century rabbis, in favour of Zionism and the pioneering settlement movement, the majority of rabbis and their flocks were apathetic, and a large and vocal minority were stridently opposed. The reason for this was that most rabbis conceived traditional Messianic beliefs in terms that were incompatible with secular Zionist nationalism, and viewed the latter as essentially a heresy. Moreover, the Zionist movement increasingly came to be dominated by non-practising Jews, and this coloured the pioneering effort in Palestine in secular hues, which were additionally objectionable. The main rabbinical position was altogether inimical to emigration from Eastern Europe anywhere, be it to Palestine or to the West, because of the well-founded fear that migration would erode the old style of life. Consequently, the role of observant Jews in the pioneering movement, through the Turkish (until 1917) and Mandate periods (until 1948) was secondary at best, and often insignificant.

Present-day orthodox hawkishness is all the more startling
when the political record of the recent past is considered. A fair
number of orthodox people did immigrate to Palestine in pre-
State years (before 1948), in defiance of rabbinical leadership.
Remarkably, these people organised themselves mainly in two
sets of political parties. Predominantly they joined the religious
workers' party; to a smaller extent they joined ultra-orthodox
parties which were stridently anti-Zionist. The religious
workers' party in Mandate times elected not merely to be a
junior partner of the leading (and presently much-discredited)
Labour-Mapai Party, but itself actually had some attributes of
socialism. Thus groups of religious workers followed the lead of
secular pioneers and established their own kibbutz (pl.
kibbutzim) communes, which differed from most kibbutzim
only in the fact that the members observed religious orthodoxy.
The standing of these religious kibbutzim among religious
people was generally high, a model for emulation (at least in
theory), just as was the case among the secular socialists.

In the 1920s the religious workers' party seriously considered
disbanding and actually joining the federation of socialist
workers, and in fact did so for the duration of two years.
Through the Mandate period orthodox workers were suffered
among their socialist colleagues only as subordinates.
Economically, those were often hard years. At times there was
unemployment, and orthodox workers were openly
discriminated against in the allocation of work. This sometimes
led to incidents of violence. Yet the political partnership of
religious and secular workers held for nearly fifty years, from
the 1920s to the 1970s. The height was in 1937 when the British
recommended partition of the country, granting the Jews only a
small slice of territory. Labour accepted the proposal over the
objections of the right-wing Revisionist Party – and most of the
orthodox sided with the former or remained neutral.

By the 1970s the orthodox position had changed dramatically,
and attained the present contours. The reasons for this shift are
essentially rooted in the turmoil engendered by the Holocaust.
The events of the times clearly vindicated the classical Zionist
position in the eyes of all survivors, including the orthodox, who
had previously been apathetic. Even where the anti-Zionist
position remained, it lost its élan. Instead of the pre-Holocaust
position there developed among those who remained aloof from

Zionism a pragmatic attitude toward the Israeli state. They accepted it on condition that it extend aid toward rebuilding orthodox communities and institutions in Israel, to replace those that had been annihilated (for a sensitive and full exposition of the mutation of orthodox views about Zionism, in the context of the Holocaust, see Friedman 1990). Actual opposition to the state remained only in insignificant fringe groups. By and large, as long as the orthodox obtained material government support for their talmudic educational institutions (*yeshivot*), and the students of those institutions were exempted from military conscription, the orthodox could be relied upon to support the government.

Among religious workers another factor operated: In Mandate times the religious workers' circles had not, for reasons that are beyond our present scope, been very successful in raising their children as observant Jews; many of the younger generation left the fold of orthodoxy. However, in the 1950s the balance of educational success changed dramatically, and there arose a stratum of youth that were markedly more careful in religious observance, than their older siblings. On the other hand, secular socialism had begun to flounder, under the impact of reaction to late-Stalinism, such as the anti-Semitic Moscow 'doctors' trials'. This dual development heightened the self-confidence of the orthodox, just as it systematically eroded that of the secular socialists. At a time when orthodox people of all shades were establishing yeshivas for their youth who clamoured to enter them, the socialist school system shed its unique ideological character. There developed among the orthodox a view of the socialists as decadent and failing, and this latched on to the old bitterness at having been, for many years, treated shabbily as second-class citizens, by the dominant Labour establishment.

The late 1950s and 1960s was a period when orthodox people felt themselves becoming emancipated and equal, and they began to flaunt proudly their particular identity. In the 1950s, for instance, there began the fashion of orthodox youths walking about in public with knitted skull-caps, whereas previously they wore innocuous berets and other caps.[2] In the 1950s there also

2. It is a traditional orthodox Jewish practice for males to cover their heads with hats or at least small skull-caps at all times.

began to emerge the phenomenon of young orthodox people
linked with the youth movement of the religious workers' party,
who sought to make their political mark in a new way, not like
their elders, who were just satisfied with matters of specific
practice (such as securing public Sabbath observance and state
religious education). Rather, these youths sought to develop, in
the context of their religious resurgence, religious policies in
areas of general public interest, such as in social welfare and,
most crucially and ominously, in external and security affairs.

These incipient developments came to a dramatic head after
1967. The defeat of the coalition of Arab states in the June 1967
war led to major territorial changes. The youth generation came
to dominate the religious workers' party and imposed upon it a
hawkish agenda. Further, these same circles of young people
spearheaded the Gush Emunim movement for Jewish settlement
in the newly conquered West Bank and Gaza territories. This
movement had a powerful religio-mystical source, that came to
be newly formulated, but it also had a source, rooted in the
vicissitudes of mundane relations between the orthodox and the
secular-socialist strata. Because of the latter's ideological
troubles the orthodox felt that the major role-model of Israeli
society, that of the pioneer, was slipping out of the hands of the
socialists, whereas in the past it was precisely the latter who had
produced the major exemplars of pioneering, in terms of both
numbers and excellence.

After 1967 and through the following decades, the orthodox
developed a view of themselves as having picked up the mantle
of self-sacrificing, devoted pioneering, which the socialists had
discarded. One of the motives for the settlement élan of Gush
Emunim, aside from the religio-mystical factor, was the urge to
make the statement that the orthodox had indeed replaced the
discredited socialists, who in the past had proudly dominated
Israeli society. The settlement drive was an emphatic statement
that the orthodox had finally arrived, and were now first-class
citizens. The drive actually to settle the territories is unique to
only a segment of orthodox people; it is not shared by the ultra-
orthodox, nor by Israelis of Middle Eastern background, the
Sephardim. However, it is crucial to note that virtually all
sectors of orthodoxy favour activism and settlement in the
territories. They are sympathetic bystanders. The differences
between the various sectors of orthodoxy pertain to personal

commitment to activism, but in principle there is accord with and admiration for the new pioneers. This view of the Israeli scene requires emphasis, for the surface developments often lead observers to mistaken conclusions.[3]

Among the ultra-orthodox there operate processes that are basically similar to those operating among other orthodox people, such as the religious workers' party. Among all of them there is a sensation of heightened self-worth, of moving into what they consider their rights as citizens. The orthodox conceive of their styles of life and viewpoints as increasingly vindicated by the erosion of secular socialism. Whereas many young people have left kibbutz life and embraced materialism (not to mention that kibbutz life itself has become much more bourgeois than it ever was), the ranks of the ultra-orthodox are bursting. The rate of self-reproduction is high, with families of eight and more children quite common. More, there is a very small but vocal segment of ultra-orthodoxy, composed of people who have shifted there from a style of secular living, and this phenomenon is another cause of high morale and pride for all orthodox people.

One expression of this morale is the increasing phenomenon of self-help organisations, in ultra-orthodox circles in particular. People innovate imaginatively so as to be able to offer philanthropic service. A multitude of tiny volunteer organisations provide for a great variety of needs: loans of bedding and cutlery for people hosting and celebrating, loans of loaves of bread and cartons of milk and baby's dummies for

3.   Thus it is incorrect to interpret the ongoing bickering between the hassidic ultra-orthodox and their 'Lithuanian' opponents (specifically, Rabbi Schneersohn, the head of Habad hassidim, and Rabbi Schach, the head of 'the Lithuanians') as implying significant foreign policy differences, with the hassidim being hawkish and their opponents moderate. In fact, all major factions of ultra-orthodoxy are highly pragmatic in the terms outlined. The infighting is focused on internal matters of religious nature (such as the role of the hassidic leader in society and in respect to Messianism), and on most mundane matters connected with resources of funds and followers. Rabbinical infighting, and social and intellectual discourse generally in Eastern European Jewry in the eighteenth and nineteenth centuries, gained an increasingly abrasive character, and this is carried over also to contemporary life. Thus, infighting among the ultra-orthodox is maintained in strident tones. Insiders do not take the colourful abusive idioms and metaphors literally, but outsiders (as most political commentators are) often do so. This observation about the nature of debate among the ultra-orthodox applies also to the topics that are chosen for dispute. Thus, to return to the analysis of positions over the Jewish-Arab conflict, shades and nuances of different positions of ultra-orthodox faction-leaders are conflated and brought to extremes. In confronting his rival, Rabbi Schach minimises all points of agreement and emphasises points of disagreement. Therefore, he and his followers present him as a dove of kinds, to contrast Rabbi Schneersohn's articulated hawkishness.

people who suddenly find themselves in a predicament at a time when stores are closed, not to mention loans of interest-free cash, and many others. It is remarkable that these ventures do not cater exclusively to the particular in-group of the orthodox activists. On the contrary, activists often pride themselves in providing service to one and all.

There is an element of patronizing here: orthodox people see themselves as superior *vis-à-vis* others whom they consider decadent, and being in a position to assist those aliens bolsters their sense of religio-cultural status. This phenomenon dovetails with the pioneering drive in the West Bank settlement effort. Both activities are, *inter alia*, expressions of the enhanced self-image of the orthodox as well as means to sustain that image. In contemporary anthropological parlance, these doings are both models of and models for the new existential reality of inverted statuses, as experienced by the orthodox. The overall effect of all this is a significant, salient and general shift of the orthodox strategy, away from isolation, centrism and leftism – towards the right-wing pole.

The discussion so far has been focused on the orthodox of Ashkenazi (Northern European) background. Pertinent developments among Sephardim are different from those we have followed in matters of detail only. However, these differences are sufficiently salient to warrant separate discussion of the two social strata. Moreover, the nature of Sephardic religiosity is somewhat different from that of the orthodox Ashkenazim. Therefore, I now reserve usage of the term 'orthodox' for people of Ashkenazi background, and when referring to people of Middle Eastern background, even when clearly observant, I use the general term 'Sephardim', although that term encompasses people of vastly different levels of observance.[4]

The Sephardim appeared massively on the Israeli scene only with the onset of unrestricted immigration, after 1948. In Israel they found themselves in a setting that was clearly dominated by Ashkenazim, and in particular by those of secular-socialist persuasion, the Labour-Mapai establishment. The nature of ensuing relationships between the latter and the immigrants has been recounted many times, and need not be repeated (see, for instance, Smooha 1978; Ben-Rafael 1982; Weingrod 1985). The

---

4. I cannot, in the present context, elaborate on the considerations that underlie these statements. This is offered in my article cited in note 1.

point to be emphasised in the present context is that the orthodox experience had much in common with that of the Sephardim, in terms of subordination to and sometimes discrimination by the socialists. The major difference between the orthodox and the Sephardim lay in the fact that the former came to assert themselves in the mid-1950s, one generation in time before the Sephardim, in the course of the process that I have outlined. The Sephardim, on the other hand, remained dominated by Labour-Mapai institutions, and largely quiescent, until the mid-1970s. In terms of both culture and politics the Sephardim long remained passive, content to be junior partners in socialist-run institutions, much like the old religious workers' party. Because of details unique to the situation of the Sephardim, the change, when it came in the late 1970s, was dramatic. Sephardic personalities were propelled to prominent positions, instead of the socialists who were then replaced by a right-wing government led by the Likud Party.

Crucially, in common with the orthodox, the Sephardim to this day nurture bitterness toward the socialists. There is also a parallel between the development of pragmatism *vis-à-vis* the State among the ultra-orthodox, upon which I remarked earlier, and developments among the Sephardim. In the course of the 1980s there emerged a politically articulate group of ultra-orthodox Sephardim, the Shas Party, that has become a significant political factor. The agenda of Shas is to establish schools and yeshivot which would revive old Sephardic traditions and lead people to heightened ethnic-orthodox observance. In a fashion parallel with that of other ultra-orthodox groups Shas maintains a pragmatic attitude towards the State, as is exemplified in its tactics for coalition formation. Matters of state, security, economy, and so forth, are of relatively minor consideration for Shas politicians.[5]

The dialogue of the deaf

This review of religious and social developments affords us a fresh perspective on Israeli positions concerning Arab–Jewish

---

5. The phenomenon of Sephardic religious resurgence is described in Weingrod (1990), Ben-Ari and Bilu (1987) and Goldberg (1987). For the beginnings of the phenomena, see Deshen and Shokeid (1974). On the Shas phenomenon in particular, there is a Hebrew article (Deshen 1989).

settlement proposals. Israelis holding hawkish positions, whom I introduced at the beginning of this paper, view their opponents who maintain dovish positions in a particular way. As an outcome of the developments that I have traced, right-wing Israelis of many shades – orthodox, ultra-orthodox, Sephardim – view the doves negatively. In the eyes of right-wing Israelis the latter are morally tainted. Most of the doves are of Ashkenazi secular background, and this implies that they will tend to be of middle-class standing materially. Since they have relatively few children, the doves are conceived as being relatively secure in terms of standard of living, income and social status. At the same time, the doves make claims of a humane and social nature, in the context of the international conflict, on behalf of the Arabs. This complex combination causes the hawks to view the doves as hypocrites. They are conceived as mouthing leftist slogans while personally remote from, and insensitive to, the needy in their immediate environment. They are seen to agitate about injuries done to Palestinians, but apathetic when their fellow Jews are hurt.

The doves are seen to nurture alien values, because they present their positions as founded on considerations of human rights, civil rights, minority rights, academic freedom, democracy. In the eyes of contemporary popular interpreters of Judaism in Israel, such as most rabbis, all these values are seen as foreign and clashing with orthodox religion.[6] To take a concrete instance. Two private radio stations in Israel, Kol Ha'shalom and 'Arutz Sheva, propagate the left and right wings' positions respectively. Both stations are similar in mostly featuring light music and songs, thinly interspersed with explicitly ideological rhetoric. There is, however, a glaring difference in the style and covert atmosphere that the two stations convey. Kol Ha'shalom offers a diet of American peace

---

6. These statements are consistent with findings of the American Jewish scene. The following summarises a recent synthesis of research: 'In many ways, non-Orthodox American Jews have deservedly acquired a reputation for adopting social, political and sexual attitudes more liberal than their non-Jewish contemporaries . . . In contrast, the most traditionalist Orthodox generally espouse the most conservative orientations in these areas . . . they are typically more nonliberal on public policy questions for reasons having to do with religious law, institutional concerns, and private morality . . . Between these two poles stand the modern Orthodox who express views between the liberalism of the non-Orthodox and the conservatism of the traditionalists' (Heilman and Cohen 1989: 178–9). To this I would add that the Israeli parallels of the American 'modern Orthodox' are in retreat. In terms of both numbers and moral salience, they have become weaker over the years.

songs and much of the verbiage is hence in English. The rival station offers an exclusive diet of Israeli songs, in particular those with themes of patriotism and attachment to land and nature. 'Arutz Sheva also offers popular religious songs and Sephardic songs, both of religious and of pop nature. This selection leads to an exclusively Hebrew language programme. The covert message that the stations convey is therefore that dovishness is associated with alienness and lack of roots, while hawkishness is associated with the opposite. Clearly, the effect of this image of the dovish station, in terms of moving public opinion, is one of unmitigated self-imposed defeat.

Being popularly seen as both distant from Jewish yearnings and beliefs, and as actual hypocrites, the doves and their agenda altogether lack credibility. In effect, the different positions over the Arab-Jewish conflict become vastly ramified and heavy with symbolic meaning. In the eyes of the orthodox the positions of the doves and the hawks are associated with diffuse cultural differences. It is part of the great clash between those faithful to the heritage of Jewry on the one hand, and the rootless on the other hand, between 'Guardians of the Torah' and detractors of the Torah, between goodness and corruption. This magnification by right-wing partisans of a particular political stand, on an issue that is essentially political, is an important social fact. Though the magnification may be unfounded in terms of reality beyond that of orthodox-hawkish beholders, the fact that they view the situation in this way is itself a crucial element of the social reality. This has important ramifications for internal Israeli foreign policy debates, and ultimately also for overall chances of a non-violent Arab-Jewish settlement. To these we now proceed.

In the prevailing political debate, both outside Israel and within the country, moderate-dovish positions are promoted primarily by left-wing moral and ideological considerations. Thus, for instance, the management of the intifada, the Israeli handling of West Bank schools and universities, the policy towards the establishment of a Palestinian state, are all faulted as being brutal, injurious of human dignity and national rights, violating freedom, and so forth. These criticisms may or may not be valid. But the crucial point, which flows from the foregoing analysis, is that these criticisms do not engage the minds of precisely those protagonists to whom they are addressed, right-wing Israelis. Moral arguments are resonant primarily to Israeli protagonists of dovish convictions. But the latter do not require convincing. Among hawkish people who are secular such arguments might indeed be effective. However, I argued earlier that the hard-core of the right wing does not lie among them.

Hawkish positions are currently not founded on any secular étatist-type ideology. Secular hawkish people maintain an ideological partnership with the orthodox, and it is from the latter that they obtain moral and symbolic support for their positions. The core of the right wing is among the orthodox, who offer to the pragmatic hawks ideological grounding for their positions, primordial images and visions of history. This grounding is combined with pragmatic considerations, such as the risks entailed in permitting or forbidding the operation of West Bank schools, of retaining or retreating from territories, of a Palestinian state – in short, the tragically realistic dangers of compromise.

An attempt to influence Israeli public opinion to move beyond the present tie and deadlock of political views, must be tailored to reach the hawkish position at its crux. Namely, it must be articulated in terms that are reasonable to orthodox people, and not in terms that are obnoxious to them. Paradoxically, it is precisely the richness of dovish positions, in terms of liberal ideology, that causes these positions to be repugnant to orthodox people. On the other hand, it is the shallowness of hawkish positions, in terms of lacking an étatist and fascist ideology, which enables them to be accepted by the orthodox. The debate of doves and hawks in Israel may be summarised as follows. Much of contemporary dovish rhetoric consists essentially of sermons to the converted, and fails to engage (not to mention convince) those whom it most crucially ought to address.

My aim is to formulate a dovish mode of discourse which would overcome this problem. The formulation of such a discourse entails consideration of the various costs of a non-violent settlement to the relevant categories of protagonists. The first such category I proceed to consider is that of the orthodox right wing. Among them the premium on a non-violent settlement is not high, because of the extreme valuation of the actualisation of the ancient dream, the recovery of the entire ancestral Land of Israel. For that any price is tolerable, including armed conflict within the foreseeable future.

The second pertinent category of people is that of the principled left wing, namely people of liberal and socialist background whose secular convictions – humanism, equality, minority rights, self-determination, and so forth – lead them to a willingness to pay the costs of a non-violent settlement. Namely, to undertake the risks of compromise, such as exposed borders, the hazards of a Palestinian state, the threat of armed hostile neighbours. Crucially, however, for this dovish category of people there is a particular cost that they are not called upon to pay. Since they are remote from traditional Jewish beliefs and myths, the dream of a regained Temple Mount, Judea and Samaria (not to mention the Gilead and Bashan regions in present-day Jordan) are not meaningful. Resigning these territories to Arab domination is not very painful to them. The gulf between such left-wing people of principle and the first category of people is therefore very great.

For both these categories of Israelis, the attainment of a non-violent settlement entails accepting the risks of peace, but only for the orthodox right wing does it entail forgoing some of the great yearnings and passions of their religion. Seen from this perspective the clamour of the doves for concessions on the part of the hawks is cheap; it requires relatively little from them and much from their opponents. It is no wonder then that in over two decades of intensive and articulate debate between these protagonists the doves have not advanced their viewpoint in any significant way among the orthodox. One might indeed marvel at the fact that this dialogue of the deaf has been maintained for so many years, without realisation of its futility. This leads us to consider the position of a third category of people over the Arab-Jewish conflict, that of moderates not out of ideological conviction, but out of pragmatic considerations.

These people, pragmatic doves, are not moved by secular ideological commitments of the kind that motivate the ideological left wing. Due to their lack of secular ideological commitment the pragmatic doves may in fact be attuned to the traditional national and mythical values, that propel the orthodox in connection with the Land of Israel and the Temple Mount. The pragmatic doves, however, contrary to the orthodox, are resigned to forgo their yearnings as a part of the price to be paid for a non-violent settlement. The particular price that these moderates are willing to pay is higher than that of

their dogmatic left-wing colleagues, because for them the value
of liberating the whole ancestral territory is a serious issue, not
an inherently repelling position. We have now arrived at an
important point in the analysis. There is more affinity between
the pragmatic dovish and the orthodox positions than there is
between the latter and the ideological dovish position. Before
finally proceeding to the important practical recommendation
that flows from this analysis, and which is the main point of the
discussion, an aside must be made to introduce a pertinent facet
of rabbinical Judaism. Ever since its formation in antiquity, and
into our times, Judaism as a religio-legal system has been
positively receptive of pragmatic considerations.[7] Thus,
rabbinical principles of decision-taking include considerations,
that a particular course of action might lead to 'mortal danger',
'enmity', or 'great material loss'. Such considerations are
religiously and legally legitimate in various particular contexts.
It is important to note that those are not considerations that the
rabbinical system incorporates out of external overpowering
duress; rather, they are internal to the system.

Thus to cite a classical example, when a person is permitted,
upon rabbinical discretion based on considerations such as the
aforementioned, to perform an action that is normally prohibited
on the Sabbath, that person is viewed as having nevertheless
sanctified the Sabbath. Moreover, refraining from engaging in an
action on the Sabbath under such conditions is considered sinful.
Transposing this facet of traditional Judaism onto the political
problem at hand we are led to a second important point.
Namely, the pragmatic dovish position is more attuned to the
orthodox one, not only because the cost of a non-violent
settlement is broadly similar for both, but also because
pragmatic considerations are considered in the rabbinical
tradition as inherently reasonable and legitimate.

We arrive at the following conclusion. The prevailing debate
between doves and hawks in Israel is bound to be inconclusive,
because the discourse is formulated in the strident terms of
contrasting world-views. The orthodox consider their opponents

---

7. The literature on Jewish religion in general is voluminous. For an excellent balanced
account that spells out the role of pragmatic considerations in a particular area of Jewish
practice, see Katz (1989).

depraved, their positions equally so, and they have no reason to wish to be convinced otherwise. However, if the doves were to present their position in exclusively pragmatic terms, the orthodox, in terms of their own world-view, could not easily lend them a deaf ear. There would at least be a serious engagement of views. From the perspective of people of left-wing ideological persuasion, the forgoing of ideological and moral pathos, and the presentation of their position in pragmatic terms, would entail a significant price. Namely, disregarding some of their deep ideological commitments in the area of human rights. It would, of course, not require acting against these commitments, but it would require realisation that the ideology is irrelevant, worse – self-defeating, in the social reality of contemporary Israel. That is indeed a price to pay, but it is not greater than the parallel ideological price that is paid by pragmatic doves who forgo mythic visions (not to mention the few orthodox people who maintain a dovish position).

Two decades of injurious self-presentation on the part of the left, ever since the 1967 war, are one of the causes for the current frightening ossification in the position of the Israeli right wing. The blame for this falls not only on Israelis of dovish ideological persuasion, but also on foreign friends of Israel among the left. The damage of the prevailing self-presentation of the left *vis-à-vis* its opponents requires to be repaired. This may indeed be ideologically distressing to maintainers of dovish positions, whose convictions are fuelled by leftist and liberal values. However, moving Israeli public opinion is of such strategic importance in the quest for a resolution of the Jewish-Arab conflict, that the matter warrants that price. In short, the pursuit of peace requires a price from one and all, not only from the rightwing hawks, but also from the doves.

This analysis of Israeli doves and hawks uncovers some of the potentiality of contemporary anthropology. We have moved far from the dispassion and detachment of earlier generations of anthropologists, in the heyday of evolutionism and functionalism. The present analysis is the product of a complex commitment, both to one's home society and to anthropology, as a discipline of social commitment and critical insight. The outcome is a fresh view of mainline social positions that leads to the formulation of a new agenda.

In one sense this kind of anthropological discourse is novel. Indeed, ever since the 1960s, anthropologists have not always been satisfied to serve the establishment and to remain disengaged from the people they studied. They have often adopted committed stances in the field, in favour of the disinherited and discriminated. But in taking that option, those anthropologists acted as moral humans; their choice was not commonly fuelled by insight that was particular and unique to the discipline. In contrast, the point of the present analysis is that the practice of the discipline, in a rigorous, methodological sense of the term, can lead to committed conclusions. Chances are that such conclusions, informed with insight that is marked by conventions of methodology, and not just by moral passion and high-mindedness, will be detailed and specific. As the present Israeli example demonstrates, the recommendations are addressed to particular categories of people and take into account individual configurations of social circumstances. Such conclusions, one may reasonably hope, will be of greater applicability than others, that are fired primarily by moral passion, and formulated in generality.

Acknowledgement

I am thankful to friends and colleagues who criticised the thesis of this paper and commented in writing, particularly Aviezer Ravitzky, Ya'aqov Shavit, Moshe Shokeid and Dafna Yizraeli.

Chapter 4

Foreign myths and sagas in Japan: the academics and the cartoonists

Halldór Stefánsson

The present article[1] is a case study of the mechanism and the process involved in what is taken to be a particular Japanese way of relating to phenomena originating in the outside world. What follows is an investigation into what happened when the Icelandic classics voyaged to Japan. That adventurous trip was promoted by two remarkably different agents: first, in the form of scholarly translations into Japanese of the sagas and the Edda; and subsequently, as free adaptations and elaborations of themes borrowed from these sources by a number of Japanese authors of cartoons, whose work is the stuff on which the popular culture of Japan has thrived in the postwar period. Since the 1960s, all the major sagas and both the prose and the poetic

1. Living in Japan for any length of time one becomes keenly aware, not only of oneself observing others, but equally of others observing oneself. Over the period of eight years of returning intermittently to the study of ancestors and death rituals in a village community in central Japan, I managed to spin out a minor network of loyal friends-informants. Over the same period of time, I have also been sought out by a certain number of individuals, amateurs as well as distinguished researchers and scholars of Germanic studies with special interests in old Icelandic literature. Apart from the occasional tourist, expatriate Icelanders are an extremely rare species in the land of the rising yen; so I have become their privileged informant-friend. Some of these people have come to me with all sorts of (in-)credible questions: What was the nature of fictive kinship among the original settlers in Iceland? How did men go about becoming 'blood-brothers'? What were the acts that accompanied the use of the 'runic' writing for magical purposes among the Vikings? Did I think that there may have been real Valkyries (the Nordic counterpart to the Amazonians?) who decided to settle and cool off in Iceland?, etc.

Repeatedly finding myself, as it were, 'on the wrong side of the table', in the role of the informant, the idea occurred to me to anthropologise the Japanese anthropologising me. In other words, I decided to study and write about the gateways, however minor in importance they may be, that have opened up for and introduced the old Icelandic literary classics into Japan.

Edda have been translated into Japanese. I have studied the
writings of and interviewed two of the pioneers of this subject,
the two most prolific among the translators. In so doing I
wanted to clarify three things; first, their evaluation of the object
of their studies, the Icelandic classics. Second, the specific
technical and cultural problems they have had to tackle, in
opening up the world of the Icelandic classics to a Japanese
readership. And third, their general evaluation of the role of the
translator in the process of transmission of foreign culture.

The second part of this paper is a comparison and analysis of
the works of two further representatives of the transmission of
the Nordic classics into Japanese culture. This time, I am
concerned with what happens when this material is handled in a
way free from scruples about authenticity (problems tackled by
the scholarly translator), when the agent of transmission is fully
liberated from the burden of the obligation to preserve the
presupposed identity and integrity of the Other.

After presenting in some detail the particular nature of the
Japanese production of cartoons, I describe and analyse what
happened when the sagas found their way into them. As in the
section on the academic translations, I have, for presentational
purposes, chosen to focus on the two representative agents of
this sort of cultural transmission which, to my knowledge have
made the most noteworthy contributions. Here, I rely solely on
visual images, since they, as it were, 'speak for themselves'. I try
to show how each of the cartoonists studied applies the raw
material (the Nordic classics) in ways and for purposes that are
part and a parcel of the local cartoon genre, primarily for
relating things about Self through the manipulation of the face of
an Other.

Japanese scholars as agents of cultural transmission

The first person to introduce saga literature to the Japanese was
an Irishman of Greek descent, the globe-trotting Lafcadio Hearn
(1850–1904), alias Koizumi Yakumo who settled in Japan and
lived there for the greater part of his life, even becoming a
Japanese citizen. He spent his time writing fascinating accounts
of the exotic customs and lore of the 'yet unspoilt' Japanese,
whom he truly loved and admired. Towards the end of his life

(1896–1903), Hearn also taught a course on western literature at the English Department of the Imperial University in Tokyo (Sugawara 1976: 24). Among the texts he introduced to his pupils were Sturlunga saga and Njal's saga. In his lectures he elaborated on what he saw as some of the striking characteristics of these ancient texts. These he summarised as (1) the limited use of adjectives; (2) succinct, laconic descriptions; and (3) the concealment of emotions. He emphasised how the saga-narrative is never burdened with complicated accounts of events taking place in individual psychology. In spite of this absence of literary subtleties in the manuscripts, Hearn marvelled at their capacity to evoke emotions in the hearts of their readers.

Evidently, Hearn's teachings did not reach a wide audience during his lifetime. The number of students pursuing higher education at the time was, of course, very limited, and since he taught in English the language barrier would certainly have been a major obstacle. Hearn's lectures were rediscovered more than a half a century later when serious interest in translating the works of old Icelandic literature began to manifest itself in the Japanese academic world and his contribution was warmly appreciated by these pioneers in the new field of Germanic-Nordic studies.

During the 1960s and 1970s a growing number of academics at Japanese universities were working in areas that brought them into contact with old Icelandic literature. In two or three places, in departments of foreign languages, courses were established in Old Norse, and some departments also organised courses in Danish, Norwegian and Swedish. German, on the other hand, following English as the most popular foreign language taught in Japanese universities, has in some places been supplemented with a general introduction to the history and culture of the Germanic peoples. In the mid-1970s, at the Osaka University of Foreign Languages, Sugawara Kunishiro made the first ever systematic bibliographic survey of all there was to be found in Japanese relating to Icelandic classical literature. According to his estimate, about twenty individuals or institutions were involved in what he called 'Old Nordic studies' (Sugawara 1976: 27).

In the late 1970s, Sugawara and Taniguchi Yukio (formerly at the National University of Hiroshima, now at Osaka Gakuin University) co-founded the Japanese Association of Icelandic

Studies (Aisurando Kenky-kai). These two scholars are not only the founders of the Aisurando Kenky-kai, but are also the undisputed leaders of Icelandic studies in the country. Not only have they translated numerous sagas and related texts, but they have also published learned articles in Japanese journals, even entire books of textual analysis of the saga literature (Taniguchi 1976). My two 'subjects', being both Japanese and colleagues of the same profession, obviously have much in common. Viewed individually, however, they could hardly be more different. One, Sugawara Kunishiro, is a linguist, a specialist in Scandinavian philology. The other, Taniguchi Yukio, specialised in Germanic studies with wide-ranging interests in comparative folklore. Both scholars have spent considerable time working abroad, Sugawara in Denmark, Sweden and Iceland, and Taniguchi mainly in Germany.

On the subject of the three questions singled out for enquiry, the two translators were in perfect agreement about the first, concerning why they became interested in the saga literature. Quoting Sugawara: 'One might well wonder what most of all attracts Japanese admirers of Old Icelandic literature. Certainly its high literary quality in itself, and probably also the "Viking" morality, revealed in many poems and sagas, which has striking resemblance to the morality cherished by the Japanese in the course of the centuries' (Sugawara 1976: 25).

In Taniguchi's view the sagas have, in addition to their literary value, a vital importance as historical sources on innumerable aspects of both material and spiritual life in medieval Europe. While they are quite obviously works of fiction, they are works spun out of the real experiences of their authors, enriched by those of their ancestors, and handed down by the collective memory of oral tradition. Taniguchi stresses the degree of realism that he believes characterises the sagas and sets them apart from the rest of medieval European literature.

Taniguchi, furthermore, names some special, non-technical reasons why the sagas, as he put it, 'translated themselves so successfully' in his mind, and proceed, presumably, to translate themselves quite smoothly to the minds of his readers. He argues that these secondary reasons are of an historical and cultural nature. The plots and the general mood of the sagas call to the mind of the average Japanese reader images from their own historical fiction (Heike monogatari, Hôgen-heiji monogatari, Senki monogatari, etc.), which depict a time when clans were opposed to each other in an endless, murderous struggle for power. Japanese medieval monogatari, like the Icelandic sagas, are replete with vendettas and feuds between antagonistic groups organised around their leading families. The Japanese monogatari, just like the sagas, make use of legendary accounts of outstanding, power-hungry chieftains and of super-human endurance and fabulous exploits on the part of their heroes. In Taniguchi's view it is in many ways easier for a Japanese reader to understand the 'archaic' mentality animating the protagonists of the saga literature than the Judeo-Christian-based breed that supplanted it. The Japanese feel familiar with what they see in the sagas as a fatalistic vision of human destiny, a pragmatic view of man's relationship with supernatural powers, and a system of values strongly oriented to this world - emphasising courage, material wealth and shrewdness in the art of accumulating other people's loyalty and power.

As for the second question, with regard to the technical and cultural obstacles in the process of translating the Icelandic classics into Japanese, the two scholars hold similar views about the nature of the major problems encountered. On the other hand, they do not fully agree about how to solve them. Sugawara (1974, 1976) is undoubtedly the Japanese scholar who has contributed most to the issue of methodology and authenticity in translations of Nordic, and particularly old Icelandic, literature. He has singled out problems relating to concepts and terms of central importance in the original texts which have no exact equivalents in Japanese. He raises the difficult question of what to do with these words. When should they be translated, or glossed with Japanese approximates, and when should they be left the way they are, simply rendered phonetically in the text?

Another technical problem that Sugawara has attacked concerns the radical differences in the phonetic systems of the original and the receiving language, i.e. how to transliterate Nordic proper names into Japanese.[2] In an important paper

---

2.   He is referring to categories such as 'bóndi', 'godi', 'thingmadur', 'berserkr', 'víkingur', 'althing', etc. There has reigned an unfortunate inconsistency among Japanese translators as to how to handle these terms. For 'althing' alone there have been at least four different Japanese translations: 'Kokkai'; 'Zento kaigi'; 'Kokumin gikai'; 'Dai-minkai' (Sugawara 1976: 28).

Sugawara (1974) has attempted to lay down general guidelines for Japanese translators on how to transliterate in Japanese proper names in the sagas. He seems to recommend relying on the rules of pronunciation in modern Icelandic (IP), whereas Taniguchi, in keeping with his Germanic background, is in favour of following what is believed to be an approximation to, or a reconstruction of, the language spoken throughout Scandinavia in the early medieval age (RP).

Both Sugawara and Taniguchi consider Japanese scholarship on the sagas and Edda as having often been of a very uneven quality. Sugawara notes that 'many writings display a lack of fundamental knowledge' (Sugawara 1976: 27), and gives examples of translations so full of mistakes that the originals become hardly recognisable. There have also been authors writing on themes relating to ancient European history in scholarly journals, who have referred to the sagas and the Edda in a totally irresponsible, if not outright misleading way. Some have gone to the other extreme of plagiarising their sources, taking passages directly from them and inserting them into their own works without the use of quotation marks, as if these were their own accounts of past events. Fortunately, however, it seems the number of these abuses in 'serious' publications have been decreasing over the years.

In addition to the numerous sagas that he has translated over the last twenty years, Taniguchi has also undertaken the much more onerous task of translating, or maybe rather transcribing, poems of the Edda.[3] In his view, the ultimate difficulty in translation is presented by Scaldic poems. They were composed with a rhythmic rise and fall of stressed and unstressed syllables, totally alien to the phonetics of the Japanese language, which can only replace this with regularity in the number of characters in a poetic line. No effort on behalf of the Japanese translator can properly overcome these technical difficulties. Taniguchi reminisced about how he used to envy German and Scandinavian translators of the Icelandic classics, whose works he consulted along with the originals when translating old

---

3.   Taniguchi's translation of the Edda has come out in fifteen editions. His collection of Saga translations is now in its fifth edition. It first came out in 1500 copies, and then 500 at the time of each supplementary edition. The Edda translation was first published in 2500 copies, and then about 1000 in each of the later editions. The introductory book *Saga to Edda* has sold in the greatest numbers of exemplars, originally published in about 2500 and then 1500 in the subsequent twelve editions.

Icelandic poems, since they could often work out combinations of syllables that at least resembled the sound structure of the original verses.

Taniguchi reckons that compared to the ancient poetry, translating the sagas into Japanese was a relatively easy task. Reading and rereading them, telling them and teaching them for more than thirty years has permitted him, in his own words, to ingest them mentally, not unlike the people who supposedly transmitted them orally in the beginning. But he thinks that even after being 'immobilised' in the form of a text, the sagas still retain a great deal of their oral character. This survival of an oral element, even in its written form, is, he thinks, crucial in explaining why they lend themselves so well to translations into Japanese, or any other language, for that matter.

In translating foreign texts, Taniguchi professes to pursue the way of natural simplicity. He prefers to see his relationship to the readers of his translations as parallel to the one that originally obtained between the saga-teller and his audience. 'While striving never to diverge from the original story', he said in an interview, 'the most important thing is to tell it in language that permits the artistic work to rise again like a phoenix reborn to a new life in a different culture.'

Then there is the third question of how Sugawara and Taniguchi conceive of their role in relation to the foreign literary tradition. What do they emphasise? Here some subtle differences can also be seen to distinguish the two Japanese scholars. For Sugawara, 'it goes without saying that every translator should be well versed in Old Icelandic and have a reasonable knowledge of Old Scandinavian as a whole' (Sugawara 1976: 29). He also recommends the mastery of modern Icelandic as an aid in saga translations (Sugawara 1974: 246–7). In addition to the indispensable mastery of the language, he seems to think that the ideal qualifications for accomplishing the task of translating the sagas would be those combining a poet and a linguist in the same person (Sugawara 1976: 29). Poetic talent permits insight into the literary products of foreign cultures, while linguistic competence must be the privileged guardian of their authenticity when they are taken abroad, dressed up in the new garments of an alien language.

Taniguchi's emphasis is much more on the 'creative' aspects of the work of translation. He insists that a literary translation is not to be considered in the same terms as plain technical translation. When translating a literary text it is essential not just to cling to one-to-one correspondences between terms in different languages, but rather to seek to transmit the artistic quality that gave value to the original work at the moment of its creation and enabled it to move its audience. Thus the role of the translator is, as it were, to re-enact the original inspiration that gave life to the work, and thereby to permit it to be reborn in another language. This re-creative role obviously demands the utmost degree of self-discipline on behalf of the translator not to drift radically away from the original.

In the same vein, Taniguchi stresses that translations should be done with ordinary enlightened readers in mind. They have to be able to enjoy reading them, which requires the translator's seeking primarily spontaneity and smoothness in the transmission of their meaning. Taniguchi says:

> when working on the sagas, I try to concentrate primarily on capturing the enchanting flow of their narrative, since the ultimate goal is to enrapture the reader and send him down its stream. To put it in other words, literary translations could be likened to the performing act of musicians. The partitions are composed and written down by the composer, the author, but then they are uniquely 'translated' into the sounds of music by the performer, delivered by him and, through him, to the audience. The work of translation does not only imply the rendition of all sorts of rhythmical nuances – andante, allegro, or presto – that may carry the work at each moment, but just as much the sentiments that the performer exercises himself to lend to them in his quest for capturing their spirit. (Taniguchi 1984: 67)

To summarise, Sugawara conceives of his role as serving as a link between, on the one hand, the 'foreign' existing out there, where it should be sought out and grasped in its essence, and, on the other hand, the 'laboratories' of the different departments of Japanese universities where the findings should be further analysed in the quest for academic knowledge. Taniguchi, on the other hand, considers himself to be a mediator between the timeless products of artistic genius born on the outside, and the common people at the grass-root level of Japanese society. Instead of submitting himself to an analytical pursuit of the essential nature of the products of the Other, to accomplish his task he rather tends to stress the original 'magic' to be recreated with empathy. While he is, in his own way, a serious and accomplished scholar, Taniguchi's latter attitude can be seen as having played a key role in permitting the 'digestion' of the Nordic classics by Japanese cartoonists, who, undoubtedly, are among the most efficient agents of cultural borrowing in modern Japan.

The Japanese re-visions of the sagas

The world of manga: *Japanese cartoons*

Manga (or the somewhat more pompous *gekiga*) is the term the Japanese use for the products of their cartoon industry.[4] A typical manga is normally published as a 200–300 page thick, loosely bound paperback in large format. It is printed in black and white on recycled paper of poor quality in stark contrast to the conspicuously colourful, shiny cover. Each volume commonly contains several stories, different genres sometimes being mixed together. The more successful of these monthly or bi-monthly *manga* publications can reach astronomical sales of 2–4 million copies, and many of these are later re-edited and published in a smaller hardcover edition. There are piles of *manga* available to customers in public places all over Japan, in coffee houses, at the dentist's, at the barber's, in the laundries, etc. Anywhere the Japanese can be found waiting there is likely to be a great supply of *manga* at hand for distraction. In Japan it is a common sight to see people standing upright packed in groups in libraries reading *manga* for hours. There is even a special term for such behaviour. It is called '*tachiyomi*' ('stand-reading'). Sociologists in Japan have estimated (Pons 1988: 428) that Japanese youngsters commonly absorb as many as forty volumes of *manga* every week. And yet, this age-group does not

4. One conspicuous characteristic of the Japanese *Manga* – as opposed, for example, to their American counterpart – is their authors' strict monopoly over their own creations. *Manga* characters are normally created by individual Japanese cartoonists who then continue to draw them all along, even after having had the success of turning them into a best-selling gold mine. Of course, there are cases in Japan of cartoonists teaming up with story-writers, and successful masters of the trade using the talent and hand-power of debuting neophytes, but a Japanese cartoon is always, from the beginning to the end, in principle if not in practice, created by an individual artist, and strongly identified with him or her by the fans. In Japan, there is no question of a cartoon character 'outliving' its author. A Japanese *manga* lives and dies with its author.

constitute the majority of *manga* readers in Japan; in fact, two-thirds of them are adults.

An essential characteristic of the Japanese *manga* is the systematic and specialised nature of their production. There is a multitude of coexisting genres, each with its own characteristics and styles. This diversification is far from being limited to recreation: 'The message that it passes on is a complex one and often gives voice to profound aspirations, frustrations and hopes of certain groups ("couches") in society' (Pons 1988: 410).

Many *manga* were at one time impregnated with ideological and political, as well as psychological, meanings. Sanpei Shirato's 'Ninja bugeicho', which first appeared in 1959, was epoch-making in the modern history of Japanese cartoons. It marked the beginning of a sub-species of *gekiga* modelled after the *jidaimono* ('historical pieces') of the kabuki theatre. Sanpei's stories were based on a serious preliminary enquiry into real and legendary events from past epochs in Japanese history which he then analysed from a Marxist perspective and reinterpreted in terms of the conflict between social classes. Often, the reading of Sanpei's comics required a considerable knowledge of Japanese history. The decline of the politically-oriented *manga* set in in the early 1970s. But this did not result in the disappearance of the genre of historical *manga*. On the contrary, it survived and flourished without the original radical impetus. *Jidaimono* in *manga* tended now to idealise the truly 'Japanese spirit' of the world of the samurai, and to stage and unfold plots of sado-masochistic deliria such as Hiroshi Hirata's 'Bushido zankoku monogatari'.

In the early 1970s the historical *gekiga* expanded and came to explore dramatic themes borrowed from foreign cultures. Interestingly, that particularity was reserved for the young girls' *manga* and ended up by marking these off as an independent genre of the industry (a subject to which I shall return).

The production of Japanese *manga* in the postwar period has developed a variety of new genres which specifically appeal to different age, sex and occupational groups. They have proliferated in their capacity of catering to the most diverse tastes and interests. The first of the major distinctions is the one between *Shonen manga* (boys' comics) and *Shojo manga* (girls' comics). The boys' *manga* are commonly concerned with the world of sports, and in Japanese sports nothing equals the importance of baseball. Their heroes are, therefore, often baseball players engaged in fierce competitions, opposing different high-school teams in highly dramatised encounters. Other sports also feature regularly as well: The martial arts of kendo, judo and karate are great favourites. There are also endless boys' *manga* depicting the fantastic worlds of giants and monsters, robots and spaceships.

The *manga* aimed at young girls are normally characterised by their 'romantic effect'. The heroines in girls' 6 *manga* are often 'foreign beauties' ('wakaranai kuni no bijin'), commonly long-legged blondes. When the main hero is a boy rather than a girl, the colour of his hair is also more often than not blond, and his body tends to be drawn with delicate features and he is dressed in decidedly feminine clothes, the result of which is an androgynous, elf-like being of obscure sexuality. Lately, most authors of women's *manga* tend to be women themselves, highly specialised in appealing to the sugar-sweet taste of young Japanese girls.

This fertile ground was first broken by Ikeda Riyoko whose two voluminous works of historical fiction, both based on foreign themes, were enormous successes: 'Berusaiyu no bara' ('The Rose of Versailles'), appearing originally in instalments totalling 1700 pages between 1972 and 1974, and 'Orufeusu no mado' ('Orpheus' window') also originally published as 'a never-ending story' in the girls' magazine *Seventeen* in 1975.

The *sarariman manga* ('the *manga* for office workers') first appeared in the 1970s and have progressively gained a tremendous popularity. They tend to show an image of working conditions and life in Japanese companies as radically different from the idealised one often projected in the West. They do not present us with the world of wonder thought to have produced the miracle of 'Japan as number one'. Quite the contrary, they tend rather to depict a world filled with frustrations and humiliations but in a humorous way that can be sarcastic, though never really critical.

Yet another sort of *manga*, which has enjoyed great popularity in recent years, are those caricaturing the life of high-school and university students in modern Japan. Some of these give expression for a keen perception of many of the sociological complications that result from the straitjacket nature of the Japanese education system. It can be maintained that the *manga*

serve Japanese youth as a means of relief from the pressure that
is put on them by the educational system. The *manga* have
become their privileged 'hang-outs': a world of fantasy
progressively replacing the real playgrounds that have been
wiped away with the organisation of urban life in the big cities
in the postwar period (Pons 1988: 483). As we have seen, there
seems to be no limit to the communicative appetite of the
Japanese *manga*: it is omnivorous. Lately, *manga* for educational
purposes have started invading the market. There are now
manga for teaching mathematics and physics and for initiating
people to the world of the stockmarket. The team left behind by
the late Osamu Tezuka is working on a 26 episode animated
manga version of The Bible for television. And the life-work, as
he puts it, of the cartoonist Ishinomori Shotaro (an author I shall
return to) is to make a record of the whole of Japanese history in
cartoon form – 48 hardback volumes of 225 pages each.
Ishinomori is assisted by a team of professors from the
prestigious Tokyo University for documentation.

The cartoonists' encounter with the sagas and the Edda

Hundreds of thousands, or perhaps rather millions of young
people in the English-speaking world have grown up as
passionate readers of one of the most popular among American
comic books, *The Mighty THOR*. It is a serialised monthly
sequence of stories about the adventures of the Nordic god Thor,
who is pictured as a blond superman, flying around with his
magical hammer opposing the destructive forces of evil that
keep attacking ever more balefully the world of gods and
humans (see Plate 4.1). It has already run to over 415 issues,
which represents around 30 years of publication history. The
mighty Thor is thus a slightly younger contemporary of the
more Mediterranean looking Superman. The image popularised
by *The Mighty THOR* has presumably been instrumental in
determining many people's conceptions of ancient Nordic
mythology in the English-speaking world.

Japanese cartoonists have clearly been familiar with *The
Mighty THOR*. They may even have been tempted to introduce
in one form or another the world of this hero to their Japanese
readership. But yet, the necessary conditions for Thor's (or for
that matter any other Super-Heroes') successful passage over the
Pacific seem to have been missing.

Plate 4.1. The American vision of Thor and Loki. (From 'The mighty THOR')

Two things may be suggested to explain this state of affairs. Umberto Eco has analysed the role of 'the positive hero' in western comics. The hero is perceived as a surrogate incarnation of 'the requests for power that the ordinary citizen raises without the possibility of satisfaction' (Eco 1976: 24–5).[5] But curiously enough, these cannot be the psychodynamics animating the Japanese *manga*. There, the super-hero of the western tradition is definitely not a common character offered for identification to their readers. The Japanese hero is rather prone to be of the nihilistic kind, the loser, or the victim. It has even been held that the Japanese are much more attracted by 'idols' than by 'heroes'.[6] This may help explain why Thor – in his crudest form of a 'positive hero', as a blond, blue-eyed mountain of muscles engaged in one brief, but more or less self-contained eschatological battle in every issue *ad infinitum* – did not appeal to the understanding and the sensibilities of Japanese authors of cartoons. Then there was a second major obstacle to Thor's leaping the Pacific. It consisted of a lack of introduction to the deeper and wider cultural background that the American Thor had sprung from as a modern-day hero, without which the Japanese authors could not possibly relate to the subject in their own personal way.

All this changed during the late 1960s, and all through the 1970s, when many of the Icelandic sagas and both the poetic and prose Edda were all translated into Japanese. This material, now within reach on the shelves of bookshops all over Japan, was bound to fall under the eyes of the omnivorous cartoonist, out hunting for material to fill his or her pages. In the following, I will briefly introduce the work of two representative cartoonists who have dealt with the subject. The former, Ishionomori Shotaro, who is also one of the most established masters in the field, is the first Japanese cartoonist known to have included his vision of the North and its cultural tradition in his cartoons. The latter, Azumi Ryo, is a relatively unknown author.

A cartoon-story for boys: the Edda as Japanese science fiction

More than twenty years ago, when Ishinomori started his career as a cartoonist, he came up with a fairly conventional idea for a cartoon story, but he developed it skilfully and originally. He created his CYBORG 009, a series of adventures about a

---

5. 'Exigence de puissance que le citadin ordinaire nourrit sans pouvoir les satisfaire.'
6. Umezu Kazuo, a Japanese cartoonist quoted by Ian Buruma in *The Asian Wall Street Journal*, 20 March 1980.

fabulous, international team of characters which soon became highly popular and continued to appear for many years (Ishinomori 1960). The work is made up of a succession of episodes ('-hen'). Each episode constitutes one of the ongoing, challenging adventures encountered by this international team of fabulous heroes, which assembles every now and then and goes on expeditions into fantastic worlds of mysteries, normally to fight all sorts of danger that are lurking there, threatening mankind. This in itself certainly does not sound very original. But the way the theme is adapted and developed to suit Japanese idiom, sensibilities and tastes, and the way, in a particular instance, the author made use of the Nordic cultural tradition, are the elements that may attract our attention.

First of all, instead of the handsome, macho muscle-mountain crushing all opposition single-handed, here we are presented with a team which works perfectly together in spite of the heterogeneous nature of its members. There are seven male members along with one female. The group has six foreigners (the outsiders), joining in with two central protagonists (the insiders). The former, although sympathetic in every respect, are pictured emphasising their funny, exotic sides. They are caricatured portraits of the different racial and cultural Others. This is suggested from the outset by their striking physical features, and their imperfect mastery of the Japanese language. The latter two are stylised, cute-looking adolescent characters, a boy and a girl with delicate features, and big eyes. When they are not on a mission, they live in Japan. She dances ballet and he drives a sports car. If nothing about their appearance alone (besides their miniscule noses) could make us suspect it, their manner of behaviour and speech tell us beyond doubt that they must be Japanese.

The episode that I want to focus on is relatively short for a Japanese comic story, only 160 pages long. It is called Edda (Nordic mythology), and is divided into three chapters, Skuld, Verdandi and Urd, after the three terrifying sorceresses who decide on the destiny of all living beings in the universe. Before entering the actual story, there is a brief three-page prelude sketching the cosmogynic account of Nordic mythology. The last image shows the three sorceresses seated at the roots of the world tree, the Axis Mundi, Yggdrasill, from where they decide upon the destiny of gods and humans.

The story proper then opens with the eight heroes gathering for a new expedition to accomplish a secret mission. They all fly off together to Iceland, that mysterious place on the edge of the inhabited world. The band of heroes then disembarks in the middle of the wilderness. At first, there is no sign of life. They are greeted by nothing but threatening mountains as they struggle against a violent snowstorm. The expedition proceeds, and the snowstorm changes into a thick fog. The ensuing story consists of series of escalating battles which the members of the team are drawn into against the intrigues and attacks of monsters and robots all bearing the names of divinities from the ancient Nordic pantheon. This encounter with the world of boreal monstrosities is then finally brought to an end with a 'grandiose finale', a total war destroying all the 'Nordic gods', and as in the original Edda, it is called Ragnarrök, 'Doom of the Gods'. Yggdrasill, the World Tree, is shaken to its roots, and finally blown up in a gigantic atomic explosion revealing that a time-machine mounted by a mad scientist had been concealed within it. The madman had travelled back from the future, halting in Iceland where he had set up his camp dressing it in the gown of the ancient mythology of the region.

A cartoon-story for girls: a Viking saga of patricide and love

Azumi Ryo is the pseudonym of one of the Japanese authors who write cartoon stories for girls. She has specialised in Nordic mythology and the Icelandic sagas, and has published, since 1986, two of her major works inspired by that literary tradition. The contrast with the work of the aforementioned Ishinomori Shotaro could not be sharper. Ishinomori made use of Nordic mythology for reconstructing a perfectly hostile world into which he then sent his easily identifiable heroes from the outside on a fantastic expedition. Azumi Ryo attempts to situate her fictional stories within the world of the Nordic literary tradition itself, trying to give the impression that her heroes are 'naturally' generated out of that environment. She creates the dramatic effect of her own 'sagas' out of 'real' historical themes borrowed from the past of the Nordic peoples. The general background is the so-called Viking-age, of the Nordic conquest of parts of the ancient and the new world, the unification of Norway into a single kingdom, the colonisation of Iceland and, most of all, the radical social and cultural impact of the conversion of the inhabitants of the Nordic countries to Christianity (reorganisation of authority and power within the elaborate 'new' structure of a church, the painful death of old gods and the birth of new ones). Into this macro-landscape of historical upheavals Azumi Ryo spins her epic stories. While these are filled with totally fictional characters, the key elements that make up the substance of their life-stories are often borrowed more or less directly from one or several, if not more, of the original Icelandic sagas. Recurring motifs marking the lives of the early settlers of Iceland and Viking heroes are employed further to substantialise fictional character formations.

'Akai Tsurugi' (The Scarlet Sword) is Azumi Ryo's major work so far. It was published in four volumes, each one about 200 pages in length, between 1986 and 1988. Like the 'Edda-hen' of Ishinomori's Cyborg 009, it begins with a four-page prologue picturing the Nordic cosmogynic myth, the heathen gods creating the universe from the body of the primordial giant, Ymir. The ensuing story is then made up by the editing of two parallel, intertwined narratives. They describe the world of the heathen gods in Asgard, struggling against the onslaught of their own apocalyptic end, their Ragnarrök, and the tumultuous, conflicting destiny of individual humans in vertiginous limbo, suspended between different world-views: the heathen and the Christian. The tension in that leitmotif oscillates between scenes unfolding dramatic action among the society of gods in Valhöll, the palace of Odin, and the society of mortal men in the Viking world, centring on Iceland.

Part I of the Scarlet Sword is called Ultima Thule. The era is towards the close of the tenth century. The first scene uses a well-known motif from several sagas ('the pursuit of revenge in foreign territories') to introduce the main hero of the story, Rŷu. He has disembarked on some small island (Shetland? Orkney?) for the purpose of taking revenge for the assassination of his kinsman, Uncle Snorri. Single-handedly, he kills a number of retainers who try to hold him back to get to the 'jarl', the earl responsible for the death of his kinsman. 'For that you will have to pay with your head,' he tells him, proving his earnestness by actually chopping it off. He then rushes off to his Viking boat, jumps aboard and sails away with his mates. The destination: Iceland.

This opening, with its classic scene of dramatic action, is then succeeded by the first of many informative windows presenting 'plain historical information' meant for progressively 'feeding the illusion of reality' into the ensuing story. A map filling up two whole pages illustrates the Scandinavian colonisation of Iceland via the Celtic Isles in the north Atlantic. The map is then supplemented in the best of the saga traditions with a genealogical account (taking the form of a genealogical tree) of the direct ancestors of the principal hero, tracing his descent back to the founder who first left Norway and moved to Iceland in 875. The genealogical tree presented shows a marked resemblance to the one provided in the famous Saga of Egill.

The name of the 'ætt', the kin-group to which the central hero belongs, is 'Grasida' (a name borrowed from The Saga of Gisli where it designates a legendary sword). The hero, having reached his twentieth year at the outset of the story, is a sixth generation descendant from the pivotal ancestor, Ragnar, who emigrated to Iceland rather than submit to the authority of the King of Norway. The young hero's full name is Lutrekr, but fortunately for Japanese readers their phonetic system does not distinguish between 'r' and 'l', so everybody just calls him Rŷu. 'Rŷu' is in fact a common component in Japanese names, often written with a Chinese character that signifies 'a dragon', a masculine symbol of strength, courage and long life.

Disregarding multiple details, the major plot revolves around Sigmund, the chieftain, who suspects (but never actually says!) that Rŷu, begotten to his wife, is not really his own flesh and blood. From the time of his birth he tries repeatedly, but unsuccessfully, to get rid of this disgraceful reminder of his humiliated pride. But through divine intervention the child survives every attempt on his life, and grows up to become the most handsome of young warriors. Yet a succession of events irrevocably severs the bond between father and son, and their ways part. The father undergoes a somewhat treacherous, and eventually fatal, Christian conversion, becoming a Viking missionary for Harald the Fair-Hair, King of Norway. Rŷu, on the contrary, remains 'a healthy heathen Viking', living by his sword, seducing men and women, totally free from the knowledge of sin and promise of salvation. The two are bound to clash at the end of the story. While the personification of heathendom, the son Rŷu, prevails over and kills the personification of Christendom, his father Sigmund, the inverse result turns the world upside down around them. The army of

Odin and his proud pantheon of divinities is swept aside by 'the White Christ', his apostles and angels.

How, then, could this apocalyptic theme possibly be made appetising to Japanese teenage girls? As mentioned before, a common trait of Japanese girls' cartoons is their particular way of appropriating things borrowed from foreign, historical and literary traditions, through conventionalised manipulations of their form as well as their contents. In the Scarlet Sword, a familiar repertoire of common devices is employed, skilfully blending in to the dramatised epic of the fictional characters the most sober, informative elements from the 'real' world of the sagas and the Edda. This free manipulation of things foreign for the creation of an apparent realism in the narrative account is further impressed upon the reader by a remarkable concern for the details of daily life and material culture. Landscape, interiors of houses, ornaments, house-work, cutting of wood, work in the fields, shipbuilding, etc., all this is depicted in the most realistic and convincing fashion.

As for the contents, the otherwise purely exotic Viking motifs are punctuated by all the standard posters from the girls' comics to assure the necessary affective attachment to the *dramatis personae*. A succession of violent separations and sentimental reunions is interspersed with highly suggestive scenes of love, love-making, sexual ambiguity and sexual attraction between members of the same or the opposite sex. When Rŷu meets the Celtic Halldora, the greatest love of his life, their desire explodes and flows panoramic over the pages depicting the climatic moment of their reunion out in the open nature of Shetland. The celestial trickster Loki's sexuality in the Nordic mythology, is markedly dual.[7] So it is in the Scarlet Sword (see Plate 4.2). There, he not only takes over the role of a caring mother *vis-á-vis* Rŷu but also appears once as a beautiful young woman, a soothsayer, calling upon the home of the Grasida. Rŷu's own relationship with Kjartan, a character in the story, who was

---

7. Loki is a kind of a trickster who for the Japanese may evoke the person of Susan-no-o-no-mikoto, the naughty, rebellious younger brother of Amaterasu, the sun-goddess in their own mythology. The development of the mythological character is though totally opposed. Loki's character deteriorates gradually in mythological time from being a loyal blood-brother of the highest god, Odin, into becoming a heavenly *persona non grata*. Susano-O, on the other hand, starts out defiling and perturbing order in the universe, only to convert himself to better ways as a major divinity of the nether world, becoming a genitor of some other central divinities in the mythological pantheon.

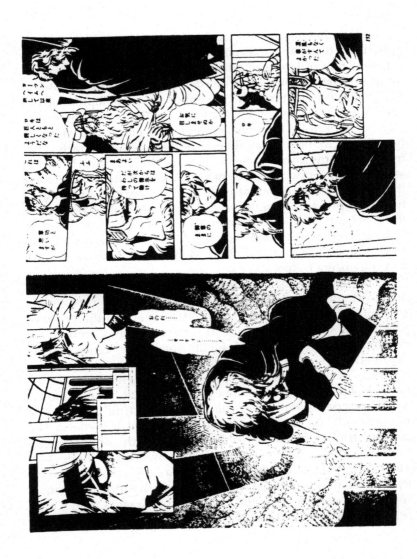

Plate 4.2. Loki confesses his treacherous mischief to Odin. (From Azumi Ryo's 'Scarlet Sword')

captured in his early youth and brought to Iceland as a slave, is fairly explicitly homosexual. In fact, with the exception of the old folks, all of the heroes and villains that appear in the illustrations are drawn in a highly stylised fashion, and are androgynous looking, such as it is the custom in Japanese *manga* for girls.

Azumi Ryo does create some remarkable Viking characters in the Scarlet Sword. If there are moments when their behaviour strikes a Nordic reader like myself as peculiar, it must be because the author occasionally feels obliged to introduce Japanese reasoning, sentiments, motivations and ways of being in the world to reinforce their appeal to their prospective readership. Just before undergoing baptism at the hand of the missionary Thangbrandur, an ally of Sigmund, Halldora, separated from the Viking-Lover Rŷu, is struck by a sudden, terrifying thought, bringing her to a standstill: 'What will happen to her already dead parents, relatives, and ancestors? Will they also be saved, along with herself?' When she is informed by the missionary that, on the contrary, they will burn eternally in Hell, she retreats horrified from 'the egocentric immorality of the act she was just about to commit'. This is, in fact, one of the standard objections that the Japanese have always raised against the very idea of Christian salvation. They see it as a selfish, individualistic rejection of the very thing that for them constitutes the main root for all moral conduct: the succession of generations from the family past. While this is crystal-clear to the mind of the average Japanese, nothing from the Icelandic sagas suggests that such was also the dilemma faced by ancient Nordic heathens when presented with the idea of a Christian conversion.

Azumi Ryo goes even further in providing her Vikings with Japanese religious sentiments. Once Rŷu reproaches his father Sigmund for having lost his temper and given him a thorough beating exactly at the time of his deceased mother's first *meinichi*, the anniversary of her death. Nowhere in the saga literature is there a mention of a specific recognition, or remembrance of the anniversaries of deaths. In addition to such direct impositions of Japanese culture into the Viking world for 'improving' its comprehensibility, the author sometimes simply exchanges the contents of the more hopelessly exotic Viking customs with the closest she can find from her own cultural tradition. An example

would be the *hestaat*, the horse-fights at the time of the General
Assembly at Thingvellir, which she depicts in considerable
detail in the form of horse races.

Reflecting on the way Japanese cartoonists appropriate and
manipulate themes, not only from the sagas and the Edda, but
from world history and literature in general, I was reminded of
Laura Bohannan's fabulous attempt to take 'Shakespeare in the
bush'. In a humorously enlightening magazine article from 1966,
she told what happened when she tried in vain to tell the story
of Hamlet to the Tiv of West Africa. The Tiv listeners, through
constant interruptions, bit by bit, inserted their own vision of the
tragic events narrated 'to make sense of them', until the original
story had been moulded into their scheme of things.

Conclusions

Writing the descriptive part of this paper required adopting a
different perspective from the one conventionally applied in
anthropological practice. I have attempted to find out what
happened to elements of my own culture when they were
'filtered' down in Japan for mass consumption in popular
culture through different levels and genres of re-creative efforts
by professional agents, transmitters of the alien culture. Tracing
what happens to elements of one's own culture when they travel
abroad results in a reversal of the habitual roles in the praxis of
anthropology. What has been depicted in this paper is how some
products of the culture incorporated in the person of the
anthropologist are studied, interpreted, and processed by
foreign specialists.[8]

8. This is not without recalling some of the more radical recent criticism levelled against
the conventional praxis of anthropology (see, for example, Fabian 1983; Clifford and Marcus
1986; Marcus and Fischer 1986; Kuper 1988). Could anthropology itself be understood as the
ultimate instance of cultural borrowing? Anthropology has developed as an academic field
in the western world engaged in the construction of the category of Other as distinct from
Self. For that purpose it has developed forms of discourses (schools) and a methodology,
validating its knowledge about the Other. The descriptive efforts in the ethnographic
present can be seen as striving to 'reflect' the world of the Other as it 'appears', and the
academic labour at home excelling in 'recreating' it as it 'is' according to Self's own
conventions of scientific methodology and discursive practices. From this perspective, the
anthropological praxis consists on the one hand in collecting 'texts' in the field, and on the
other in 'rewriting' them at home. Lévi-Strauss, for one, has described anthropological
discourse as being 'a myth upon a myth' (Lévi-Strauss 1963: 6).

The general purpose with pursuing this issue was to demonstrate how even the most apparently alien of worlds can be apprehended if not appropriated within an age old tradition of cultural borrowing. Pollack (1986) suggests that the Japanese accommodate things of alien origins in a particular manner and that this accommodation goes back to the opening of historical times in the country.[9] It started out as a reaction – a way of coping with acculturation, overwhelming waves of influence sweeping the country from China and Korea across the ocean. Later, little by little, it became an institutionalised mechanism in the radically transformed society and culture permitting maximum exposure to and emulation of things from the outside. This mechanism involved a pairing off of the foreign in a new semantic relation to the native world, and thereby contextualising what had been their cultural significance in the place of their origin. Foreign things could thus be freely incorporated into the Japanese way of life by a splitting operation which added a new meaning to borrowed cultural items.

This particular way of solving acculturation problems, which gradually became one of the distinguishing features of Japanese society, probably reached its highest degree of sophistication with the introduction of literacy and organised religion from the mainland of East Asia. In adopting the Chinese form of writing, the Japanese resorted to giving each sign two different kinds of reading (*on/kun*), a Chinese one and a Japanese one – a distinction later expanded and generalised with the development of a supplementary double system for phonetic writing – *katakana* and *hiragana*, respectively employed for representing foreign and native vocalisations. In taking over a foreign form of a great tradition in religion such as Buddhism, Japanese spiritual leaders found, in their turn, a way of making it their own while at the same time projecting it onto the world of indigenous cults and beliefs in local spirits and gods (*honji/suijaku*).

It has been my contention here that what Pollack identifies as 'the fracture of meaning' at the opening of historical age in Japan has survived and thrived up to this day as one of the most fundamental, deep-rooted cultural institutions in the society. It was therefore no coincidence that the Japanese idealised the

9. 'The very way that meaning would be structured in Japan was determined from the outset by the primacy of the dialectical relationship between the antithesis of alien form and native content' (Pollack 1986: 6).

efforts at modernising their society at the close of the nineteenth century under the slogan 'Japanese spirit/Western technology' (*wakon-josai*)! Revolutionary westernisation of material culture was to be accompanied by the revival of an archaic, untainted spirit of an imperial *Gemeinschaft*. After the crushing defeat in the Second World War, Japanese authorities mobilised the population once more, this time for reconstructing their world after an American model. Once again, as if spontaneously, the same mechanism of cultural borrowing initiated 1300–1400 years earlier came into motion, permitted an extraordinary success in adapting to entirely new conditions. Democracy, human rights, free enterprise, freedom of expression and belief, and sexual equality were some of the principal 'western values' officially enshrined in the new constitution introduced during the occupation years in the aftermath of the war. Now they were taught as the golden rules of society, and apparently with the instant approval of the population. The English language soon followed to become a major cornerstone in the new educational programme.

As it turned out, the Japanese, as if spontaneously, were engaged in their own age-old practice of domesticating the trauma from acculturation, the excessive influx of foreign phenomena. Foreign practices and their underlying ideals were, of course, thoroughly studied by Japanese administrators and scholars and their general principles understood and retained for educational purposes, but as they started 'sinking in' for local application they came to acquire supplementary, native meanings with reference to lived experiences.

When Japan then became the centre of world attention for its 'economic miracle' in the 1970s and 1980s a whole new chapter was opened in the history of Orientalism with an avalanche of publications on Japan by its admirers and its critics. The common denominator characterising the discourse of the latter has been the accusation that Japanese society is masked to look as if it abided by the same principles as 'ours', while in reality it closes in on itself due to inherent double-standards. Hence, we are told, the 'unfair trading practices', the 'corruption in the stockmarket', the 'enigma of Japanese power', etc.

The postwar history of the English language in Japan reveals another major instance of the Japanese way of domesticating the foreign. Titanic and ever-growing efforts have been put into the scholarly teaching of English at every level of the official educational system. And even so, there remains a tremendous extra demand for schooling catered to by private language schools, strictly speaking all over the country. To the great dismay of all concerned, native as well as foreign instructors, the harvest from all this educational labour remains remarkably meagre. On the other hand, the indirect influence that English has had, and continues to have, on Japanese language and culture in general is monumental. English terms are constantly being introduced into the daily use of the native language in Japan without the slightest sign of collective restrictions or displeasure of any kind (unlike, for instance, in France and Iceland). This is done by naturalising them entirely through the sound system of Japanese so they can fit perfectly in the flow of speech. In writing, these words of foreign origin are then again distinguished by writing them in the phonetic alphabet of *katakana*. The noteworthy thing in this context is that the meaning that these 'loan words' come to acquire is often remarkably different, if not entirely different, from their original meaning. Of course, English written in the Roman alphabet is also widely used in popular culture in Japan. Here English words and phrases are primarily employed as mystifying icons for decoration, adding moods and emotions for selling commodities. English words and phrases are used in a limbo out of linguistic context, alienated from their 'normal' application. Endemic occurrences of the violation of orthographic and/or grammatical conventions catching the eye of the foreigner in the country do not in the least bother the sensibilities of Japanese consumers, if they notice them at all.[10]

This is, then, the global context into which I aimed to situate the descriptive part of my chapter on the sagas in Japan. It relates a case of minor importance in the ceaseless stream of cultural borrowing from the outside world (see Hannerz, this volume). It was selected for scrutiny for the sole reason of its relation to my own cultural background. Multitudes of other examples could have served just as well or better for showing the mechanism at work in the Japanese art of embracing and digesting alien phenomena.

10. One of the more subtle instances that I have come across recently of 'Japlish' (as the idiosyncratic uses of English in Japan are sometimes called) was in a mountain hut 2400 m above sea-level close to the peak of the sacred Mount Hakusan. There I had the opportunity to chat with a lovely Japanese woman with the intriguing suggestion 'Let's enjoy your life!' written in big letters across the bulging breast of her tee shirt.

Chapter 5

The anthropologist as shaman: interpreting recent political events in Armenia

Levon H. Abrahamian

When trying to gain an understanding of traditional customs, of festivals, for example, anthropologists must resort to the help of a native expert for interpretation, as long as they do not know the language of the rites they are witnessing. A traditional festival is a kind of stable text (in the broad semiotic sense of the word), and the anthropologist is in fact trying to 'translate' it into his or her own language to be able to understand it. The anthropologist approaches the problem much like a linguist trying to decipher an unknown text – proceeding from translation to understanding, especially if the text consists of ritual fragments and those who used them or possessed detailed knowledge of them are long dead.

In this paper I mean to discuss the position and functions of a native anthropologist who, by chance, encounters a very different situation and becomes a witness to, and part of, stormy national and political processes – something unstable, changing and dramatic (cf. Deshen, this volume). In this case the anthropologist is not merely a distant observer, but rather a passive participant in the drama. How should anthropologists proceed in such a situation? If they remain outsiders they miss a number of important features which can be revealed only from the inside, failing to grasp the vivid nerve of the event. On the other hand, while being entirely on the inside means complete existential dissolution, it makes observation an impossibility.

After all, the phenomena anthropologists are witnessing have to be distanced from them, even if only a little. A similar problem in fact arises when anthropologists try to look at a traditional rite from the inside. While the rite is something that takes place right now, it is a repetition of the sacred past and at the same time a guarantee for the future. Thus the traditional ritual drama is something known and expected (at least for ritual experts), whereas the political ritual drama, as a rule, is uncertain and unknown to everybody. In any case, the anthropologist must be both on the inside and the outside of the event at the same time. And though the measure of this ambivalence cannot be defined exactly, it is a necessary condition for any anthropological translation, especially if the text to be translated is 'written' in the mother tongue of the anthropologist.

The uncertain, ambivalent position of the anthropologist is well reflected in the attitude of the people, the subjects, towards his or her work. During my fieldwork in a crowded square, when studying some of the events discussed here, I encountered a broad range of such attitudes – from irritation to euphoric excitement. The anthropological project was apprehended partly as an ethical problem. Stepping from the inside to the outside involves a transition from one's own familiar world to a strange, new world. I was told that the phenomenon I was involved in could not be translated, that it was a kind of mystic experience which loses its significance the very moment it is looked at from outside. A patriotic Armenian reader of my work even felt insulted by the structural analogies suggested by my analysis. But though some of the informants very much disliked the idea of becoming objects of investigation, others, in contrast, were intrigued and satisfied by the realisation that they were a part of a sacred text, of which they were only vaguely aware, and unable to grasp, through not knowing its language.

In this sense, the anthropologist is transformed into a person who knows a 'secret' language which enables him or her to pass from this world to some other world. The ambivalence and marginal position, which is a part of the profession and which is something gained automatically and unconsciously, this time becomes a well-realised instrument for attaining special knowledge. Thus the anthropologist approximates to a shaman who passes into the sacred world to gain the knowledge and prophecy necessary for society at critical moments in its history.

And just as this sacred world is the primordial mythological world of the shaman's community, the world of its Beginning (let us remember that the shaman is travelling this passage by descending to the *roots* of the inverted cosmic tree), the anthropologist has to look for a similar primordial world, where the roots of his or her own society (or the phenomena under investigation) lie, in order to gain the ability to prophesize after returning. The scheme is the same as in any anthropological research: the anthropologist is 'passing' to a familiar world to make comparisons and conclusions afterwards, but this time he is using the same features of the profession (ambivalence and knowledge of the second language) in a special way and thus can expect some special results, though these differ from anthropological comparison, just as a shaman's journey differs from an ordinary journey, be it even much more adventurous and cognitive. To understand the situation the anthropologist in fact tries to consult a certain ancient text, thereby undertaking a special type of translation. Of course, anthropologists do not use the trance techniques shamans employ for their mystical passage. I am only suggesting there are structural analogies between the two kinds of translation.

What kind of a sacred proto-text do anthropologists have at their disposal for their passage? Each case, perhaps, demands its own proto-text, just as in a comparative analysis the anthropologist makes analogies with the cases judged to be of greatest relevance. But the proto-text has to be a real original text and not an arbitrary one, and indeed there is a way of checking its authenticity: a number of independent but parallel codes (etymological, spatial, royal, etc.) or specific auxiliary languages which have to provide the same type of translation as the proto-text would do if chosen rightly. Even some mystical coincidences, or rather regularities, come to keep the anthropologist in check.

The Karabagh movement in Yerevan

Now I want to present you with one example of such a translation, which I tried to perform in 1988 during a sudden burst of national activity in Armenia, now known as the Karabagh or Artzakh (the Armenian name for Karabagh) movement. It is not my task to discuss here the roots of this movement and all the political and humanistic problems arising from it. I would like to note only that the movement was not something monolithic all the time. Sometimes it revealed even polar tendencies. Thus in Nagorno-Karabagh, *perestroika* and *glasnost* were used only to gain reunion with Armenia, while on the contrary in Yerevan, the capital of Armenia, the Karabagh problem was mainly used to strengthen the idea of *perestroika* and *glasnost*. But at the beginning there was no such polarity in the movement, all its participants were really forming a very monolithic crowd.

The Karabagh movement in Yerevan began on 19 February 1988, when several thousand people, mainly students and representatives of the intelligentsia, gathered in Theatre Square to support the Armenians of Karabagh who were demanding reunion with Armenia (see Plate 5.1). During the first three days, these meetings were simply a reflection of a political trend and would hardly attract a social anthropologist's attention, even though the roots of the movement lay in an ethnic sphere. But very soon the situation changed abruptly and the meetings involved all social groups. On 22 February, when about 500,000 people gathered at the building of the Central Committee of the Communist Party to demand a special session of the Supreme Soviet, many workers joined the demonstrators. And two or three days later, when masses of peasants came to the town to attend the demonstrations, the movement became really nation-wide. I am not going to discuss here the concrete reasons that transformed an ordinary national, political manifestation into nationwide protests and meetings which in turn brought about a tremendous burst of national consciousness. Here I am interested more in the results of this outburst than its development.

The people were joined in a kind of united body, much like that of the medieval European carnival keenly characterised in a famous study of Michael Bakhtin (1965). This immense body, which probably amounted to a million people at the peak of the demonstrations (and this is in a city with a population of a million), was not created mechanically. It had a united spirit, a common thought and finally a common sense of ethnic self-consciousness. According to the statements of many participants, they had a wonderful feeling of being present everywhere, in every place occupied by that huge body of people.

Plate 5.1. One of the first demonstrations in Yerevan in February 1988 (Photograph by G. Harutunian)

Being a student of festivals and ritual, I found myself suddenly in the midst of an 'archaic' proto-festival much like one of the festivals of the aborigines of Australia I once tried to reconstruct (Abrahamian 1983). The sacred text I chose to consult naturally lay in the roots of human society, and as I knew its language well, I tried to perform a kind of translation, to open a passage to the proto-festival. Of course, I did not use any shamanistic trance techniques, I simply did intense field-work in the crowded square.

The principal traits of the 'archaic' festival are the inversion, undervaluing and, in general, the elimination of the main structural oppositions of society. During a medieval European carnival, the highest and the lowest, the king and the jester would exchange places and social positions. And during a primitive festival in societies with dual organisation, the two halves would change places – together with a set of oppositions such as 'right/left', 'high/low' and 'masculine/feminine'. These inversions weaken the oppositions and even result in their disappearance during a chaotic festival.

In accordance with this principle, during our 'festival' in Theatre Square important polarisations in Yerevan society disappeared, in particular 'townsman/villager', 'man/woman', 'adult/youth', and 'Armenian language/Russian language'. The opposition of town and village is one of the most important for Yerevan, because its existence is the result of a very strong urbanisation process. On those February days, villagers were greeted by local citizens with great enthusiasm, each new column of villagers entering the square breathed fresh energy into the huge body of the people. One evening, after it was proposed in the meeting to provide lodging for the night to villagers who came from remote districts, a large group of local citizens who had gathered at the place invited the villagers by chanting: 'You are welcome, dear guests!'

The second opposition (men/women) disappeared due to the fact that any young man could freely address any woman, but before the events, this could have been regarded as a violation of ethical norms. For instance, a small demonstration of young women were given heart by a youth: 'Girls, don't be afraid!' he cried to them, referring to the soldiers who had appeared near the women. Normally, a young man would not have tried to talk to them, or he would do it only with a certain unsocial aim in mind. An anecdote from the same year underlines these essential changes in the 'men/women' opposition. A mother reprimands her son for not marrying. She says: 'Can't you find a good girl to marry?' The son replies: 'Where can I find one? 'Don't you know that by now we are all brothers and sisters?' Spencer and Gillen mention (1904: 378–80), one may note, an analogous case from Central Australia where during a festival men violate traditional norms regarding how to address women.

The polarisation of bilingualism also disappeared completely. This occurred on the first day of the February meetings, when a Russian-speaking leader made a speech. One would guess that in the larger national and political context of these events, the people in the square would have expressed their discontent concerning the Russian language of the speaker. But on the contrary. 'A Central Committee secretary addressed you before me', our Russian-speaking leader said, 'and he was speaking Armenian. And what did he say to you?' This speaker, in contrast, had many things to say, though in Russian. From that moment on and till the end of the February meetings the opposition between the two languages in fact vanished. Age differences, another important opposition, were also smoothed away in the uncertain age of the huge body of people.

Even such an unimportant opposition as 'healthy/disabled' was done away with. One could see the blind and the deaf coming to the square in groups together with their interpreters. On one occasion a handicapped man, who had lost both of his legs, arrived from a remote district in a primitive cart and asked to make a speech. Out of respect for him the people squatted to be on the same level with him. It was as though they had got rid of their legs to break the opposition. In short, a specific chaotic festival structure was created: the orderly cosmos of everyday life turned into a kind of festive chaos.

The connection of the events in Theatre Square with the archaic proto-festival is not limited to these structural similarities. As I mentioned earlier, the proto-text must provide a number of parallel codes to prove its authenticity. One of these codes is the etymological one. The Armenian word for *glasnost* is *hraparakaynut'yun*, derived from *hraparak* meaning 'a square'. And, perhaps, it is not by chance that the people performed the 'archaic' festival in the *square*, and not somewhere else. Let us remember that a square in the centre of a town has always been the place for mass festivals. The fact that the people refused to transfer their meetings to the outskirts of Yerevan, as the authorities had suggested, says something about the centripetal force reflected in the planning of many cities of the world. Led by this principle, Alexander Tamanian, the architect of the general layout of Yerevan, sited a large square in the centre of the town. Evidently, it was not by chance that the people's festival took place just where, according to an earlier proposal, the architect intended to erect the House of the People, where the 'people-onlooker' were to watch the festival demonstrations of the 'people-performer'. In other words, according to Tamanian, the opposition 'performers/spectators' was to disappear at this very place, where it eventually disappeared during the days of our festival. This is also one of the main features of the 'archaic' festival.

The connection between the Armenian words *hraparak* ('square') and *hraparakaynut'yun* ('glasnost') is so close that one can look at the first and so judge the second. Thus one could find out much about *glasnost* in the country simply by watching the events in Theatre Square. A certain spatial code, then, a specific language of description, accompanied the political one. Strangely enough, the uneven progress of *glasnost* seemed to be reflected in the events in the square. Take, for example, the blocking off of the square and gaps in the 'wall' surrounding it. From time to time, for unknown reasons, the people were allowed into the square through a side entrance, just as *glasnost* sometimes found its way through the wall of totalitarian prohibitions. There are parallels as well in the attempts to relocate the meetings from the centre to the outskirts and in the fluctuations in the strength of the blockade – the variation in the nature and degree of military involvement, the army, special troops, different types of armoured cars, etc. Thus, we can see how some specific auxiliary translation seems to work in parallel to our process of translation.

The etymological code – another language, which provides a parallel translation – also provides a test of our main translation. Thus the stem *glas* also shows the festive character of the political events referred to by the Russian word *glasnost*. *Glas* is the old Russian for 'voice'; that is, it implies a listener, a dialogue – a question which presupposes an answer. It doesn't have the independence and abstractness of the 'word' in the concept 'freedom of speech' (namely 'freedom of word' in Russian). The difference between the two ideas is often noted, but only as a theme for political criticism and satire. The 'voice' hidden in the *glasnost* is the sound component of the word, its vowel part (the Russian word *glasnyj* meaning 'a vowel', by the way, is derived from the same stem) which demands a response. According to the Armenian variant of the word, the response is expected to be heard in the square. And our festival came to support such a prognosis; the participants of the meetings and processions created a number of word games having ritual question-and-answer characteristics. For example, the leading man asks loudly: 'Whose is Karabagh?' to which the crowd responds in chorus: 'Ours'. This is repeated three times (with various endings constructed as puns). Sometimes these question-and-answer repetitions were used to conclude some other newly-created ritual. It wasn't by chance that the song that turned out to be the most popular chorus-song during those days was an old song, 'Who are they?', a song with a typical question-and-answer structure about *fedayis* (the Armenian avengers of the era of Armenian massacres in Turkey). In this chorus-song, every question of the refrain was answered by a many-thousand 'Hey!' (It is interesting that after more then two years of the movement, the question-and-answer dichotomy of the song attained a new, dialogical semantic in anecdotes reflecting the modern *fedayi* movement.) Demonstrations also acquired the question-and-answer construction, though their aim, as the word suggests, is to *demonstrate* something. But the Yerevan demonstrations demanded very often an immediate answer to their demands and/or questions, thus giving a direct 'dialogic' trend, in the Bakhtinian sense, to the demonstrations. Curiously enough, the authorities, against whom the demonstrations were directed, sometimes became involved in the dialogue by giving an answer, thereby reinforcing the ancient question-and-answer archetype. The question-and-answer form is characteristic of the most ancient rituals, especially those dealing with a borderline situation (e.g. the New Year Ritual), when the world fallen into Chaos is to gain a new Cosmos.

Thus both the Russian *glasnost* and its Armenian variant meaning, 'a square', each in its own way shows a deep connection between the phenomenon denoted and the festival; that is, with the proto-text we are consulting. The etymological code adds yet another festive colouring to the situation discussed. The word 'democratisation', a twin concept to *'glasnost'*, implies a *process*, a movement of essential mass character. Democratisation is often opposed to the concept of democracy (in the way that *glasnost* is opposed to the liberty of the word), also without seeing the 'archaic' features that inspired the spirit of the proto-festival in the events I am trying to represent.

'Emotions and reason'

There is another essential feature of the February meetings which reveals their connection with the festival. This is the deep feeling of solidarity, unity and mutual love that is unlikely to be forgotten by those who experienced this emotional state (cf. Wikan, this volume). This unique feeling alone makes the participants remember the February meetings with nostalgia and pride, as a contrast to the tense and sometimes violent nature of more recent meetings. This provides good evidence that the festival is over. A mass display of solidarity was a rather rare thing in our country. The mutual consideration, strict discipline and distribution of food free of charge during the February meetings were qualified by the authorities as the work of sinister forces. This idea was discussed in a notorious article, 'Emotions and reason', published in *Pravda* (21 March 1988). From that day on, the 'emotions/reason' opposition became a key-phrase, something like a ritual incantation for any official interpreter of the Karabagh movement – be it a provincial reporter or the future President. With its help – that is, by calling for the suppression of emotions – attempts were made to solve all the problems that were raised.

It is quite true that, generally, emotions play an important role in the structure of the festival. It is precisely emotional tension that makes the proto-festival proceed according to its specific rules. Contrary to the destructive actions of a furious mob which are also a result of emotions, the proto-festival (and its descendant represented by events in Theatre Square in February) gives birth to principally *positive* emotions. As the Nyakyusa of Africa point out, a rite will be ineffective, even fatal for society, if its participants keep 'anger in their hearts' (Wilson

1957: 8). Besides, during such mass meetings the emotional factor does not stand alone and does not govern other factors. It does not subdue reason; rather, it creates a new consciousness directed inwards, to the roots of the community. The archaic festival is an event that allows its participants to communicate with their sacred history. And everyone who was involved in the events I am discussing here remembers the sudden awakening of ethnic self-consciousness and the keen awareness of history.

One additional feature of the proto-festival is represented by the name of the place where our festival occurred – Theatre Square where the Opera is located. (The square was given this name only during the period of the festival and later on people referred to it as 'Independence Square' or 'Freedom Square'.) Festivals tend to have a theatrical character, and elsewhere I have discussed in some detail the theatrical features of our mass meetings and our Parliament sessions (see Abrahamian 1990a). Here I want to mention only one noteworthy point. The late architect Tamanian, it is said, was quite sure that in the remote past there stood a temple of 'Song and Love' right on the spot where he erected his Opera House. Even if the history of the square does not go back that far, during the last two and half years the square has been a kind of stage, where real dramas have been performed. One such drama was the highly ritualised funeral ceremony of a youth who perished in July 1988 (alas, it was not the only funeral to take place there). At first sight, the tragedy and grief that the square has witnessed have nothing to do with festivals. This is the point which offended the feelings of some of my opponents. Nevertheless, the tragic aspect is one which brings the Theatre Square phenomenon close to the proto-festival. The fact remains that the archaic festival, as a rule, unites within its limits, laughter and weeping, joy and sadness, birth and death – be it a real death (for example, the final part of funeral ceremonies among Australian aborigines) or a symbolic one, performed during initiation rites.

We have already mentioned the spatial code – a special language the anthropologist could use to check the process of translation. Thus the round shape of Theatre Square adds new nuances to our festival. This shape demarcates a space where communication becomes easy and spontaneous. It is as if the circle creates a shapeless, movable structure inside its area. The chaotic character of the traditional people's festivals is, in a way, provided by the round shape of the central 'square' of a town. Thus, a lot of invisible threads lead us from the present-day square to the archaic festival. This specific leap towards the proto-festival is characteristic of the Armenian situation only. Of course, some proto-festival features are present in all national movements in the (former) USSR, but one hardly finds the complete set of these features elsewhere but in the Armenian 'festival'. Strangely enough, the name and features of the place where the first burst of national consciousness occurs often become a key to future processes in the society.

We have already seen how the festival aspects of Theatre Square worked in Armenia. In Estonia the first national manifestations took place in the so-called 'Singing Field', where the people sang Estonian folk-songs and danced national dances during their political meetings. This made their 'festival' look like a local folk-festival. If the Armenian 'festival' was a kind of leap to the universal past of humans, the Estonian 'festival' was directed towards more recent times of national realities. Another example could be Lenin Square in Baku, where the first mass meetings of the Azerbaijanians took place in November 1988. The name of the square shows that the political orientations of Baku and Moscow coincide. And though this coincidence was later transformed into an opposition and strident confrontation, the native Azerbaijani movement preserved a lot of ideas ('words') from the Soviet imperial ideology ('dictionary'). For example, everybody in Armenia recognised Moscow's involvement in the continuous blockade of Armenia by Azerbaijan, when in April 1990 Moscow began the economic blockade of Lithuania. One can also compare the term 'internationalist', often claimed by Azerbaijanians to be an essential feature of their national frame of mind, with the term 'internationalist' which the Soviet occupiers of Afghanistan used to refer to themselves. It is worth noting that in Estonia the force that opposes itself to the national Popular Front bears the name 'Inter-Front' (International Front).

Sometimes, one may note, the Lenin Square of Yerevan was also proposed as a place for national demonstrations. But while it really became such a place once or twice, the idea was not welcomed by the people, who preferred the 'archaic', pagan Theatre Square to the official communist Lenin Square. During

the celebration of the 1990 New Year festival, a real competition
even took place between the two squares, official and non-
official festivals seeking to obtain the tallest and the most
splendid of the Christmas trees erected in each square.

The semiotic shaping of the square became a new,
inexhaustive talking point of the festival occurring there. Thus
traditional tents where demonstrators were camping in the
Yerevan Theatre Square became a kind of fairground sideshow
with all its attributes. The tents for similar demonstrations in
Baku's Lenin Square in November 1988 revealed a quite
different ethnic and cultural reality. In the latter case, the square
resembled a nomadic camp with sheep entrails strewn around.
Even the central press, which avoided criticising Azerbaijani in
those days, noted that such insanitary conditions could bring
about epidemics. From time to time this 'camp' was a base for
aggressive groups, which made brief, menacing raids into the
Armenian quarters – as some kind of prelude to the pogroms of
the future.

Any act of demonstration during the 'festival' was highly
symbolic, and semioticians would, no doubt, find it a fertile field
for their interests. For example, in September 1988, when
armoured cars were brought to Yerevan, a picket of young men
blocked their way to Theatre Square, which was 'guarded' by a
chain of demonstrators holding hands. The pickets were sitting
across the street with their backs to the tanks, except for three
boys who faced them with a ritual gesture of a fist raised over
their heads and the national tricolour in their other hand.
Volumes of Lenin's works were placed across the street a little in
front of them, so that the tanks had to crush Lenin's ideas before
smashing the picket. Interestingly, a side street free of pickets
led to Theatre Square only 30 metres away from this symbolic
obstruction. I have tried to analyse, with a colleague of mine
(Abrahamian and Maroutian, n.d.), the language (or, rather, the
many languages) of posters produced during the 'festival'. These
were very sensitive devices, which reflected almost every
change in the situation. One more sign language was created in
response to the communication needs of meetings with many
thousands of participants: the 'dumb' masses were speaking to
the casual 'tribune' installed with loudspeakers by means of a
newly invented sign language.

Order and chaos

Let us now return to our festival. Like other ritual drama, it cannot last forever. The chaos created during the festival is pregnant with a new cosmos and the anthropologist can divine this new condition, using the form and peculiarities of the ritual drama – that is, its language – as a key. There are two types of society depending on the way in which ritual dramas are performed (see, for example, Crumrine 1970). In the first type, the ritual drama demolishes structural oppositions but afterwards restores them again – sometimes in an even more rigid form. In the second type of society, the ritual drama implies a structural transformation with lasting consequences for the social and cultural sphere. In the first case, the ritual drama, in fact, provides society with a mechanism for withstanding transformations of any kind. In the second, by contrast, it provokes society to change its structure. Therefore, by observing how society gets out of the chaotic festival-state one can establish the type it is drawn towards and, more than that, anticipate its future development.

First, let us see what the etymological code tells us. Earlier I discussed the concept of democratisation and *glasnost*. At this point it is relevant to introduce the third concept of the triad declared by Gorbachev. This concept is the famous *perestroika*. The Armenian word for it is *verakaňuc^{c}um*, which literally means 'reconstruction'. The new construction is supposed to be the same; it is a reconstruction (cf. the semantics of the prefix 're'). But in Russian the prefix 'pere' in *perestroika* means something new, not the same as before. As I argued above, both languages reveal a chaotic festival hidden in the concept of *glasnost*. And just as cosmos appears in ritual chaos, so the third member of the triad appears, bringing with it the idea of construction. But unlike the first two members, the third is uncertain and ambiguous, as in fact is the situation itself to which the concept refers.

The spatial code also showed some signs of a new cosmos created to replace the chaos of the festival. I have already mentioned that the people refused to move to the outskirts when Theatre Square was banned as a meeting place and blocked off by the military. Deprived of their 'archaic', pagan centre, the people chose a new centre – a spiritual one. This was the

Matenadaran – the place where ancient Armenian manuscripts
are kept. It was, perhaps, mere chance that the mass of people
formed an elongated rectangle, as a result of the layout of the
Matenadaran building, but interestingly the form supported and
supplemented the general scheme. Now the amorphous and free
meetings in the round square were transformed into something
rectangular of the Gothic type. And at the same moment the
festival features were reduced to a minimum – meetings lost
their theatrical mood and communicative spirit. As the circle
was transformed into a rectangle, the meeting immediately lost
its festival features.

But more important transformations began in the inner
structure of the movement. We have seen that during the festival
the main oppositions were destroyed. Now nearly all the
oppositions of the structure of the society which had vanished
during the chaotic festival came back to life again – in an even
more expressive shape than before. The polarity of bilingualism,
now contrasting Armenian and Russian schools, was revived.
The age opposition became expressed in the activities of the
radical wing of the movement which was mainly represented by
the young generation. The men/women opposition returned
with the special feminine (mostly emotional and aggressive)
branch of the structure of the movement. The opposition
between town and village came back a little later – during the
constituent conference of the All Armenian National Movement
in November 1989 and military self-defence activities on the
border in January 1990.

So we can see that the system is tending to return to its
previous, pre-festival state, but with a more dynamic inner
structure. That is, our ritual drama gravitates towards the first,
traditional type in Crumrine's classification. But at the same
time a new opposition appeared, which was not present in the
previous system. This was the opposition between the old and
the new in the social structure – in general, between those who
support the traditional Soviet totalitarian structure and those
who try to make *perestroika* a reality.

The oscillation of our system between the two types –
traditional and transforming – is revealed very clearly by one
more important code – the royal code. The king (the ruler, the
president, the image of the First man in general) is the
personality who, in the most tangible and sometimes tragic way,

carries all the festival transformations within himself. Elsewhere, I have tried to analyse the mythological aspects of the first persons in the carnival history of my country (Abrahamian 1990a, 1990b). The details of this analysis are not of relevance in the present context. For our discussion it is worth noting, however, that the mythological image of President Gorbachev, the initiator of our 'festival', also came to support the scheme of the oscillating system mentioned above. It was expressed in the essential ambivalence of Gorbachev, which was revealed in the eyes of my informants even in 1988 according to his attitude to Nagorno-Karabagh and Armenia. This ambivalence coincided with the ambivalent nature of President Gorbachev's *perestroika* – as we have already seen with help of the etymological code.

The social system, then, has some chances of breaking the vicious circle of eternal repetitions. After journeying to the roots of the festival the anthropologist can reveal the real meaning of the events witnessed, even make some predictions. The voyage to the proto-festival – the attempt to understand the modern, festival-like situation – brings forth such deep-level realities, however, that one may doubt whether the anthropologist is doing a real 'translation' at all. The predicament of the anthropologist is more like that of the interpreter, in the hermeneutical sense of the word, who interprets a text using the language of the text itself than of someone who moves from one language to another (cf. Hairapetian 1991). Of course, it depends on whether the anthropologist really regards himself or herself as being in touch with a proto-festival, i.e. does its language become his or her *own* language?

Finally, I shall give one example which shows, I hope, how mystical coincidences (or, rather, regularities) come to support the 'archaic' scheme we are discussing here. An informant told me of an interesting principle he had discovered: the unity and rallying of the Armenians coincides inexplicably with the erection of a temple with a circle in its ground plan, and the end of the solidarity and the dispersion of the people all over the world coincides with the destruction of such a building. Armenians began to erect a round temple, Zvartnotz, in the seventh century just on the eve of the Arab invasion, and in the tenth century, after the destruction of the temple, a great mass of Armenians left their native land. According to the same pattern the building of a Zvartnotz-type temple, Gagikashen, in the medieval Armenian capital Ani, became a sign of the rallying and prosperity of the people. And after the fall of Ani and destruction of the round temple, the people scattered across the world once again. When my informant, the author of this mystical pattern (who prefers to stay anonymous), saw, on the eve of the Karabagh movement, the stones of the Zvartnotz ruins being set out round the base of the temple as a first step for probable future reconstruction, he prophesied that Armenians would be united once more in the near future. This scheme suddenly materialised again in connection with dramatic events in Zvartnotz airport which also has a circle in its ground plan – the picketing of the airport, and the destruction of the live 'wall' round the building by soldiers who descended from the sky (Zvartnotz means 'a temple of awoken heavenly powers'). And, lastly, one more coincidence: both Zvartnotz and Gagikashen were destroyed as a result of earthquakes, and the solidarity and unity of the people was shaken after that. Hopefully, the terrible earthquake in December 1988 did not completely destroy the round temple of the people's spirit erected in Theatre Square.[1]

1. The main part of this chapter was written in January 1989, just after the earthquake and during the repression. Reaction (the state of emergency) began at practically the same moment (24 November 1988) the people in Theatre Square joyfully greeted the unofficial Parliament session, which took place at the same square, in the Opera House. It was claimed to be invalid and illegal by officials. But nearly two years later (on 9 October 1990) this 'round temple of the people's spirit' was restored once again, when the new Parliament of Armenia (which is the first one to be elected, really and not fictitiously as in the past) passed a resolution considering the November session and its decisions to be legitimate and true.

Chapter 6

Household words: attention, agency and the ethnography of fishing

Gísli Pálsson

Defining the 'household'

In this article I attempt to show how representations of nature and economic production are constituted in social discourse, particularly representations of agency, gender and social honour, drawing upon both the ethnography of fishing and my own fieldwork in an Icelandic fishing community (see Pálsson 1991). More specifically, I want to show, employing a social theory that emphasises praxis and change, how people attend to different aspects of social life in different contexts. Nature, I argue, has many languages and dialects, but each of them has a social logic or 'grammar'.

The modern notion of ecology – derived from the Greek word *Oikos* or 'household' – emphasises connections and dependencies in the natural world. Ecologists often speak of the habitat and niche of an organism, the former denoting the address or the home of the organism, the latter its profession or function. Humans, of course, have addresses and professions in the ecological sense, being part of nature, but since humans are social beings – endowed with self-consciousness rooted in social relations – there is much more to human ecology than purely 'ecological' relations in the modern sense of the term. In the course of our 'household' activities we talk about our 'homes' and 'functions', investing them with meaning. To address the members of the human household properly, to make sense of their activities, therefore, it is not enough to refer to their habitat and niche; their accounts, their 'household words', must be considered as well. Such accounts are often an important part of the information elicited by anthropologists in the field, but how they come about, how to make sense of them, and how to reconcile the ecological and the discursive, are matters of much theoretical debate. It is impossible to take part in that debate without committing oneself to a particular theory of both social life and ethnographic fieldwork.

The economy, it is often argued, occupies different positions in different societies. If this is the case, an 'economic' approach to natural discourse is bound to be anthropologically inadequate. In his recent critique of economic explanations, Godelier (1986) goes even further. For him, the shifting place of the economy in the real world is not the only problem. He argues that a general translation problem is involved, pointing out that the terms 'infrastructure' (or economic base) and 'superstructure' fail to capture the meaning of *Grundlage* and *Überbau*, the terms used by Marx. Such translations, he argues (1986: 7), often suggest a model of society as a stratified structure with unequal layers (as a 'cake'), reducing superstructure to 'an impoverished reality'. Godelier, however, fails to clarify the nature of the human household. For him, the mental 'can under no circumstances be simply reduced to reflections in thought of material relations originating outside it, prior to and independent of it' (ibid.: 10–11). Accordingly, he suggests: 'The *Überbau* is a construction, an edifice which rises up on foundations, *Grundlage*; and it is a house we live in, not the foundations' (ibid.: 6–7). I would argue, employing a similar metaphor, that *Grundlage* (not the *Überbau*) is the household itself – social life or the human *Oikos* – while *Überbau* encompasses representations of it in social discourse – in short, what it means to live in the household and be part of it.

Godelier seems to abandon the analytical priority of the social, asserting that 'every social relation exists both in thought and outside it' (ibid.: 11). To humanise the architectural view expressed by Godelier, we need to redefine the household with social beings – the members of the household – in mind, rather than the dwellings. This demands that we adopt a *social* model of the producer and the speaker (see Pálsson 1991: Ch. 1). Such a model does not require that we abandon the distinction between the symbolic and the real. On the contrary, we reaffirm it: 'culture alone is symbolic in that it represents conduct, furnishing a set of ideal "meanings"' while 'social relations . . . *are* the reality' (Ingold 1986a: 336–7; see also Ingold, this volume). In such a scheme, the Marxian concept of Grundlage is rendered as 'social relations' while *Überbau* becomes 'culture'.

The discourses discussed in this article embrace diverse kinds of phenomena – the words that people use in face-to-face interaction in the process of making a livelihood, the commonplace statements they exchange about their productive efforts, their 'folk' theories of human-environmental interactions, and the general paradigms within which they cast their theories about nature. In the present context, then, the notion of the 'discursive' is to be understood in a very general sense – as 'the broadest and most comprehensive level of linguistic form, content, and use', to borrow Sherzer's (1987: 305) definition. On the more theoretical level, it is through social discourse that people define what to attend to and what to ignore. Discourses are historically-grounded, social practices, which inform human modelling of their world, 'practices that systematically form the objects of which they speak' (Foucault 1972: 49). While some accounts, whether folk models or scholarly schemes, are more illuminating than others, any scheme is inevitably a product of social history. Accounts of the natural world and human-environmental interaction, I hold, are based on a fundamentally social logic. To understand why a particular kind of discourse is more appealing or 'contagious' than others (see Sperber, this volume), we need to consider social relations and production systems. Given such an anthropological perspective, discourses on nature are neither to be regarded as inert, independent 'traditions' in Redfield's sense nor as 'loose talk' or 'mere' household words, but rather as Malinowskian 'long conversations' firmly rooted in social life.

Fieldwork, ethnography and 'finding one's sea legs'

What happens during fieldwork and what to make of anthropological reports is an important theoretical issue. Some of the advocates of 'post-modern' anthropology suggest that ethnographic realities are essentially *manufactured*, for aesthetic or therapeutic purposes (see, for instance, Tyler 1986), emphasising that the making of ethnographies is 'creative' writing. And no doubt, the predicament of the novelist and the ethnographer has something in common. To do ethnography is to familiarise oneself with local action, to participate in the social life of a particular place, and to report the experience in writing. And the way one does the reporting depends on a host of personal and contextual factors, some of which also pertain to the writing of a novel. The discourse of the anthropological monograph, therefore, much like that of the novel, is located within a specific historical context. Clearly, modern writing about 'the Other' is a very different kind of enterprise from what it used to be during the heyday of western colonialism. And since the discourse between 'informant' and ethnographer is a dialogue carried out in a specific context, not simply the stating and recording of 'objective' facts, ethnographic 'truth' is far more elusive than strict empiricists like to think.

Some anthropologists, however, abandon any idea of ethnographic truth and representational authority. In the 'interpretive' approach of Geertz (1973), culture is a 'text' offering different kinds of interpretations. If anthropology is an 'art of translation', interpretive anthropology seems to assume that there is no single 'source' or original to translate. On the other hand, the advocates of interpretive anthropology rarely leave much room for translations for their readers. As Spencer points out (1989: 149), in filling the dual role of the maker and the analyst of ethnographic texts, the interpretivist tends to adopt a style of ethnographic writing which eliminates alternative understandings of the ethnographer's material (a style Spencer calls 'ethnographic naturalism') – in other words, legislating on interpretation. Interpretative liberalism turns out to be an authoritarian ethnography. It is one thing, I would argue, to recognise the limits of objectivism and naive realism and quite another to abandon the real altogether. Fiction may be better to read than anthropological monographs, but what distinguishes the most incompetent ethnographer from the best of novelists is that the former strives to represent a particular reality, a finite world, while the latter is free to attempt to create independent worlds of fiction. To understand that 'final world' it is necessary to partake in local discourse.

The present account of Icelandic discourse is based on my fieldwork in Sandgerði (near Keflavík on the south-west coast) in 1979 and 1981 and my general experience as a native Icelander. Not only did I work in my native country, I grew up in a fishing community in a family with deep roots in the fishing industry.

This fact inevitably affected my fieldwork – the kinds of questions I addressed, my relations with local people, and the answers they gave me. Since I spoke the 'same' language as the people I talked to, I was unlikely to ask some of the most stupid questions that a foreigner might pose. And, no doubt, my prior knowledge of the language and context of fishermen and fishworkers enabled me to grasp the nuances of the expressions I recorded and act more appropriately than would otherwise have been possible. On the other hand, had I been a foreigner my identity might have been somewhat less problematic. Perhaps, I would have been more likely to ask some of the interesting questions that fieldworkers are said to ask at the beginning of their work when they, supposedly, take nothing as given. And I might have been granted the licence to ask some of the dimwitted questions I kept to myself until I felt it was safe to pose them to others.

At the beginning of my fieldwork I felt hampered by the fact that much of the information I thought I needed seemed to be kept in closed quarters. While local people found the general topic of my research – changes in conceptions of fishing – a legitimate one, some of the questions I asked – especially those concerning fishing success, competition and fishing techniques – were seen to be both idiotic and too personal. While this is a reaction many fieldworkers are bound to experience early in their work, it may be somewhat stronger in the case of a native fieldworker. Why would an academic from the capital city, I was asked, make an effort to understand this particular fishing community? Why would an anthropologist talk to fellow Icelanders, for months and mostly about relatively obvious matters? For quite some time I felt as if I was not making much progress, isolated as I was on the margin of the discursive community. I knew that some important issues were not elaborated upon in my presence and I found it very embarrassing to see some of them discussed in greater detail in newspaper accounts. The process of establishing the necessary trust and rapport, gaining access to the local community, seemed painfully slow.

At one point, however, during the winter season in 1981, my relations with local people underwent a dramatic, positive change. A highly respected local skipper invited me to join him on one of his fishing trips. 'If you *really* want to know what the

fishing industry is all about', he said, 'you must go fishing.' I
guess he saw his offer as a test or challenge, knowing that
academics and other landlubbers who rarely go to sea
(*landkrabbar*, literally 'land-crabs') are prone to seasickness in
Icelandic waters. I accepted his challenge, and shortly after we
left harbour we were in rough seas – indeed, one of the worst
storms of the winter season. For several hours, while the skipper
and his crew patiently waited for the weather to improve to be
able to draw the nets they had placed in the sea the day before, I
was busy emptying the contents of my stomach. I did not have
the stomach, in a literal sense, to do anything except adjust my
body to the movements of the boat, attending to the sea. No
doubt my seasickness confirmed the skipper's belief that
academics were hopeless at sea. Then, miraculously, it seemed,
the weather suddenly improved and, fortunately, the feeling of
seasickness vanished. I found the movements of the boat
pleasant and relaxing and for the rest of the trip I plagued the
skipper and his crew with a variety of questions, about boats,
gear, skippers and fishing tactics. Quite suddenly, my nausea
had been replaced with a sensation of alertness and well-being,
an 'oceanic' feeling. Later on, when ashore, I found out that the
attitude towards my research had changed. My questions
seemed to acquire a new force and they were no longer easily
avoided or ignored. I had the feeling of having suddenly become
accepted as a legitimate participant in local discourse.
Apparently, then, the fishing trip was a rite of passage. I never
bothered to ask for an explanation of what happened, but
several people addressed me by reminding me of the fishing
trip: 'So, you've been feeding the fish!'

While for some existentialist philosophers the feeling of
nausea is a tragic and almost inevitable part of the human
condition (see, for instance, Sartre's novel *La Nausée* (1938),
which largely deals with troubled relationships and isolation
from other people), for fishermen - and no doubt many others –
it usually represents a temporary and even beneficial phase. For
Icelanders, the metaphor of nausea combines emotional and
cognitive aspects. To be 'seasick' (*sjóveikur*) is to be unfamiliar
with the rocking movements of the world. As nausea is replaced
by well-being, a quantum leap in learning is supposed to take
place. Getting used to or adapting to something is referred to as
recovering from seasickness, 'getting one's sea legs' (*sjóast*). And

those who return to 'life' after a hectic experience are said to have *found* their sea legs (*vera sjóaðir*). For me, the experience of the fishing trip served as a useful metaphor for a critical stage in my fieldwork. I had gone on this trip not only to accept the challenge of the skipper but also to learn about fishing – about models of success, skippers' decisions, interactions among crew men and the community at sea. While I was almost paralysed by nausea at the beginning of the fishing trip, later on, when I had, at least temporarily, adapted to the irregularities of the seascape, I was able, as a fellow passenger, to attend to the social world aboard, the tasks of the crew, and the issues they attended to. And fieldwork experience, in fact, often involves similar 'gut reactions'. Fieldworkers usually begin their 'trip' on the margin of the discursive community, nauseated by their status as alienated outsiders. As they become involved in the activities of others, they move towards the centre and begin to attend to the social world around them – to feel 'at home'.

Normally, such a feeling develops gradually (see, for example, Edelman, this volume). In my case it did not. The reasons have probably to do with the peculiar nature of the 'household' involved, the fishing crew. Not only is the crew a 'total institution' in Goffman's sense (a relatively complete and exclusive social world rather like those of prisons and hospitals), newcomers are immediately presented with a test of their belonging. 'Passing' (or 'failing') the test, however, is not the issue; what is important is *taking* it – claiming publicly, so to speak, one's immediate eagerness to participate and belong. To join such a household, therefore, is likely to involve sudden development of communion. For me, the fishing trip was both an important step in the process of social learning and a meaningful lesson on the nature of fieldwork. I came to the conclusion that to engage in fieldwork is not just to 'observe' and record but to participate in local discourse – to 'tune in' to others until one's attentiveness 'resonates' with theirs, to paraphrase Wikan (this volume). I should, perhaps, have 'known' this somewhat obvious fact from the beginning; the radical empiricism which suggests that the knower and the known live in separate worlds and treats experience as 'something passively received rather than actively made, something that impresses itself upon our blank minds or overcomes us like sleep' (Jackson 1989: 5) is not, and was not, the model of the day. But lessons of this kind only tend to sink in as a result of personal experience; indeed, they are not 'passively received'. From now on, I increasingly left my tape recorder behind and abandoned arranged, formal interviews, listening instead to 'natural' discourse and engaging in free conversations with others.

Attention and agency in Icelandic discourse

Attending to the world is no less important for a fishing skipper than a fieldworker. And for Icelandic skippers, the folk concept of 'attentiveness' (*athygli*) is a central one. Not only must the skipper be in complete control in order to co-ordinate activities – the operation of fishing equipment such as electronic gear and modern deck technology (longlines and gill nets) requires synchronising several operations – he must also be a skilful decision-maker. Skippers use a wealth of detailed information to decide both when and where to fish (see Durrenberger and Pálsson 1986). They must choose times and places to fish on the basis of their knowledge of currents, the behaviour of different kinds of fish, bottom features and past seasons, their ideas about fish breeding and feeding patterns, and their interpretations of weather reports. They compare their observations and theories of stock movements and concentrations on the inter-boat radio and in discussions between fishing trips. By memorising past observations and keeping diaries, each skipper stores relevant information and uses it to make predictions.

While the decision as to which location to visit is affected by a number of 'natural' variables, guessing where the fish are likely to be is only part of the skipper's decision. Of no less importance is attending to *other* skippers – estimating where they will be and how much they will catch. Indeed, the skipper's position or 'seat' in the local competitive hierarchy is a central concern. Being at the bottom of the daily catch records is a particularly humiliating position. Skippers who know that they have done exceptionally badly fear the comments of others when they reach harbour. Being at the head of the fleet for the season, on the other hand, being *aflakóngur* (literally, 'catch-king'), brings a high degree of honour and prestige. Prestigious skippers tend to have larger boats, more sophisticated equipment and sounder financial backing. If the skipper improves his position, he has a chance of commanding a larger boat, which is an important component in fishing success. If, on the other hand, he has a low position he risks losing his job. One of the local skippers with the lowest prestige was fired at mid-season by his company because 'he did not fish enough'. The better a skipper's reputation and the greater his prestige, the more stable and experienced his crew. When competition is tough, only a small difference in prestige and reputation can make all the difference.

In the absence of direct, visual clues, skippers try to learn as much as possible about their colleagues (especially about catches and locations) through the use of the inter-boat radio, a device fishermen call 'the spy'. While to the newcomer inter-boat communication may sound like a classic example of what Malinowski called 'phatic communion' (1923) – the lengthy and repetitive exchanges between skippers, and the gossip, teasing and joking they contain often seem to be simply an end in themselves – one should not underestimate its social and discursive significance. Such exchanges not only maintain communion in the local fleet (the crews of 46 boats of varying sizes, ranging from 10 to 200 tons), they also provide subtle information on fishing. What skippers say is interpreted on the basis of an extensive prior knowledge of catch records, fishing locations and fellow fishermen. Skippers know, for instance, that some of their colleagues are more prone to lie than others and that different meanings may be attributed to statements made on the radio, or the lack of statements, depending on the personalities involved.

A skipper's trust and prestige is not given once and for all from the moment he begins to fish. Rather, it is negotiated and maintained in the context of social discourse. The hierarchy of skippers emerges and changes in a context of flux and movement of boats, skippers and crewmen. The arena of prestige negotiation is not, however, restricted to the sea, for often it extends into the larger sphere of local relations. For instance, many of those involved in the fishing industry ashore – particularly boat owners and operators of fishing plants – regularly listen to the inter-boat radio, waiting for 'fishing news'. Local people often compare the performance of skippers, discussing the successful and unsuccessful, the old-timers in relation to the young, and in the process evaluating the relative potential and prestige of individual skippers. Some skippers 'really do fish', while others are 'fish deterrents' (*fiskifælur*).

When ashore the skipper has to build up his reputation in a highly sensitive manner, since modesty is regarded as a virtue and public staging of self is not tolerated. Typically, skippers' accounts of dangers at sea contain few references to emotional states. Their style is often strangely objective, given the nature of the events described. One skipper whose ship had been caught twice by life-threatening breaking seas during the same fishing trip commented during a chat the next day with fellow fishermen ashore that everything on deck which could possibly get damaged had been smashed – adding, laconically, that one could 'take it like snuff'.

Given the competitive context described above, it follows that both fishermen and the general public construct their own theories to account for differential success. According to the dominant theory of recent decades, the production value of the skipper overshadows that of everyone else. This theory is *hierarchical* in that it emphasises differences among a group of producers, normally within a local fleet. Catches are said to vary from one boat to another because skippers differ in their ability to locate and catch fish, an innate ability supposedly 'in the blood'. Some skippers catch more fish than others due to their cleverness, being particularly attentive and able to memorise minute details, and because they follow other procedures when making decisions about the locations of prey. This is the idea of the 'skipper effect' (see Pálsson and Durrenberger 1983, 1990). The skipper himself is not supposed to elaborate on his knowledge, decisions and fishing 'tricks', and skippers who have been at the top of the hierarchy of success for several seasons are particularly reluctant to comment upon their own performance. If skippers comment upon their own performance, they usually modestly create the impression that their success is due to the co-operation of the crew or sheer luck. When explaining exceptional catches during single fishing trips, they often refer to intuition and hunches, peculiar experience beyond their understanding and control. Several skippers have described how a dilemma regarding fishing locations was solved by a strange message or intuition, some kind of 'whisper'.

In the hierarchical model, as we have seen, fishing is not only a struggle with fish, it is also a competition amongst skippers. Such a model is in stark contrast to the model of the household economy of earlier centuries (see Pálsson 1990). The latter was an *egalitarian* one in that it minimised differences among producers. The modern skipper is a 'strong' leader fighting for his place in the hierarchy of prestige, whereas the 'foreman' (*formaður*) in charge of the rowing-boat during the era of the peasant economy was a 'weak' one, or simply one among equals. While modern fishing records are public documents which compare the catches of *different skippers* or boats for the same season (*aflaskýrslur*; literally, records of catches), the records of the past were personal or private ones, comparing the number of trips of a *particular boat* over several seasons (*róðratöl*; literally, records of trips). Foremen, of course, attended to each other, but not to keep track of the differences among them in terms of productivity. Individual differences in 'fishiness' (*fiskni*) were not ignored, but they were relatively unimportant and an ordinary fisherman might well possess more 'fishiness' than his foreman. Fish were said to be allocated to humans according to an unpredictable system of rationing, as the 'gifts of God' (guðsgjöf). Such an idea sounds strange to modern fishermen for whom economic productivity is a matter of human agency. Also, the modern model is highly gender-specific whereas the peasant model was not. In the past, women's fishing was quite common and some women were well known in their capacity as foremen. Nowadays, in contrast, economic productivity is largely seen to be restricted to the activities of males; women often work in fishing plants, but they rarely go fishing and in the folk model fishing is the most 'productive' activity of all. Women's participation in fishing is regarded as unnatural, and they are never employed as skippers.

The hierarchical model of fishing success developed at the beginning of the twentieth century, when the domestic economy gave way to entrepreneurial fishing and large-scale capitalist production for an expanding foreign market. Labour became a commodity and the previous ceiling on production was lifted. With new kinds of social relationships, the relative power of fish and humans was reversed. The focus of production discourse was shifted from nature to society. The model that emerged emphasised human agency and the role of the individual in the production process. While the model of the household producer regarded fishing as a struggle against the elements, the model of the modern skipper holds that the competition with fellow producers – other skippers and their crews – is central. In order to appropriate fish, skippers had to become fishers of men.

More recently – especially after the introduction of a quota system in 1983, two years after my 'proper' fieldwork – a new model has been emerging. This is the model of 'scientific' management. With increased integration of the fishing industry with the agencies of the state, a new succession has taken place. Given the competitive nature of the expansive fishing described above, each skipper attempted to maximise his catch. This demanded remedial action, a co-operative implementation of a scientific policy which put a new ceiling on production. In an attempt to exploit the reproductive potential of fishing stocks fully, Icelanders first claimed the fishing territories as their own (during the so-called Cod Wars) and then allocated catches among themselves, this time obeying a secular or social quota system. The system of quota management allocates a given annual catch, a transferable quota, to each boat, largely on the basis of its catches in the past. Not only has a permanent right to fish been given to an exclusive group, but this right is increasingly being turned into a marketable commodity. As access has to be bought, and prices of boats and quotas are subject to the mechanism of the market, it becomes increasingly difficult for newcomers to enter the industry.

With institutionalised capitalism, scientific fisheries management and the quota system, the resources of the sea have been redefined once again; production discourse has become centred on both ecological and social relations. Humans are not only seen to depend on fish, but fish are seen to depend on humans. This new rationality often challenges the wisdom of fishermen. On the public level some important aspects of folk discourse are increasingly being silenced on the grounds that they are inadequate and irrelevant. Confronted with the details of scientific research, fishermen have become powerless, in their word 'mute' (klumsa). From their point of view, management has become increasingly the business of wise men who speak a 'strange' language. Fishermen and managers agree, however, that the hunting element of fishing (veiðimennska) is rapidly disappearing. Fishermen sometimes express the view that with increasing governmental control of the industry the custom of awarding the most successful skipper of the year a particular prize on Fishermen's Day (a standard custom in most fishing communities for decades) is a little archaic. As fishing is being 'reduced' to business transactions, success becomes less a matter of fishiness than capital and economics. The top skippers are simply privileged 'quota-kings' (*kvótakóngar*). Significantly, after the winter season of 1989 the skipper highest on the national records of catches (the 'catch-king'), one of the most celebrated skippers in the fleet, publicly declared that he would not accept the prize to which he was entitled. The competition, he argued, was 'unjust' since some skippers were barred from the competition due to the small quota assigned to them.

Not only have recent changes in the production system of the fishery brought with them changes in the discourse of fishermen and a 'scientific' rationality of fishing. National discourse on the distribution of wealth has begun to change too. Some people (fishworkers in particular) have called for a redefinition of the prevailing notion of 'interest group', questioning the privileged access of either fishermen or boat-owners, the 'lords of the sea' (*sægreifar*) as the latter are sometimes called, to the most valuable national resource. The 'interest groups' of those involved with fisheries management are no longer unanimously seen to be restricted to owners of fishing plants, boat-operators and fishermen. Processing workers, many of whom are women, are demanding their share of the cake, protesting against unemployment and refusing to be treated as 'outsiders', as economic and political 'invisibles'.

The modelling of nature and economic production has not ceased with the hierarchical notion of individual success and the concept of 'scientific' fisheries management. What Icelanders attend to will continue to be negotiated. Discourse is always continuous, and new models will continue to be subjected to debate. The decisive battles over agency, resources and economic power, however, are no longer fought primarily in face-to-face encounters in the local arena, in the fishing communities, but in a public, national and even international context – in the mass media, in national organisations and interest groups, in the academy and Parliament.

A sea of difference

While discourses are situated in time and space and one would not expect to find exact parallels in different temporal and social contexts, the radical claim, informed by 'substantivism' and 'historical particularism', that there are as many discourses as there are societies and contexts allows no comparison whatsoever. To engage in ethnographic comparison, moving from local context to a larger one, is to involve oneself in global discourse, in the 'long conversation' of humanity across ages and continents. Moving from Icelandic issues to the global context, focusing on notions of agency, gender and social honour in the ethnographic record, we may distinguish between four kinds of production systems - allowing for two modes of circulation (production for use versus production for exchange) and two modes of access to resources (systems where fishing territories are non-ownable versus ones where areas of the sea are subject to relations of property). Such a scheme may help us to understand the variability in the ethnography.

In one kind of system resources are non-ownable and production is focused on use values. Such systems may be represented by societies of hunters, gatherers and fishers. Given the ceiling on production and the emphasis on use values in these societies, the domestic mode of production, differences among individual producers are unlikely to be emphasised. Among the Dobe !Kung in the Kalahari, for instance, the news of a successful kill is typically met with indifference, even hostility. While men are encouraged to hunt, the successful hunter is expected to be modest and to understate the size of his kill. There may be short-term differences in hunting success, but they tend to be levelled out by joking, insults and gossip. Hunter-gatherer society, then, is characterised by an egalitarian ethos – sharing and generalised reciprocity. Lee (1988: 267) defines this ethos as 'primitive communism'. If each producer *expects* to succeed and differences among producers are suppressed, as is typically the case among hunter-gatherer-fishers, one can reasonably expect to find passive notions of human labour. Examples of such modelling abound in the literature. In general, the animals are said to be offered to humans. Humans, animals and spirits are said to engage in a complex series of transactions; see, for instance, Tanner (1979: 139) on the model of the Mistassini Cree. The hunting and killing of animals, consequently, does not simply involve the application of human skills and energy *upon* the animate world, but rather a dialogue or exchange which is often patterned after human relationships.

Hunting activities are regarded as love affairs where hunters are 'seduced' by their prey. Similarly, in Chipewyan society hunters must enter into relationships with game animals in order to have any success (Sharp 1988: 185). Prey animals may refuse to be killed, and to make the animal consent to its death, the hunter must possess a particular magical power, *inkoze*. Only if properly applied will the animal offer itself to the hunter. The model of the Icelandic 'foreman' during earlier centuries closely resembles such a model.

In the second kind of system, production is geared for subsistence, as before, but in this case the resource-base *is* defined as property. In Sri Lanka, where access to fishing grounds is divided between local lineages by a system of rotation, fishing grounds are similarly regarded as property. Alexander (1977) describes this form of tenure applying the concept of the 'estate'. Once access to the resource-base is divided, differences in success and influence can be translated into a permanent power-base. In such production systems, the leaders of fishing operations tend to fill an ascribed position – more like chiefs than Big Men. In Micronesia, those who lead fishing operations and practise magical rites in fishing sometimes occupy a formal status as Chiefs of fishing, a status which is assigned to particular estates. Their authority and contribution to the production process reside more in their office than their person. In systems of this kind, production models still tend to assign a passive role to human labour. Both land and sea tend to occupy a central place in folk models as domains of fertility and value, while human labour tends to be treated as a secondary factor. In this case, however, unlike that of the hunter-gatherer-fisher previously mentioned, the producers are unlikely to be concerned with the mutual bond or contract between the individual and his or her prey. Success is not so much regarded as a personality attribute as a political and economic fact. In Sri Lanka, for instance, people do not find it necessary to account for any personal differences there may be in effort and success: 'the fishing expert is normally the oldest man in the crew, for this is the least physically demanding task and the fishermen place little emphasis on differences in skill' (Alexander 1977: 238). While in this system individual differences in catches tend to be ignored or assumed, being simply a fact of life, production discourse tends to emphasise social distinctions, justifying the privileged access of particular groups to the resource-base in 'ideological' terms.

The third category pertains to market economies with open access to fishing territories. In this case, unlike those previously mentioned, there is no ceiling on production targets. Labour is a commodity, accredited with a particular force or 'power'. As we have seen, Icelandic skippers have fought each other for decades, competing for necessary facilities, equipment and crew. Where this is the case, differences in fishing ability have to be explained. Models of production not only emphasise the generative power of human labour, differential success is conceived in personal, psychological terms. In the western state of Oregon, where catches declined as a result of more boats fishing the same stocks, many fishermen emphasised that this 'affected each fisherman differently because of . . . different degrees of fishing success' (Smith 1974: 375-6). The most successful skippers (the 'highliners'), it was argued, continued to be successful while others experienced reduction in income.

The fourth category in the model represents market economies where the resource-base is subject to rules of ownership. Many fisheries have seen spectacular developments during the last years. Fishing territories are appropriated by regional or national authorities which divide the total allowable catch for a season among producers, often the owners of boats. Production is being subject to an intricate, institutionalised apparatus which limits the scope for free competition between boat-owning fishermen-entrepreneurs. Many kinds of quota-systems and licensing schemes are being introduced in different parts of the world in an attempt to put a ceiling on production. This kind of production system fosters a notion of homeostatic fisheries. At the same time, folk discourse is likely to pay less attention than before to individual differences in catching-power and to emphasise instead the role of capital and equipment in the production process. While the implications of scientific management for production discourse have rarely been explored by anthropologists, some recent studies indicate potential conflicts and changes in folk models of success. Miller and Van Maanen (1979) suggest, for instance, that the prevailing ethos of fishermen in Massachusetts in the east coast state of the United States – summarised in the slogan 'Boats don't fish, people do!' – negates the rationality of the quota system instituted by the authorities. Under quota systems, access is no longer free. For each skipper, the annual catch is decided upon in advance. The utility of catches, therefore, only increases exponentially up to a certain point. As competition between skippers declines, a new model of fishing is likely to emerge. Such changes are going on in the Icelandic context, as I indicated earlier.

Engendered discourse

Notions of gender do not remain immune to transformations of production systems. As the emphasis within production discourse changes from the passive to the active, from the medium to the agent, discourse sometimes becomes heavily 'gendered', establishing a particular stress on the male/female boundary. Women tend to be presented as unproductive, less active than men. Cole (1988) provides an interesting description of such a conceptual change in a Portuguese fishing village. Early in this century, during the period of the Portuguese maritime household economy, women participated in a number of activities which gave them autonomy and authority. Women were defined as productive workers (*trabalhadeiras*). Later, however, with increased wage employment and consumption of manufactured goods, women lost their economic independence. The woman's role was redefined as that of consumer and housewife (*dona de casa*). A comparable redefinition of women's roles has been observed for many fishing communities in other parts of the world.

Some anthropologists have attempted to account for gender-specific notions of production and agency arguing that women, being closer (or generally seen to be closer) to nature than men, tend to be socially invisible (see Ortner 1974). While such a generalisation may have some merit, it hardly applies to the peasant economy of Icelanders. If anything, women were closer to the *cultural* end of Ortner's continuum than the natural one. In Icelandic peasant society female muteness did not exist in the sense that women no less than men participated in the discourse of the 'inside', the realm of culture as opposed to nature. But while women were insiders in the peasant economy, they were not excluded from fishing in the realm of the 'outside'. Both men and women participated in fishing. Even though women's roles and responsibilities within the household – particularly in relation to pregnancy, breast-feeding and caring for young children – often ensured that they stayed home while the men went fishing, there were no cognitive barriers preventing them from joining fishing crews on their expeditions into the 'wild'. With the growth of capitalist fishing and urban centres, however, women *did* become muted.

The binary concepts of culture and nature, the tame and the wild, the public and the domestic, are problematic constructs. As Strathern (1988) has argued, they need not be equally salient categories for different groups of people. And where they *are* meaningful categories their definition may vary from one period to another. Traditionally, Icelandic household producers defined membership in the category of the 'inside' in terms of both the territory of the farmstead and the social relations of the domestic economy. With the decline of the domestic economy, the inside lost its spatial connotation; the spatial inside and the social one no longer coincided. Women remained insiders in the sense that they still belonged to the domestic unit, but according to the new cultural model they became social outsiders, devoid of power and economic productivity. Social membership, belonging to the inside, became independent of space and redefined in social terms alone, in terms of the emerging relations of the market economy.

In market economies the 'domestic' labour of women tends to be presented as private labour on the grounds that it takes place internal to the household, and that its consumption products are 'perishable' use values, requiring immediate use. Conversely, only the non-domestic work of men is regarded as socialised since it alone involves co-operation between households, the production of exchange values and durable commodities. This view of labour, shared by many professional theorists – both classical economists and Marxist critics – is reminiscent of Durkheimian dualism. Domestic labourers are presented as natural beings outside the social life of the market economy. But while in a Durkheimian interpretation of the work process found in hunter-gatherer economies the natural is represented by the extractive activities of autonomous individuals in the 'outside' world (see Pálsson 1991: Ch. 1), in dualistic theories of capitalist economies the natural is located within the sphere of the domestic, in the privatised but often crowded home. In the capitalist economy women only become social or visible insiders to the extent that they engage in non-domestic production, outside the sphere of reproduction. Clearly, one may speak of the shifting place of the natural and the outside in dualistic thought.

While Icelandic peasant society made no fundamental distinction between the economic contributions of men and women, the folk model of the market economy defined domestic roles as economically unproductive, thereby making a new distinction between work and production. About the same time as the idea of the super-productive labour of the male skipper emerged, the related idea of women's labour being *un*productive entered the conceptual universe of Icelanders. Just as some early social theories used the durability of the end product of the labour process to identify productive activities and to separate them from unproductive ones – the 'menial tasks and services [which] generally perish in the instant of their performance and seldom leave any trace or value behind them,' as Adam Smith put it (in Arendt 1958: 89) – so the folk theory of the Icelandic market economy degraded strictly domestic roles as 'passive', apparently on the grounds that they were not embodied in lasting commodities. The change from subsistence economy to capitalist production involved a change from dependence on nature to dependence on commodities. Women were confined to the domestic sphere and, therefore, regarded as unproductive. Men, on the other hand, were regarded as the sole 'providers'.

The devaluation of women's work is not restricted to market economies, but often the change from a subsistence economy to markets has important implications for the social construction of gender. With the development of market economies gender often becomes a particularly salient social category. Models of production are usually gender-specific, treating women's domestic contributions as 'private', 'unproductive' and secondary to those of men. But just as extraction is a social activity whether or not it takes place in a group or by isolated individuals, labour is necessarily a social activity whether or not it takes place in a domestic or non-domestic context. As Mackintosh (1988) argues, the household is not a private place devoid of social content but a social institution constituted by a particular set of relations – the 'social relations of domestic production' involved in the creation of use values, particularly cooking and childcare. Strangely enough, economic theory, which originally defined economic space in terms of the household (*Oikos*), restricts its definition of productive labour to that taking place outside the domestic sphere. Formerly the universe of economic theory, the household is reduced to an empty space.

Conclusions

Students of natural discourse inevitably face the 'problem of reference', or how to relate discourses to the world of which they are a part. The nature of the connection between the symbolic and the real is an age–old topic in western discourse. Plato's dialogue the *Cratylus* discusses the problem in terms of the relation between names and things. Cratylus offers a natural theory of names, arguing that 'everything has a right name of its own, which comes by nature', and that 'there is a kind of inherent correctness in names, which is the same for all men, both Greeks and barbarians' (in Harris 1988: 9). Cratylus' opponent Hermogenes disagrees, asserting that names are entirely arbitrary, being a matter of convention and habit. Most anthropologists would probably agree that folk models are a matter of convention. But if that is the case, how do we account for them?

According to the cultural determinism of Sahlins, culture is 'an order that enjoys by its own properties as a symbolic system, a fundamental autonomy' (1976: 57). In such an approach, culture is seen to be reproduced by one generation after another independent of context – as a reified phenomenon independent of the social, something pre-existing to be 'lived' or 'practised' by the producers in the course of their everyday life. Reality is constituted by meaning. Similarly, in the interpretive approach of Holy (1987: 5–6) social phenomena 'do not exist independently of the cultural meanings which people use to account for them and hence constitute them'. French superstructuralists, including Althusser and Baudrillard, carry this tradition to its extreme, deliberately inverting the base-superstructure model. Humans are seen to submit themselves as servants to the forces of language and culture. Not only is the *category* of nature invested with meaning; nature itself is regarded as a cultural construct. The analysis presented above offers an alternative approach to natural discourse. It assumes that discourses are generated in the context of social practices, in the bedrock of the social. In the course of human life, discourses and activities interweave as people involve each other in mutual relations. Discourses and social relations vary from one case to another, but while each model of human-environmental interaction is the product of a particular historical context, there are different *kinds* of context and discourse. Comparative anthropology looks for similarities and parallels in the apparently boundless variety in ethnography, attempting to contextualise them.

Discourses, however, are not cut off from each other. They are the products of communities of modellers and their boundaries or compositions are problematic (see Gudeman and Rivera 1990). Nor are they static phenomena; each discourse contains the seed of a new kind of discourse, a new paradigm which redefines the issues that people address and attend to. As we have seen, at the beginning of the twentieth century Icelandic discourse on production, gender and agency was radically transformed as Icelanders involved each other in the relations of the market economy. The relatively egalitarian models of the peasant gave way to a 'hierarchic' model with new conceptions of social honour. More recently, with the quota system in fishing and increased government control, a second transformation has begun. The prevailing rationality of the skipper persists, but its credibility diminishes as it loses its social significance. Local discourse is increasingly being silenced by the more public discourse of marine biologists, politicians and state bureaucrats. The contracting for tenure or property rights is at the centre of a fiery, national discourse on various issues; fishiness, the environment, gender and equity - the distribution of wealth and income. Such shifts in natural language, as Foucault (1980) points out in his 'genealogy' of knowledge, are rooted in relations of power; some discourses are suppressed, but others attain the status of an established 'episteme' in the 'regime of truth'.

The indigenous producers referred to above may not regard the preceding account of production systems and discourse on agency, gender and social honour as truthful or convincing. Bird-David suggests that anthropological models of reciprocity and sharing in food-gathering economies, phrased in terms of modern economic and ecological ideas, are 'unlikely to be acceptable to food-gathering people themselves' (1990: 189). She suggests a revision of earlier models, drawing attention to 'a particular type of economy that has not previously been recognized' (ibid.: 189). Some anthropologists go much further and suggest that for a social scientist a false or naive folk model is a contradiction in terms. But just as some ethnographies are more trustworthy than others, some elements of natural discourse are more authentic than others (see Hanson 1979). Lakoff (1972: 650) points out that 'in the gap between the way the universe is and the way people conceive of the universe, there is much philosophy.' There is much anthropology too. However, the most important question regarding the folk model is not whether it agrees with 'reality' but the extent to which it encourages people to act in accordance with the rationality of their social system. Natural discourse serves many purposes beside making true or false statements; people do things with words (Austin 1975). There is no need, then, to assume that informants are always right in their claims. Nor should one assume that people's conceptions are inevitably mystifications of reality, to be decoded by intellectually privileged observers. The important thing is to examine how different kinds of discourse are initiated and reproduced.

A similar argument may be developed for *scholarly* discourse, the household words of the academy. McEvoy emphasises that ecology is discursive praxis, arguing that Hardin's thesis of the 'tragedy of the commons' represents a 'mythology' of resource use, a model 'in narrative form for the genesis and essence of environmental problems' (McEvoy 1988: 214). In this view, the theory of the tragedy of the commons is an important means for making history, an authoritative account with a social force of its own, and not simply an attempt to describe and understand the world. The argument of the tragedy has been forcefully used by governments, companies and individuals when pressing for leasehold or freehold rights to be granted to individuals on areas formerly used by local producers, on the assumption that the users of commons – where access is 'free' for everyone – are autonomous, selfish individuals. 'The farmers on Hardin's pasture', as McEvoy aptly puts it, 'do not seem to talk to one another' (1988: 226). Such an approach illustrates the persistent tendency in western discourse radically to separate systems and activities, the social and the individual. Given such a tendency, different political theories often have more in common than one might expect. For instance, those who advocate 'external', governmental solutions to social problems and those who favour the free-market often seem to be trapped within the same kind of discourse. Despite their differences in other respects, both groups present the political and economic actor as an irresponsible and asocial being, devoid of agency. On the one hand, we have a state apparatus which has nothing to do with individuals, on the other, an individual who has nothing to do with society. In the first case all responsibility is removed from the actor to the state – where it eventually evaporates, given the experience of state dictatorship and military governments. In the second, individual responsibility seems to disappear as well, not because it has been appropriated but simply because it is seen as irrelevant or beside the point.

The members of the household – whether it be in 'real' life or the academy, laypersons or scholars – do not meet on an equal basis in the making of the discourses that come to prevail. Nor is their making based on any absolute standards or criteria. As Bourdieu points out, a prevailing system of prestige and social honour is 'an arbitrary way of living', imposed as 'the legitimate way of life which casts every other way of living into arbitrariness' (1984: 57). What counts is discursive power – in other words, access to symbolic resources. And academic models are no more a straightforward or 'factual' representation of reality, independent of the social context in which they are produced, than the indigenous models of the producers. Discourses on the household of human life and the art of economic production – the issues that people attend to, where they locate agency, and how they define social honour and distribute it among themselves – are, thus, inevitably situated in a larger social context, the art of living.

Acknowledgements

The main arguments developed here are to a considerable extent presented in Pálsson 1991, particularly chapter 3, and some passages of the present text have been directly reproduced from the latter work. I thank Manchester University Press for granting permission to use this material.

Chapter 7

Acting cool and being safe: the definition of skill in a Swedish railway yard

Birgitta Edelman

It is hardly surprising that employers and employees in a company embrace different opinions about how particular tasks should be performed, what skills are needed for the performance, and how one should go about them in order to obtain such skills. This article discusses conceptions of skill among shunters in a large marshalling yard in Stockholm, as well as the conceptions of skill the national railway company displays in regulations and management. In the past differing definitions of the skilled shunter have coexisted, but recent changes in technology and work organisation in addition to the new company policy of regarding skills and abilities, as opposed to seniority, as the grounds for promotion, have now brought the definition of skill *per se* into focus.

Much of the ethnographic material presented here was collected in 1989 and 1990 during fieldwork carried out in Stockholm, at Hagalund railway yard (Hgl). My research was fieldwork 'at home' in a double sense (cf. Abrahamian and Pálsson, both in this volume). First, the people of 'my tribe' spoke my mother tongue, several shunters lived in the same suburb as I did, and, although I am Finnish, I was partly brought up in a Swedish country town. Most of the shunters do indeed come from such small towns, only a slight minority – the youngest ones – being Stockholmers. Secondly, I worked as a shunter for about two years prior to my fieldwork, learning the ropes, not in order to study my comrades but to earn wages and fulfil my place in the team. During the three years I was away from the railway yard I still had occasional contacts with shunters who provided me with the latest news and stories from Hgl, keeping me up to date. When I started my fieldwork I was thus personally acquainted with most of the shunters and many of the new ones were familiar to me through the accounts of my old mates. I was familiar with the jargon, with the jokes and with many of the old stories that were repeated from time to time. It turned out that I even figured in some of them myself.

When I came to do fieldwork I was constantly met by the question: 'Are you coming back to work or are you just visiting?' Visits by old work-mates are common and expected, and there is always time for a chat. It was quite natural, then, that I turned up and I was informed about changes and news even without putting any questions. Matters of work are seldom discussed with outsiders as the shunters find that their job seems to be a mystery to the general public. The insights I had, or was expected to have, from my work experience made it possible and meaningful for them to discuss changes at work with me. As days turned into weeks, my presence became more puzzling, and every so often I was asked what I was really doing. 'You know everything already.' I also repeatedly had to explain that the railway company (SJ) had not paid me to do this 'job'. Hints were made about my intentions, but suspicions were seldom made explicit. This happened in spite of my writing a letter to everyone explaining my plans. I was eventually nicknamed 'the spy'. This name did not, however, catch on very well, but I used it sometimes jokingly myself.

There were straightforwardly positive reactions, too. Some people saw me as an investigator whose report would take issue with inconveniences or problems at work. For this purpose they considered it an asset that the study was made by 'one of us'. Managers and office workers also showed an interest in my work. One person said enthusiastically that my study could be of 'good use' to the company, while another suggested that I compare the shunters – a problem-free group – to other less smoothly working ones at Hgl. As I understand it, they wanted my work to be a kind of 'key to success', a recipe for decreasing turnover of labour and absenteeism among those problem groups.

Although I was 'at home' in the sense of being within my own society, as well as knowing the work and the workplace intimately, due to other circumstances I was still labelled a stranger among the shunters. Apart from being a foreigner, I was a woman, I was 'educated'; I came from an intellectual, middle-class background. Indeed, through my behaviour, language and style, or simply because of what I said, I must have signalled a social position different from the rest as soon as I started working as a shunter at Hgl. It was assumed that, because of this different background, I could not possibly have the same reason for working there as everyone else; to earn a living. I was out of place - not at home. To me, the male, working-class environment suggested values stressing physical strength and forceful action. My survival as a shunter, I felt, depended on coping with the most arduous tasks and distinguishing myself through excellent performance. However, in this my definition of skill and manual labour differed from the ones prevalent among the shunters. What mattered was not heroic contributions or single-handed exploits but the ability to take part in a team, at work as well as in social interaction. My sex turned out to be of very little significance, indeed, but my – no doubt class-bound – conceptions of work and workers were a greater obstacle to learning the ropes and getting the hang of it.

Learning a skill is also learning to recognise what counts as skill, which again means that I improved as a shunter and changed my definition of shunting skills simultaneously (cf. Ingold, this volume). The process was slow, gradual and difficult to grasp as it was not formed by a series of incidents but rather by the daily experiences of and at work. There was no one point that I could call the moment I finally was 'at home', if ever I was.

The problem for the anthropologist 'at home', in the double sense discussed above, is not so much to 'create a distance' from the familiar, nor to overcome 'home blindness'. It is rather, I suggest, a matter of tracing back the steps, of formulating the intuitive and implicit knowledge that so invisibly has been generated in and through the work process, the joking, the mockery – the social interaction – and then to convey convincingly these insights to the anthropological community.

The organisation of work and the shunting career

Swedish passenger trains at the national railways, 'SJ', are composed of a large variety of coaches. The different types (*littera*) have, for a long time, numbered about a hundred, but SJ has aimed at decreasing their number in order to make the 'train-picture' (the composition of the trains) more uniform. A large number of *littera* calls for a much larger stock of coaches and much more complicated and time-consuming shunting, with higher risks of injury to railway workers and damage to materials.

The risks involved in shunting train coaches are not difficult to imagine. Indeed, they are one of the reasons why passers-by often stop to watch shunters at work, to see how they go between the buffers as coaches clash with relentless force. The imminent risks are naturally reflected in the rules and regulations that determine how and by whom the work is to be done, but also in the conceptions of the shunter about the proper attitude to work. Risk versus safety constitutes an idiom in which negotiations of other aspects of work, such as skill and commitment to the group, are veiled. One of the terms the shunters use to describe a good shunter is *säker*, which means 'confident', but also 'safe' and 'cool'.[1]

The traditional way to work is in teams of three to five shunters. The shunt leader (*A-turen*) plans the work on the basis of the work schedule for that particular shift. Leaders give orders to the members of the team, often in an indirect form, before the team go out. In the yard the leader is also, in most cases, responsible for the signals that are given to the engine driver. The heavy responsibilities of the shunt leader are often stressed, perhaps excessively, and this aspect of the work is seen as its biggest drawback. The 'second man' of the team, the B-member (*B-turen*), makes sure that the coaches are stopped properly on the side tracks. Often the B-member works far away from the shunt leader and, therefore, has to possess good knowledge of the work-process as the shunt leader sometimes is

---

1. Douglas and Wildavsky (1982) have discussed risk as a culturally relative concept. My perspective is more limited. I discuss the differences that are represented by SJ and the shunters respectively.

---

obliged to make sudden changes in the plans. Depending on the amount of work, there may be two or three B-members in the same team. In this case, they divide the tasks informally between themselves.[2]

The last person in the team is the C-member (*C-turen*) who normally works entirely according to the orders of the shunt leader. The heavy part of the work, to disconnect and connect coaches, can be done rather mechanically, though not, however, without vigilance. Perhaps the most important task of the C-member is to keep the line of signals between the shunt leader and the engine driver unbroken. With the tracks being considerably bent, this connection is, for the most part, dependent on the C-member and it is considered to be a severe sin to neglect this duty. If C-members stand in the wrong place when a coach is to be disconnected, they are likely to be considered stupid, ignorant or lazy. On the other hand, if they fail to repeat the signals they will be judged more seriously as this jeopardises the lives of other team-members. While the B-member is relied upon by the shunt leader, and sometimes takes on the role of a co-leader, the C-member more often is given redundant orders and reminders.

When ordinary members become ill or go on leave, teams are filled up with people from the deputy-list. While deputy-list workers may qualify as leaders, they may nevertheless be ordered to work as C-members. Almost all shunters begin their career on the deputy-list, joining shunting teams as opportunities arise, but some prefer the unpredictable deputy's life, enjoying the rotation of tasks and work-mates. Becoming an ordinary member of a team is partly a matter of seniority. Within the teams, the rule of seniority has been rather strict as far back in time as one can piece together the system.

One's position in the team, or whether one is working in a team or as a deputy, does not, therefore, unambiguously signal one's skills. It is rather the individual progress through the different tasks that is indicative of differences in skill and performance. In order to become a B-member or a shunt leader in a team, one has to train with a supervisor. The selection process is informal and the amount of training one is given

---

2. Shunt leader, B-member and C-member broadly correspond to 'engine foreman' (or 'yard conductor'), 'fieldman' and 'pin-puller', respectively, in North American terminology (Frederick Gamst, personal communication).

varies. Trainees complain that they are offered few training shifts and irregularly. When there is no shortage of staff, very ambitious persons can, however, influence their own promotion by asking for training shifts and by bargaining with the staff delegator. The staff delegator may also informally consult the senior members of the team in order to find out whether a person is 'ripe' enough to go on to the next stage. In the opposite case, a person only reluctantly accepts a training shift. It is often said that the best job in a team is that of the B-member. The biggest step in the career within the team is the one from being a B-member to becoming a leader and the progress of the trainee during this stage is the thing that is most eagerly observed, discussed and commented upon. It is also at this stage one finds most cases of reluctant trainees.

It is recognised that a number of persons – particularly women – have quit the job when they have been on the verge of becoming shunt leaders. In some cases shunters see this as a form of natural selection, arguing that some persons are not suitable for the job, being too nervous or too indecisive. In the case of the women, however, the shunters express disappointment at the fact that they leave at the moment they are making railway history. One of them was considered to be an extraordinarily talented shunter and her fellow shunters found no explanation for her resignation. They even tried to blame themselves: 'What did we do wrong?' One shunter argued that women were too ambitious and perfectionist; in general, women were better than men in the beginning, but later on, when the complexity of the task was such that one invariably made a lot of mistakes, they tended to break instead of bending. The work of the shunt leader was the watershed, according to this view.

Next above the shunt leader in the career ladder are the outdoor boss and the indoor boss. The former acts as a co-ordinator between the shunt team and the other parties concerned. The outdoor boss is seen as ultimately responsible for the outcome of the work of the team, but a boss who interferes too much is not appreciated by the team. The most popular boss is the one who keeps the team informed and is able to avoid unnecessary work. The same holds for the indoor boss. To take out a coach from a train-set and bring it into the repair shop, rather than having it repaired on the spot, only because a toilet-pedal is out of order, is an example of a 'stupid' task that a good boss refuses to take on. Otherwise, the indoor boss is mostly concerned with paper work - keeping track of coaches in the shunting yard and outside office-hours, making sure that absent staff members are replaced. It is considered to be an important asset to 'have psychology', as one shunter put it, and be able to influence reluctant persons, sometimes even their spouses, in such critical situations.

Team pressure is important. When someone becomes ill immediately before an unpopular shift, especially a night shift, there often is suspicion that the illness is not that serious. Some shunters drag themselves to work regardless of fever and illness, purely to avoid being accused of letting the team down. Filling in for unpredictable gaps in the teams is meritorious. A distinction is made, however, between shunters who take on the shift for the sake of the team and those who are known as notorious *gnetare* ('overtimers'), who will take on any shift for the sake of money.

According to the promotion scheme, the progress from being a C-member to becoming an indoor boss is a slow but certain one. Persons who feel incompetent or uninterested are sometimes able to avoid promotion, but it is almost impossible to halt the advancement of those who are insensitive to group pressure – hints, jokes, criticism or open condemnation – if they have been employed for a given number of years.

Safe shunting: skills, strength and regulations

Skilled shunters are *säker*, cool and secure. Beginners are nervous and, therefore, not *säker*. They do not master the situation and may behave in unpredictable ways. It is often claimed that the problem with the new ones is not that they cannot perform their tasks properly, but rather that they require constant supervision. In addition to the shunters' view on safety, there is an official definition – the safety regulations. These regulations apply to all categories of workers that are in the security service, although different paragraphs are applied to different categories.

'Security service' is a term that refers first and foremost to the safety of passengers and the public (for instance, it is forbidden to kick loose coaches carrying 'persons', i.e. passengers, but not 'personnel'), but it naturally refers to the security of shunters and other workers at SJ. Furthermore, in the case of war SJ falls under military command, and the responsibilities of the railroaders will then include military ones. Negligence or carelessness could become a very serious matter, classified as sabotage. While the presumptive military obligations are, for natural reasons, hardly ever mentioned, except in the introductory course, the term security service has a serious overtone that no doubt gets part of its strength from this very fact.

In discussions about work conditions or pay claims, shunters often refer to themselves using the expression 'we who are in the security service'. Responsibility for the safety of passengers is a natural ingredient of the expression, but often it is obvious that the speakers are chiefly referring to the dangers they submit themselves to in their work. While the security regulations and the shunting instructions describe the proper execution of different tasks stressing the dangers involved in careless and overdaring behaviour, shunters emphasise the risks posed by defective materials and external conditions. New and inexperienced shunters are a risk and should be carefully selected, but nothing can be done about beginners in the sense that they will always be around. The ones that 'fit' the ambience and the demands of the work will stay, while the ones that do not will quit. It is sometimes said that if you stay seven years, you are in it for good.[3]

New shunting regulations were enforced on 1 June 1987. These regulations are founded upon accident statistics and mainly concern the speed limits for the shunting movement as regards jumping on and off and coupling coaches. Formerly, these components of the work process were unregulated and up to the judgement of the individual shunter (within the general speed limit of 30 km/h). Speed was considered a matter of skill and freedom of judgement and beginners are often reminded to show the 'slow-signal' as soon as they feel uncertain or alarmed:

3. The statistics confirm such a view. Of the 87 persons listed in the register of persons that left the group in the seven years between 1982 and 1989, 23 either retired, died or were granted sick pension. Of the remaining 64, only one had been employed for more than seven years in active service. The average length of employment in the case of the 23 persons that died, retired or went on permanent sick leave was 38 years!

'Don't jump off at high speed. It's better to remain on the coach
than risk ones life.' 'Give a slow-signal before you jump, in the
long run you will ruin your knees if you go on like that.' Such
comments are familiar to every beginner. The new regulations
do not, of course, distinguish between old and new shunters. In
the statistics that form the basis for the new rules, only fatal
accidents are related to age and seniority.

Skill, then, is a very important concept for the shunters in
judging risk and danger while it is completely ignored by SJ in
the formulation of the regulations. It is not surprising that this
should be the case, but for this reason the safety regulations take
on an air of a 'beginner's manual' and can, therefore, be
neglected to a certain extent. The controversy between blaming
external factors versus individual judgement as the cause of
accidents is thereby increased. If someone falls and gets hurt
while jumping off the engine, the shunters are likely to blame
uncleared ice or pot-holes in the gravel while SJ rather will
explain the accident in terms of speeding or carelessness.[4] This
will undoubtedly often be a good guess as the speed limit of 0.5
m/sec (half walking-speed) is easily transgressed.

Figure 7.1 illustrates some important shunting concepts. The
vertical line ending in point 'A' represents a continuum going
from the 'perfect' conditions in 'O' to progressively more chaotic
external conditions. This includes everything from tools and
snow-clearing to falling cables and poisonous substances. At 'C'
we have the lack of knowledge that distinguishes the beginner,
the *kabyl*, from knowledgeable shunters whose knowledge is
engraved in the 'spinal marrow' (*ryggmärgskänsla*).[5] The *kabyl*,
according to this view, would be the person who, for example,
tries to stop a rolling coach by putting gravel on the tracks. By
being enlightened, or by experiencing the effect of this action,
the person will presumably avoid doing it again. Finally, point
'B' stands for careless shunters; the ones who use tools for
purposes other than those which they are devised for, who
decide to go between buffers despite the speed being 'too high'
or the tracks being 'considerably bent', and the ones who kick

4. McKenna (1980: 180) writes in relation to the difficulty British railway workers had in
obtaining compensation for accidents up to the 1950s: 'For many years, accidents to railway
staff were attributed to acts of God or personal negligence.' In the case of SJ, however, no
economic gain is to be had by blaming the victim.
5. Kabyl is old railway argot meaning 'beginner'.

out the electric cable of a coach that is 'too close' to the electric post.

To sum up, the security regulations of SJ delimit 'B' in describing the proper uses of technology, the handling of the trains, and all that belongs to the train traffic. It is more or less assumed that the risks involved in 'C' will be eliminated. Training in the correct handling thus involves a 'safety margin', so that unexpected events are included in the work-process. From the viewpoint of the railway company, 'B' has been the problem. This has led to new regulations and a greater emphasis in the education of newcomers on eliminating 'cowboy attitudes'. For the shunters, the perspective is rather different. To them, the balance between 'B' and 'C' describes the real skills of the trade. They think it is their duty to teach the new ones to work 'properly' and to rub out all the tendencies of idiosyncratic Wild West fads that young men tend to develop after the initial stupefaction. This is part of both the process of fitting into the group and learning the ropes, and neither of these can be taught through courses or regulations. Informal condemnation – jokes, stories, ridicule or a shake of the head – are the shunters' weapons against cowboy attitudes. It is, therefore, easy to understand that shunters think there is a connection between the first signs of sociability ('starting to talk') in the behaviour of beginners and the promise that they are becoming *säker*.

Managers stress the importance of formal education, courses and training. Their picture of the shunter's progress is one of steady advances which can be pushed forward to a certain extent. Shunters acknowledge the impact of formal training, but only as an initial measure towards becoming a cool and experienced worker. The everyday events and routines, repeated endlessly over days, months and years, are even more important as it is these that build up the necessary 'feeling in the spinal marrow', and without which, knowledge and formal training would be of little use. This *ryggmärgskänsla* transforms pondering and hesitation into automatic and instinctive behaviour. For shunters, the right attitude to work is something that cannot be taught, only learnt through the process of fitting into the crew and then slowly absorbing good judgement.

The fact that the correct attitude according to the shunters comes from fitting in rather than from instructions can be exemplified by their reactions to a film that is used in the

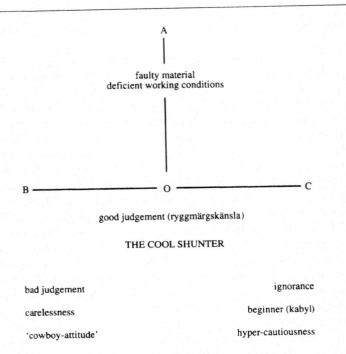

Figure 7.1. Safe shunting: a schematic presentation

introductory course. This film uses a cowboy as an example of the careless shunter. This unlikely figure – wearing a cowboy hat, a fringed suede jacket and high-heel boots – sneaks around in a shunting yard, hits his head on buffers and leaps off a train at high speed. The old and experienced shunters who happened to see the film at the same time as I did thought the film was not only corny but 'inapplicable to the conditions at Hgl'. 'It isn't like that here,' they said. The film built on an assumption that an atmosphere of 'cowboyism' prevails in the marshalling yard. This is something that the shunters would never subscribe to.

To do things calmly – in your own style, and not slavishly follow the instructions of a teacher - but still safely and efficiently, is indeed a sign of skill. To break the rules without proper knowledge is dangerous, but to do it with complete control is a show of skill and personality. The reason why the cowboy image is rejected is that it collapses the two into one, presenting every step away from the rules as a Wild West fad, while the shunters eagerly protect the border between them.

They can tell skill from ignorance, and cowboyism from moderate and safe bending of the rules. The border that the shunters protect is thus the one between the nonplussed helplessness of the beginner and the indiscriminating foolhardiness of the cowboy. The skilled worker and the *säker* shunter are in between 'B' and 'C'.

As regards institutional measures to prevent accidents, the attention of the shunters is almost exclusively turned 'upward', towards material factors 'A'. Complaints concerning the working environment - insufficient lighting, ungreased couplings, unheated switches and lack of working telephones, clocks in the marshalling yard, bars at the road-crossings, snow-clearing and reliable portable radios, etc. – have been the response from shunters to complaints from the company about accidents attributed to careless shunting. While the company seeks the causes of accidents in 'B', the shunters answer by blaming 'A'. A constant ping-pong game of accusations takes place between these points. Balancing on the border between 'B' and 'C' we thus find the cool and experienced shunter, the shunter who has developed good judgement and whose spinal marrow is impregnated with the right feeling. Naturally materials, too, must work, or be made to work, to perfection, so we may place the *säker* shunter in the centre of the figure; 'O'.

When asked about the necessary abilities and skills good shunters should possess, the answers invariably include that they should be calm and have the ability to grasp several moves simultaneously and anticipate the moves ahead. Other properties often mentioned are 'split-vision' (perhaps a rephrasing of seeing several moves simultaneously, although it includes more, for instance being on the look-out for possible dangers), the ability to work in a team, and to be able to take the tough jargon. One old man said: 'Well, you mustn't be an intellectual', but quickly corrected himself to: 'You mustn't act like an intellectual.' 'Fitting in' is the term I have used for the social requirements that signal sensibility to prevalent values and judgements, while, strictly speaking, not being part of the work-skills. Shunters are reluctant to admit that strength is important. When asked they answer: 'I have never used any strength', or 'It is only people who are inexperienced who use strength – I use technique', but none the less you can see the muscles of the young boys swell after a few months of work.

Even old and experienced shunters happily admit (in other contexts!) that their muscles ache when they return from a fortnight's holiday. Shunters also admit and even stress that certain shifts, such as cold winter nights, take a lot of endurance.

Several of the shunters have rather heavy jobs beside shunting, in gardening, boat repairs, stores, etc. Beginners may admit they are exhausted at the end of the shift, but as shunters sometimes work two shifts in a row, even three, the complaints are met with jokes and little understanding: 'How can you be tired? I haven't seen you do a thing today', or 'I can't remember having been tired when I was your age'. Such comments stress that the cause of a beginner's exhaustion is to be sought not in the work but elsewhere. Technique and timing, then, are considered more important than physical strength. Instead of lifting up the coupling you give it a push and catch it at the right moment when it swings back. You don't waste strength on a coupling in a bend, but let the engine push the coaches to a straight part of the tracks. Fighting with frozen couplings is useless so you just put a newspaper on top and set fire to it. The little tricks are considered to be many and no one will give you credit for using your hands instead of your head. 'You mustn't be stupid!' is the triumphant phrase used when someone wants to make sure another has noticed the smart tricks needed to solve a problem. Generally speaking, beginners have the heaviest tasks. By stressing the importance of the right technique the elders thus camouflage that they themselves have an easier job, displaying at the same time their know-how and competence.

Things 'you just learn'

Both tricks and fitness are part of the make-up an experienced shunter has accumulated over time. Another asset that 'comes with time' is the mass of local knowledge that is never taught in a sequence, but rather portioned out in occasional comments that the beginner is simply expected to heed himself – the tracks and their branching, the different *littera* of the coaches, the manoeuvring of gates, etc. All of this is learnt little by little before, during and after the training period. Although shunters sometimes claim there is 'nothing to learn', one should not underrate the amount of knowledge involved. Some of the most elementary tasks, such as reading the work-schedule, demand a great deal of knowledge.

No one will expect a beginner to be able to read the work-schedule, 'the slips' (*lapparna*), and there are, in fact, several ways to read them. The shunting team gets information about how the trains should be assembled, with every coach marked with numbers indicating whether or not it is arriving as part of another train, whether it is to be collected from the reserve, the repair shop or somewhere else. Shunters in jobs other than the shunt team proper get the 'reverse' information from the slips. By checking incoming trains they can see which coaches are to go together in the new train and which ones have to be prepared for shunting by 'knocking holes' in the train – i.e. by clearing bridges and cables. These 'knockers' are said to have the benefit of learning to read the slips as a side effect of their work. It is, however, quite possible to learn to knock without getting the hang of how shunting is done. I think that this is yet another instance of the underrating of the information you need in order to be able to lead a shunting team. The knockers learn the numbers and the compositions of the trains, the times and tracks of arrival, and the places to which the coaches will go after shunting. They also learn certain manipulations that make shunting easier – for instance, 'stealing' coaches from one train, knowing that they can be replaced by coaches that are to arrive later on. Such knowledge is necessary but hardly sufficient in itself for the shunt leader. Shunt leaders have a rather intricate jigsaw on their hands, and there is no shortcut to getting the hang of it. They have to know the timetables for tracks as well as for trains, be able to 'read' a train composition at a distance, in order to save the team from superfluous moves and unnecessary work. And all of this has to be considered simultaneously.

Good shunt leaders are thus characterised by their ability to plan and to see ahead. Although plans are, of course, invisible, and superfluous moves and clumsy solutions may pass unnoticed, the behaviour of the shunt leader, or the B-member, will not do so. As long as the shunt leader is calm and confident and things run smoothly, there is a tendency to read his planning as good, even if the solutions are not as smart as they could have been. Calmness is connected to safety and ideal shunting is conducted without shouting, running, hesitation or changes of mind.

To have the hang of it (*att ha greppet*) means to have sufficient knowledge to shunt without making a complete mess of it all, but it also includes possessing good judgement. Having good judgement is, however, less important than making everyone else believe that you have it. In trading the image of yourself as a good shunter every question or uncertainty that might signal deficient planning or foresight means a little crack in a polished and calm surface.

Composure is the hallmark of the good shunter and therefore situations of crisis are also critical situations for the image of the shunter. Calmness can be brought too far. To be calm when an accident is imminent displays lack of good judgement. Composure is the first thing the fledglings learn to imitate. Indeed, beginners sometimes have to be shaken out of their false composure by an experienced shunter. Little incidents – involving, for instance, removal of a train-set with the electric cable still connected or a coach running wild – call for speedy execution. The necessary leaps and manipulations in such situations do not call for composure and the comrades are unlikely to mock a shunter for unstylish or clumsy behaviour as long as it is successful. The unstylish leaps that one makes from a coach due to misjudged urgency will, however, be noted and possibly commented upon. Excuses, explanations, rationalisations and fully fledged lies – and plain silence, if no one observed the mistake – are needed to protect the image of the shunter. The ultimate criterion for good judgement is the outcome. Returning to Figure 7.1, in the grey areas of uncertain cases on either side of the centre, an accident would switch behaviour on the B-leg over to the C-leg in one instance. But while behaviour may be condemned as risky and lacking good judgement long before it results in an accident, the margin of 'negotiation' is rather large. Complaints about laziness or neglect are often dressed up as arguments about risk and danger. Being able to define the clumsiness of someone else as dangerous ensures that a condemnation is taken seriously, but if one fails to do so criticism turns back upon oneself. Good judgement comprises the ability to detect *real* dangers – to define possible outcomes and to give sound advice. The personal work-style of the shunter is recognised and valued. Personal style, much like the good taste described by Bourdieu (1984: 169), indicates that rules and regulations have been internalised and moulded into the personality so that no traces of effort or nervousness prevail.

Personal style, too, has a tinge of the safety aspect, as consistency and repetitive behaviour allow for prediction. Teams are said to work well because members know the work-style of each other and can, therefore, predict what the others are up to. Being used to a team and a certain style consequently means that one often prefers a particular way of working. While the shunt leader who never makes any mistakes may be held in esteem and be described as the best, one may nevertheless prefer to work with less perfect ones because it feels less demanding, because one enjoys the jokes and the atmosphere, or because one is given more responsibility in the planning, thereby learning to read the slips.[6]

Competence in timing and time-saving are very important in shunting. The amount of work on the day's agenda, the weather conditions, and the amount of repairs that have to be done influence the time it takes to get the job done. By increasing the work-speed, minutes can be saved. The extent to which the team can speed up the process is limited, however, partly because of safety considerations. Accidents are easily identified, but exactly when safe and sound shunting is surpassed by rushed or risky shunting is arguable. Shunt leaders set the speed, but as they are dependent on all members of the team and, furthermore, the engine driver, a one-sided attempt to speed up the team would be met with irritation and criticism. Speed is thus a result of the co-operation of all the individuals in the team. A gain in work-time means that the team can spend more time at breaks and leave early. Collectively gained 'slip-off time' (*smit-tid*) at the end of the shift is a matter of pride – an objective proof of the skill of the team, in particular the shunt leader. A team entering the coffee room after work is sometimes met by a comment like: 'Have you already finished?' The shunt leader will smile, saying 'Yes, we are very early, but then we had such a good shunt leader today', or just modestly point out that there was little

6. I do not consider it a universal human trait or a prime mover to strive for esteem, work-satisfaction, or material advancement, as Hatch (1989) does, for instance. While I agree with him that 'the qualities of the participants' achievements are noticed and evaluated by others' (Hatch 1989: 348), I doubt that such an evaluation automatically leads to a hierarchy, as this seems to build on the assumption that participants in collective activities not only share the same values but, furthermore, that these values do not come into conflict with each other. My view of a 'cultural system', I think, is much more chaotic than that of Hatch.

work that day. Workers will answer by complaining about extra
work or the useless driver they had. In the long run, external
factors should even out. Certain teams are considered to be
always slow while others regularly manage to get a reasonable
slip-off time. The time gained is a gain for everyone in the team.
A work-speed that allows the shunters to express their skill in
timing, planning and co-operation without bargaining with
safety is the ideal of every shift.

Individual slip-off time is suspect or outright condemned.
Shunters on the fringe of the teams – including trainees and
extra B-members – sometimes take the opportunity to slip off
instead of helping the team. If there is little work this is
considered acceptable, but if the work-load is heavy, everyone
should stay until the job is finished. Those who are repeatedly
late or generally leave their team with a lot of work will quickly
get a reputation as *smitare* or, if notorious, *strulare* – a messy
person or trouble-maker. The stress on punctuality and
reliability is a stress on the importance of group solidarity. Skills
and strength are highly valued, but as the shunters say: 'What's
the use of it if the person isn't here?'

Skill, as we have seen, is to a large extent the ability to co-
operate, to do one's duties in the team and not to slip off. To do
something over and above the necessary, however, to excel and
show off, has little value. The path between speed and safety,
between *kabyl* and *cowboy*, is the narrow path of proper shunting
– shunting with flow and perfect co-operation.

The new order: a redefinition of skill

The Swedish labour market had become very competitive and
low-paid jobs were increasingly difficult to fill. In 1988 and 1989
there was a constant shortage of twenty persons in the shunting
group at Hgl and it turned out to be impossible to recruit new
shunters. The situation was all the more serious due to the fact
that many old shunters were about to retire. The constant
shortage of staff made it impossible to train younger shunters to
fill the gaps as everyone was needed to keep the teams going
and the trains rolling. The annual limit of overtime seemed to be
reached before the beginning of the summer holidays. In the
midst of this it was difficult to maintain that the teams were

working at their full capacity. Even older shunters admitted that things were beginning to become 'too slack'. In order to deal with these problems, the manager of the shunters introduced a new order.

The first part of the reform was the introduction of remote controlled engines. The engine driver was replaced by a shunter. As this new engine driver could stand on the ground far from the engine, and still operate it by remote control, there was no longer any need to allocate one person to the job of mainly repeating signals. By reducing the number of engines from four to three and the number of teams from nine to six, further savings were accomplished. The new teams were, however, enlarged and it was said that the work should now be organised in a more flexible way so that everyone would do the task that was closest at hand. The strict division of tasks was to be abandoned. This was, however, later rephrased as an optional reorganisation. Every team was to be given full autonomy to work out its own routines. Team solidarity was seen as all-important.

The replacement of external engine drivers with internal shunters, in addition to cuts in the teams, meant a gain for the shunting group of approximately 19 million Swedish kronor annually. In order to make the shunters accept such drastic changes, each shunter was offered a bonus of 100 kronor per shift, thereby returning about 5 million kronor to the shunters. Apart from raising a lot of envy among other workers at SJ, this bonus had the effect of stopping the drain of the workforce. One of the unintended consequences of this was that the already low rate of absenteeism decreased even further. Staff are now abundant and several persons have been trained as engine operators and shunt leaders. The shunt group that formerly discussed the end of the shunting division at Hgl are now in the mood to expand.

There are, however, unforeseen complications within the group. While some of the teams have retained the old way of shunting, other teams have developed a new model which is consistent with the intentions of the team reorganisation as they were first expressed. The new model is a direct result of the fact that the remote-control operator stands on the ground rather than on the engine. Standing in strategic spots the operators can see the buffers meet, making the signalling of the C-members superfluous. This way of working is considered, at least by those who are in favour of it, to save a lot of work and to be much safer. The 'traditional' shunters are working as before, but there has been much animosity between contesting groups, even threats and aggressive behaviour, which is difficult to understand given the voluntary nature of the new arrangement.

To return to my earlier argument, the 'new order' – where the operator that drives the engine is simultaneously a shunter – is a model that favours innovative and daring shunters. The double-checking and omnipresent style of shunting is on the losing end. The former ideal shunters, reliable and predictable in every inch, have been reluctant to change and divide tasks in a new way. They cling to their old styles as far as possible and refer to 'the principle' of shunting, according to which one person should not do two jobs, i.e. drive and shunt simultaneously, or they refer to the security risks that are involved in the new order. The more flexible and easygoing shunters, however, have been able to accustom themselves to the wind of change. They delegate tasks freely and boast about how well the team-members co-operate and how much safer the new working practices are. While they admit that it will be more difficult for beginners to partake in the new teams, they emphasise that the work has become more interesting as everyone in the team is more qualified and knows what is going on. Since the engine operator is unable to handle the rather heavy hand-control for more than half a shift, several persons in the team must take turns at operating and giving orders.

There is, thus, an obvious 'democratisation' in teams that work in the new way, as opposed to traditional ones where a strict hierarchy prevails. The end-result of all of this is that while earlier there were various styles of doing the job, there are now two different methods, each demanding different kinds of skills and a different allocation of responsibilities. The definition of the skilled shunter and good judgement, then, is changing. Some shunters are considered to be 'old-fashioned' and their way of working 'outdated'. This would, perhaps, not be so serious had it not been for the general uncertainty among shunters about the future. There is a feeling, even by the proponents of this scheme, that standing on the ground when operating the engine will be introduced by force and, as a consequence, the team-members reduced in number. This will lead to a rather heavy work-load, unless there are cuts in shunting – due to new fixed high-speed train-sets or some other unknown future changes.

Another uncertainty concerns the reformed promotion scheme. Earlier, promotion was granted on the sole ground of seniority, but this is no longer the case. Management is now, in principle (the union has a say, too), free to choose among the employees and grant promotion according to 'skill and ability'. The work-process, then, has undergone a fundamental change which has led to a redefinition of skill. The 'best shunter' of Hgl has suddenly discovered that his reliable way of shunting is labelled old-fashioned by the management and authoritarian by the shunters.

At present, to talk in the terms of Figure 7.1, the border between 'B' and 'C' is under dispute. A group of cowboys has appeared on the scene. And as long as they manage to redefine the correct way of working, which indeed they seem to be doing, the former ideal shunter is relegated to a position on the *kabyl* side. Skill and good judgement are no longer what they 'always' used to be. This will not only influence the esteem and informal position of the individual shunter but most likely salaries and future prospects as well. This allows one to understand why the question of whether someone else in another team prefers to operate the engine from the ground, rather than standing on the engine, can cause such animated feelings and so much disturbance. The discussion about whether the new way of working is risky or whether it is the old way that is the risky one is, then, a discussion about skills, future prospects and group solidarity and not primarily a discussion about how to drive a remote-controlled engine.

Time and flow

Time has, since Cottrell's classic article 'Of time and the railroader' (1939), been one of the most important aspects when discussing railway work from a sociological point of view. While Cottrell (1939: 195) stresses the time-consciousness of the railway men, the demands of the system that make the workers slaves to the clock, a more recent study, made by Kemnitzer, extends the time aspect to include 'the ability to integrate time, distance, and subjective estimates about weight, slope, and speed in making

decisions about the movements of cars and engines in switching'
(1977: 27). He describes this time-sense, which he calls
'switching time', as the most important one regarding
competence and safety. Such skill in timing and estimating
speed in varying weather conditions is more closely related to
the skill one needs in order to catch and throw a ball than to the
'tyranny of the clock'. Timing, as I call this skill, has few social
connotations and is basically a matter of skilful estimations of
the combination of force, weight, speed and friction.

A high work-speed and perfect timing gives the work the
good 'flow' the shunters at Hgl constantly strive for. Flow, as
opposed to timing, is completely dependent on the
achievements of the entire team. Planning, co-operation and
consideration for the skills of every team member, then, are
obvious prerequisites. Here safety aspects enter the picture.
Higher speed means greater flow only as long as all links of the
chain, all members of the team, are competent to handle the
situation. There can be no guessing or explicit risk-taking, and
the policy is consequently to avoid pushing the weakest team-
members into situations beyond their competence. Safety calls
for tolerant behaviour. Telling someone off is not ruled out, but
it should be done swiftly, leaving no lingering grudges.

Stressing the 'flow' of work, the friendly co-operation and the
ability to put up with dreadful weather conditions with a sense
of humour implies that the attitude towards work and
workmates is of more importance than individual skill or
strength. As long as one meets the demands of team-work,
idiosyncratic ideas and behaviour are allowed and even
encouraged.

My initial understanding of the skills in shunting was
founded on the assumption that they were assessed on the sole
basis of individual achievement. I regarded it as a natural set-
back to be a woman and not a particularly strong one. The
shunters, on the other hand, stressed co-operation and the
importance of standing in the right spot at the right moment,
and, consequently, my middle-class assumptions about
'distinguishing myself' were a greater obstacle to my being
accepted than my sex.[7] However, I was beset, just as the

7. Gamst (1986: 251ff) reports on the situation in the United States as radically different in
the way women, in similar jobs, are accepted. He refers this fact to the physical handicap women
represent. My material shows that strength is not considered to be of importance at Hgl.

shunters were, invisibly but forcefully, by the reciprocity of the demands and obligations that spring from the daily toil, the constant efforts to co-operate and create a 'flow' in the work, the 'logic' of the work-process, and the interpretations and meanings that were attached to individual actions. As a shunter among the rest, I absorbed my lessons too.

The experience of work and the comradely interaction during breaks taught me the shunters' dialect. I could now understand the jokes, get the hints, read between the lines, and sense hurt feelings and embarrassed silences. I was 'at home', in the sense that I was expected to know and to understand. I could not pretend to be ignorant. Nor could I ask stupid questions or inquire into self-evident things. I had no stranger-identity for protection. There were no excuses for breaking the rules of decent conversation and normal sociability. I was not only let into the world of implicit meanings and communication; I was very much immersed in it. I can only hope that I have been able to translate some of my spinal knowledge into terms that the reader can grasp.

Acknowledgements

This article is based on research for my doctoral dissertation. My research has been made possible by a generous grant from the Swedish Work-Environment Fund. I thank Tim Ingold for his comments concerning the acquisition of skill and Kristina Bohman for her patient attempts, both during and after my fieldwork, to make me organise my observations and passing fancies. Needless to say, I alone am responsible for the ideas presented here.

Chapter 8

Interpreting and explaining cultural representations[1]

Dan Sperber

A representation sets up a relationship between at least three terms: that which represents, that which is represented and the user of the representation. A fourth term may be added when there is a producer of the representation distinct from its user. A representation may exist inside its user: it is then a *mental representation*, such as a memory, a belief or an intention. The producer and the user of a mental representation are one and the same person. A representation may also exist in the environment of its user, as is the case, for instance, of the text you are presently reading; it is then a *public representation*. Public representations are usually a means of communication between a user and a producer distinct from one another.

A mental representation has, of course, a single user. A public representation may have several. A speech may be addressed to a group of people. A printed text is aimed at a wide audience. Before recent techniques such as printing or magnetic recording made the strict duplication of a public representation possible, oral transmission allowed the production of representations similar to one another: the hearers of a tale may, for instance, become in turn its tellers. It must be stressed, however, that oral transmission is not a reliable means of reproduction; it generates a fuzzy set of representations which are more or less faithful *versions*, rather than exact copies, of one another (cf. Wikan, this volume).

1. This article expands and corrects Sperber (1989).

Consider a social group: a tribe, the inhabitants of a town or the members of an association. Such a group and its common environment are, so to speak, inhabited by a much larger population of representations, mental and public. Each member of the group has, in his or her head, millions of mental representations, some short-lived, others stored in long-term memory and constituting the individual's 'knowledge'. Among these mental representations some – a very small proportion – get communicated, i.e. cause their user to produce in the environment a public representation which in turn causes another individual to construct a mental representation similar in content to the initial one.

Among communicated representations some – a very small proportion again – are communicated repeatedly and may even end up being distributed throughout the group, i.e. have a mental version in most of its members. When we speak of *cultural representations*, we have in mind – or should have in mind – such widely distributed and lasting representations. Cultural representations so understood are a fuzzy sub-set of the set of mental and public representations of a given social group.

Anthropologists have not converged on a common view of cultural representations, a common set of questions about them, or even a common terminology to describe them. Most authors approach the various genres of representations separately and talk of beliefs, norms, techniques, myths, classifications, etc. according to the case. I would like, nevertheless, to reflect on the way anthropologists (and other social scientists) represent and attempt to explain cultural representations in general.

Interpreting cultural representations

Suppose you want to produce a representation of a basket: you may produce an image of the basket, or you may describe it. In other terms, you may either produce an object that resembles the basket, for instance a photograph or a sketch, or else you may produce a statement. The statement in no way resembles the basket, but it says something true about it. (Truth, of course, is a necessary, but not a sufficient condition for a description to be adequate.) It might seem that the situation is the same when what you want to represent happens to be a representation, the tale of Little Red Riding Hood, for instance. You might record or transcribe the tale (or, rather, a particular version of it), that is, produce an object that resembles the tale in the manner in which a photograph or a sketch resembles a basket. You might also describe the tale by stating, for instance: 'It is a tale found throughout Europe, with one animal and several human characters, etc.'

Yet, there would be something missing in these representations of Little Red Riding Hood: the recording or the transcription in themselves only represent an acoustic form, while the description suggested tells us little more about the *content* of the tale, which, after all, *is* the tale. All you need do, one might argue, is describe the tale in greater detail. You might state for instance: 'Little Red Riding Hood is a tale found throughout Europe, which tells the story of a little girl sent by her mother to take a basket of provisions to her grandmother. On her way, she meets, etc.' You could, of course, in this manner recapture the content of the tale as closely as you would wish, but notice what would be happening then: instead of *describing* the tale, you would be *telling* it all over again. You would be producing an object that represents the tale, not by saying something true about it, but by resembling it: in other words, you would be producing yet another version of the tale.

Let us generalise: in order to represent the content of a representation, we use another representation with similar content. We do not describe the content of a representation, we paraphrase it, we translate it, we summarise it, we expand on it, in a nutshell, we *interpret* it.[2] An *interpretation* is a representation of a representation by virtue of a similarity of content. In this sense, a public representation, the content of which resembles that of the mental representation it serves to communicate, is an interpretation of that mental representation. Conversely, the mental representation resulting from the comprehension of a public representation is an interpretation of it. The process of communication can be factored into two processes of interpretation: one from the mental to the public, the other from the public to the mental.

Interpretations are just as ordinary in our mental life as are descriptions; they are a form of representation produced and

---

2. On the distinction between interpretation and description, see Sperber (1985a, Ch. 1) and Sperber and Wilson (1986, Ch. 4).

understood by everyone. To express oneself or to understand other people's expressions is, implicitly, an act of interpretation. Moreover, we are all producing explicit interpretations when answering questions such as: What did he say? What does she think? What do they want? In order to answer such questions, we represent the content of utterances, thoughts or intentions by means of utterances of similar content.

Needless to say, the anthropological study of cultural representations cannot ignore their contents. As a result, and whether this pleases us or not, the task of anthropology is for a large part interpretive. However, precisely because interpretation is based on a quite ordinary ability rather than on a sophisticated professional skill, most anthropologists have produced interpretations just as Molière's Monsieur Jourdain produced prose: without being aware of doing so, or at least without reflecting much on it.

As long as interpretation is about individual words or thoughts, the degree of freedom that the interpreter grants herself is often manifest and unproblematic. You inform me, for instance, in one sentence and with a sneer, of what the Prime Minister said in his press conference; I have no trouble understanding that while the gist may be the Prime Minister's, the conciseness and the irony are yours. Similarly, ordinary anthropological renderings *of individual words and thoughts* are, often enough, easy to understand and to accept (as long as not too much depends on exact formulation, and, even in the latter case, a carefully glossed translation may still do).

In anthropology, however, what gets interpreted is often a *collective representation* attributed to a whole social group ('The So-and-So believe that...'), and which need never be entertained, let alone expressed, by any one individual member of that group. There is neither a clear commonsense understanding of what such collective representation might be, nor a straightforward way of assessing their faithfulness. The lack of a clear methodology makes it difficult to evaluate and therefore to exploit these interpretations. Nevertheless, they are given an important role in anthropological accounts and, as we shall see, are even sometimes offered as ultimate explanations.

Here is an illustration. The scene, reported by the French anthropologist Patrick Menget, takes place among the Txikao of Brazil:

At the end of a rainy afternoon, Opote came back home carrying a
fine *matrinchao* fish he had caught in his nets. He put it down
without a word next to Tubia, one of the four family heads of his
house. Tubia cleaned it and put it on to smoke. Until the fall of night
he ate it, by himself, in small mouthfuls, under the interested eyes of
the other inhabitants of the house. No one else touched the
matrinchao, nor showed any desire to have some of it. Yet the hunger
was universal, and the flesh of the *matrinchao* is among the most
highly praised. (Menget 1982: 193)

So far, this is essentially an ordinary description: every sentence
in it expresses a proposition presented by the anthropologist as
true. The situation described is, however, quite puzzling: 'Why',
asks Menget, 'this general abstention?' And he goes on to answer:

The fisherman, Opote, possessor of fishing magic, could not
consume his catch without the risk of damaging this magic. The
other family heads avoided the flesh of the *matrinchao* for fear of
endangering the health and the lives of their young children, or their
own health. Since their wives were nursing, they had to abstain for
the same reason. The children, finally, would have absorbed the
particularly dangerous spirit of this species. (ibid.: 193)

This time the anthropologist – who does not himself believe
in magic or spirits – is not presenting as true that Opote was
running the risk of damaging his magic, or that the children
would have absorbed a particularly dangerous spirit. He is
presenting these statements as similar in content to the beliefs
motivating the abstinence of Opote's people. These are
interpretations. Such interpretations of individual thoughts are
neither harder to comprehend, nor more suspicious than the
interpretations we all use all the time to talk of each other.

However, the anthropologist's ultimate goal is not to report
particular events. Menget's aim, for instance, in reporting the
anecdote of Opote's *matrinchao*, was to illustrate some hypotheses
on the 'couvade', first among the Txikao themselves, then among
the South American Indians, and ultimately on the couvade in
general.[3] Menget proposes a subtle analysis of the relevant
Txikao views on life and its transmission and concludes:

3. 'Couvade', it will be remembered, refers in anthropological literature to a set of
precautions a man is expected to take during and just after the birth of a child of his,
precautions similar to those imposed on the mother of the child for more obvious reasons.
For a discussion of the couvade, see Rivière (1974).

everything happens as if two antagonistic principles ruled over the life processes. . . . A strong principle, tied to blood, to fat, rich meats and fermentation results from the constant somatic transformation of weaker substances, water, milk, sperm, white flours, lean meats. But inversely, the human body, in rhythms that vary with age, sex, and condition, anabolizes the strong substances and neutralizes their danger. . . . In the couvade, the whole set of occupational, alimentary, and sexual taboos comes down in the end to avoiding either an excess of strong substances . . . or a loss of the weak somatized substances. . . . The creation of a new human being activates the whole universal process of transformation of substance, but also the separation of a part of the somatized substance of the parents and the initiation of an individual cycle. (ibid.: 202–3)

Again, the ethnographer is interpreting: he does not himself, for instance, believe or intend to assert that 'the human body anabolizes strong substances' the non-assimilation of which 'leads to swelling diseases'. He is offering such formulations as similar in content to cultural representations underlying the Txikao couvade practices.

However, while it is easy enough to imagine Opote thinking or saying, in roughly similar terms, that he could not consume his catch without damaging his magic, it is hard to conceive of Txikao thoughts or utterances involving notions of, say, the 'somatic transformation of weak substances', or the 'anabolization of strong substances'. The resemblance of content between the interpretation and the representations interpreted is manifestly weaker here than in ordinary interpretations of individual thoughts or utterances, and the degree of resemblance is hard or even impossible to evaluate. (What is at stake is not the work of an individual anthropologist: on the contrary, I have chosen to discuss Menget's essay because I see it as a good example of today's best ethnography. At stake here are the limits inherent in the interpretive approach to cultural representations.)

An ethnographer is faced at first with a great diversity of behaviour which she progressively manages to understand by discerning underlying intentions, that is by becoming able to conceptualise this behaviour as actions. She becomes adept, in particular, at discerning the intentions governing speech acts, in other terms, at comprehending what her interlocutors mean (cf. Edelman, this volume). Intentions thus understood still call for further and deeper understanding. Let us accept that 'the family heads avoided the flesh of the *matrinchao* for fear of endangering the health and the lives of their young children, or their own health', but how are such means supposed to serve such ends? A deeper understanding of intentions involves grasping how they could be rational, or in other word, seeing how they might follow from underlying desires and beliefs. If, for the Txikao, the flesh of the *matrinchao* is 'strong' and hazardous for one's health, if father and child are of one and the same substance, a substance which, contrary to appearances, does not divide into two independent beings until some time after birth, then we begin to grasp how the behaviour of Opote's people might be rational. To grasp it further, we should try to establish the rationality of the underlying beliefs themselves, that is, not just their mutual consistency, but also their compatibility with Txikao's experience.

In our everyday striving to understand others we make do with partial and speculative interpretations (the more different from us the others, the more speculative the interpretations). For all their incompleteness and uncertainty, these interpretations help us – us as individuals, us as peoples – live with one another. Anthropologists have contributed to a better understanding and thus a greater tolerance, of culturally different others. To do so, they haven't relied on scientific theories or rigorous methods, which are not part of the anthropologist's standard tool-kit. Given the cultural distance, the comprehension goals of anthropologists are particularly ambitious and arduous. Still, the form of comprehension involved is quite ordinary: anthropologists interpret behaviour, verbal behaviour in particular, by attributing beliefs, desires and intentions to individual or collective actors, in a manner that makes this behaviour appear rational.

One might assume that the best interpretation is the most faithful one, i.e. the one whose content most resembles that of the interpreted representation. On reflection, things are not that simple. If her aim were just to maximise faithfulness, the anthropologist should only publish translations of actually uttered words. However, most utterances heard by the anthropologist make sense only in the very specific context in which they were produced; they rely on shared cultural representations which they do not express directly.

The anthropologist must, for her own sake to begin with, go beyond mere translation: only then can she hope to understand what she hears, and thus be genuinely able to translate it. She must speculate, synthesise, reconceptualise. The interpretations that the anthropologist constructs in her own mind or in her notebooks are too complex and detailed to be of interest to her future readers, and moreover they tend to be formulated in an idiosyncratic jargon where native terms, technical terms used in an *ad hoc* way, and personal metaphors mix freely. Later, writing for readers who will spend a few hours on a study to which she devoted years, the anthropologist must synthesise her own syntheses, retranslate her own jargon, and, unavoidably, depart even more from the details conveyed by her hosts. In order to be more relevant, the anthropologist must be less faithful.

Moreover, similarity of content varies with the point of view and the context. To say, for instance, that for the Txikao, the human body 'anabolizes strong substances' is suggestive and not misleading in the context of Menget's discussion: in that context, the notion of anabolisation is taken quite metaphorically. In other words, the resemblance between the chemical notion of anabolisation and the Txikao notion it interprets is seen as pertinent but quite restricted. On the other hand, the same interpretive statement would be misleading in the context of a comparative study of cultural views of the chemistry of digestion, where consideration of relevance would lead one to take the notion of anabolisation much more literally.

The intuitive and context-dependent character of interpretation does not mean that all interpretations are equally good or bad, but it does mean that our criteria of evaluation are themselves partly intuitive and of limited intersubjective validity. Some imaginable interpretations would be, by all reckonings, quite bad (e.g. that the true content of the Holy Trinity dogma is a recipe for chocolate mousse). But it may happen that significantly different interpretations of the same representation all seem plausible. The data interpreted by Menget in an 'intellectualist' manner (i.e. as involved in an attempt at explaining the world) might, for instance, be approached with equal subtlety in a psychoanalytic vein. Presented with both types of interpretations, readers would, no doubt, choose according to their theoretical preferences. Moreover, in doing so, they would act rationally. Here, however, is the rub: if it is rational to prefer one particular interpretation to another on the basis of prior theoretical preferences, then it is hard or impossible to validate or invalidate a general theory on the basis of particular interpretations.

Interpretation allows a form of understanding that we cannot do without in everyday life, the understanding of representations, mental and public, and therefore the understanding of people. In the scientific study of representations, interpretation is just as indispensable a tool as it is in everyday life. But can we use as a scientific tool an intuitive and partly subjective form of understanding?

No evidence is absolutely reliable, and, arguably, no evidence is theory-independent. However, the basic requirement for the scientific use of any evidence is not that it should be absolutely reliable and theory-independent, but only that it should be more reliable than the theories that it serves to confirm or disconfirm and therefore independent of these particular theories (or of any equally or more controversial theory).

Some interpretations are more reliable than others and more intersubjectively acceptable. If these interpretations somehow depend on 'theories' of human comprehension, these are tacit theories that human beings in general and anthropologists in particular are not even aware of and therefore not intending to challenge. Thus, we would all, I guess, trust Menget and accept his claim that Opote could not consume his catch without the risk of damaging his fishing magic as, at the very least, a reasonably approximate interpretation of part of what Opote himself or others around him might have said. That is, we would trust Menget's ability to understand and sometimes to anticipate what individual Txikaos may have said to him on specific occasions, just as we would trust ourselves if we had been in Menget's place, having learnt the language, spent the time among the Txikao, etc. Fairly literal and flat interpretations of particular utterances and ordinary intentions made by individuals competent in the language and familiar with the people are not totally reliable or theory-independent, but they are often uncontroversial.

Commonsensical interpretations of particular utterances and of other normally intelligible individual behaviours are reliable enough to be used, with methodological caution, as basic evidence for anthropological theorising. That is, these interpretations are significantly more reliable than the theories we might want to test with their help. On the other hand, more speculative forms of interpretation, such as interpretations of beliefs the believers themselves are incapable of articulating, or interpretations of collective mentalities, whatever their attractions and merits, will not do as evidence.

The question then is: can anthropological theorising rely only on the first, more reliable but also more modest, kind of interpretation? The answer depends on the kind of theorising one wants.

Explaining cultural representations

'To explain' may be taken in two senses. In a first sense, to explain a cultural representation, for instance a sacred text, is to make it intelligible, i.e. to interpret it. The previous section dealt with such interpretive explanations. In another sense, to explain a cultural representation is to show how it results from relatively general mechanisms at work in a given specific situation (cf. Pálsson, this volume). In this second sense, the only one to be considered in this section, the explanation of cultural representations has an essential theoretical aspect: the identification of the general mechanisms at work. This theoretical objective is not a concern of most anthropologists, whose main focus is ethnography, and is pursued in a scattered and piecemeal fashion. There is not even a majority view – let alone a general agreement – as to what might be regarded as an adequate explanatory hypothesis in anthropology.

Simplifying greatly (and with apologies for the unfairness that such simplification entails), I will nevertheless distinguish four types of explanation – or purported explanation – in anthropology, three of them widespread: interpretive generalisations, structuralist explanations and functionalist explanations; and a rarer type of explanation a version of which I have been defending for some time: epidemiological models (see Sperber 1985b, 1990).

Interpretive generalisations

Many anthropologists seem to think that a – if not *the* – right way to arrive at theoretical hypotheses consists in taking the interpretation of some particular phenomenon in a given culture and tentatively generalising it to all phenomena of the same type in all cultures. Thus, on the basis of European examples, the couvade was long considered as a symbolic – more precisely, hyperbolic – expression of the ties of paternity. Mary Douglas for instance suggests: 'The couvading husband is saying, "Look at me, having cramps and contractions even more than she! Doesn't this prove I am the father of her child?" It is a primitive proof of paternity' (Douglas 1975: 65). Claude Lévi-Strauss offers another generalised interpretation, inspired by American Indian examples:

> It would be a mistake to suppose that a man is taking the place of the woman in labor. The husband and wife sometimes have to take the same precautions because they are identified with the child who is subject to great dangers during the first weeks or months of its life. Sometimes, frequently for instance in South America, the husband has to take even greater precautions than his wife because, according to native theories of conception and gestation, it is particularly his person which is identified with that of the child. In neither event does the father play the part of the mother. He plays the part of the child. (Lévi-Strauss 1966: 195)

Patrick Menget, whose essay develops Lévi-Strauss's suggestion, concludes in a more abstract fashion (rendered even more abstract by out-of-context quotation): 'The power of the couvade lies in its articulation of a logic of the natural qualities of the human being and a problematic of succession, and in signifying by its progression and durability the irreversibility of human time' (Menget 1982: 208).

Such anthropological interpretations raise two issues. First, what exactly are these interpretations supposed to represent? Some would say: they represent the general meaning of the institution they interpret. Yet, any bearer of meaning, be it a text, a gesture or a ritual, does not bear meaning in itself, but only *for someone*. For whom, then, does the institution have its alleged meaning? Surely, it must be for the participating people, say for Opote and his fellows. There is every reason to suppose, however, that the participants take a view of their institution that is richer, more varied, and more linked to local considerations than a transcultural interpretation might ever hope to express. At best, therefore, these general interpretations are a kind of decontextualised condensation of very diverse local ideas: a gain in generality means a loss in faithfulness.

The second issue raised by these interpretive generalisations is the following: in what sense do they explain anything? How – and for whom – would the performance of an easy rite by the husband of every about-to-be or new mother serve as a 'proof of paternity?' How would the father's playing 'the part of the child' protect – or even seem to protect – the child from grave dangers? Who would willingly endure great deprivations for the sake of 'signifying the irreversibility of human time?' A meaning is not a cause; the attribution of a meaning is not a causal explanation. (Of course, there are cases where the attribution of a meaning to a behaviour fills a gap in an otherwise satisfactory causal explanation, but not so here.)

Interpretive generalisations do not explain anything and are not, properly speaking, theoretical hypotheses. Interpretive generalisations are patterns that can be selected, rejected and modified at will in order to construct interpretations of local phenomena. As such, and only as such, may they be useful.

Structuralist explanations

Structuralist explanations attempt to show that the extreme diversity of cultural representations results either from variations on a small number of underlying themes, or from various combinations of a finite repertory of elements, or from regular transformations of underlying simple structures.

All varieties of structural analysis start from interpretive generalisations, but then attempt to go beyond them. This rooting of structural analysis in interpretive generalisation is particularly manifest in the work of one of the founders of the genre, Georges Dumézil (e.g. Dumézil 1968). Dumézil tried to show that the myths and rituals of the Indo-Europeans are all variations on the same underlying pattern: an image of social life as constituted of three 'functions': sovereignty, war and production. This tri-functional pattern is, of course, an interpretive generalisation, but Dumézil exploited it in a properly structuralist way. He tried to show how this pattern gave rise to different structural developments, according to the type of cultural phenomena involved (pantheons, myths, epics, rituals, etc.), and according to the particular culture. He did not search for the explanation of this common pattern and varying structural development in interpretation but rather in history, building on the model of historical linguistics.

In Dumézil's style of structural analysis, just as in standard interpretive generalisations, the only relationships among representations held to be relevant are relationships of resemblance: two representations resembling one another can both be interpreted by means of a third representation which abstracts away from their differences. Lévi-Strauss (e.g. Lévi-Strauss 1963, 1973) has widened the field of structural analysis by considering that systematic differences are no less relevant than resemblances.[4] He maintained, for instance, that a myth may derive from another myth not just by imitating it, but also by systematically reversing some of its features: if, say, the hero of the first myth is a giant, the hero of the second myth might be a dwarf, if the one is a killer, the other might be a healer, and so on. Thus a network of correspondences richer than mere resemblance relationships may be discovered among representations: either among representations of the same type, myths for instance, or between different types of representations, myths and rituals, for instance.

Patrick Menget follows a Lévi-Straussian line when he attempts to relate the couvade and the prohibition of incest. The couvade, as he interprets it, expresses the progressive separation of the child's substance from that of its parents. Incest prohibition prevents a man and a woman descended from the same parents from re-fusing substances separated by means of the couvade:

> There is both a relationship of continuity between the couvade and the incest prohibition, since the latter keeps separated what the former had separated out of a common substance, and a functional complementarity, insofar as the couvade orders a communication within the social group which allow its diversification, and the incest prohibition establishes its external communication. (Menget 1982: 208)

Such a structural account does not by itself explain the couvade, but if one accepts it, it modifies the explanatory task. The *explanandum* is not anymore just the couvade; it is a complex of representations and practices having to do with the mechanism of biological reproduction (as understood by the

---

4.   For a discussion of Dumézil's approach and a comparison with Lévi-Strauss's, see Smith and Sperber (1971).

Txikaos), a complex the coherence of which the anthropologist has attempted to establish, in spite of its superficial motley appearance.

Structural analysis raises two main problems, one methodological, the other theoretical. The methodological problem is as follows: in order to establish structural relationships among representations, the anthropologist interprets them. It is among the resulting interpretations, rather than among the observable or recordable data, that systematic resemblances and differences may be manifest. However, with a bit of interpretive ingeniousness, any two complex objects can be put into such a structural relationship. One could thus show that, say, *Hamlet* and *Little Red Riding Hood* are in a relationship of 'structural inversion':

Hamlet	*Little Red Riding Hood*
A male hero	A female hero
hostile to his mother	obeying her mother
meets a terrifying supra-human creature	meets a reassuring infra-human creature
who is in fact well-disposed	who is in fact ill-disposed
and who tells him not to waste time	and who tells her to take her time
etc.	etc.

Such pastiches do not, of course, invalidate structural analysis, but they illustrate its limits: the reliability of the analysis cannot be higher than that of the interpretations it employs. And the fact is that structuralists, just as all other anthropologists, practise interpretation essentially guided by their intuitions and without any explicit methodology. Moreover, the interpreter's intuitions are themselves guided by the aims of structural analysis, with an obvious risk of circularity and no obvious safeguards.

The theoretical problem raised by structural analysis is the following: in what way does structural analysis constitute an explanation of cultural phenomena? Some defenders of structuralism see in their approach a mere means of putting order in the data, that is, a means of classifying rather than of explaining. Dumézil combined structural analysis and historical explanation. Lévi-Strauss associates in a more intricate manner structural analysis with an essentially psychological kind of genetic explanation. The structures uncovered through structural analysis are assumed to be the product of a human mind inclined to flesh out abstract structures with concrete experience and to explore possible variations on these structures.

For instance: a given cultural group makes uses of representations of certain animal and vegetable species in order to display in the form of a myth some basic conceptual contrasts: say, between nature and culture, descent and affinity, life and death. A neighbouring group may then transform the myth, by reversing the value of the distinctive features of the characters, thus symbolising, over and above the contents of the myth, the group's difference from the neighbour from whom the myth was actually borrowed. Progressive transformations of the myth from one group to another may render it unrecognisable, but the systematic character of these transformations makes it possible for structural analysis to bring to the fore the underlying common structures, which, ultimately, are supposed to be the structures of the human mind.

However, Lévi-Strauss's references to the human mind do not provide an explanation; at best they suggest where he believes an explanation should be sought. Lévi-Strauss himself has hardly tied his investigations to those of contemporary psychology. The mental mechanisms deemed to generate cultural representations are postulated but not described.

More generally, the theoretical problem raised by structural analysis boils down to this: complex objects, such as cultural phenomena, display all kinds of properties. Most of these properties are epiphenomenal: they result from the fundamental properties of the phenomenon but are not among these fundamental properties. In particular, they play no causal role in the appearance and development of the phenomenon and are not, therefore, explanatory. A structural analysis brings to the fore some systematic properties of phenomena, but, in itself, it gives no means of distinguishing fundamental properties from epiphenomenal ones. In a nutshell, structural analysis does not explain; at best, it helps to clarify what should be explained.

Functionalist explanations

Showing that a cultural phenomenon has beneficial effects for the social group is a favourite form of 'explanation' in anthropology. Functional analyses differ according to the type of beneficial effects (biological, psychological or sociological) they stress. In the Marxist improved version of functional analysis (see Bloch, 1983, for a review), contrary effects and dysfunctions are taken into account in order to throw light on the dynamics of society.

Functional analyses have been a great source of sociological insight. However, they all fall under two objections, one well-known and having to do with their explanatory power; the other less common and having to do with their use of interpretations.

Might a description of the effects of a cultural phenomenon provide an explanation of this phenomenon? Yes, but with two qualifications: first, the effects of a phenomenon can never explain its appearance; second, in order to explain how the effects of the phenomenon cause it to develop or at least persist, one must establish the existence of some feedback mechanism.

Let us suppose that a given cultural institution, for instance the couvade, has beneficial effects for the groups that have adopted it. For this to help explain the presence of some form of couvade in so many cultures, it should be shown that these beneficial effects significantly increase the chances of survival of the cultural groups that are, so to speak, 'carriers' of the institution. The onus of the proof would be, of course, on the defenders of such a functional explanation.

In practice, most functionalists are content to show, often with great ingeniousness, that the institutions they study have some beneficial effects. The existence of an explanatory feedback mechanism is hardly ever discussed, let alone established. Imagine, for instance, a functionalist, taking as her starting point an interpretation of the couvade similar to that proposed by Mary Douglas. She could easily enough argue that the couvade strengthens family ties, in particular the ones between the father and his children, and therefore enhances social cohesion. But how would she go from there to an explanatory feedback mechanism? Moreover, it would not be too hard to establish that many institutions, including the couvade, have harmful effects: food deprivation, such as that suffered by Opote and his fellows, may in some cases be quite harmful.

Most cultural institutions do not have effects, on the chances of survival of the groups involved, of a character and magnitude such as to explain their own survival. In other words, for most institutions a description of their functional powers is not explanatory. Even where such a description does provide some explanatory insight, it does so in a very limited manner: the feedback mechanism neither explains the introduction of cultural forms through borrowing or invention nor the transformation of existing cultural forms.

Another weakness of the functionalist approach is that it fails to provide any specific principle for the identification of types of cultural phenomena. Rather, it relies uncritically for that task on an interpretive approach.[5]

What is it, for instance, that is supposed to make different local practices tokens of the same general type, say the 'couvade', a type which the anthropologist must then try to describe and explain? The identification of types is never itself based on function alone: for instance, no one would argue that all the sundry practices that have the 'function' of strengthening father-children ties should be seen as constituting a distinct and homogeneous anthropological type. The identification of types is not behavioural: some behaviour may count as couvade in one society and not in another. In fact, whatever its function, whatever its behavioural features, a practice is categorised as an instance of couvade in accordance with the native point of view. However, native points of views are local, and quite diverse even within the same culture. So, in the end, the identification of a cultural type is based on the synthetic anthropological interpretation of a motley of local interpretations.

Thus 'couvade' is defined by means of an interpretive generalisation: local practices that *can be interpreted as* ritual precautions to be taken by a prospective or new father are classified as cases of couvade. As I argued before, the price for

---

5. The weaknesses of functionalist typologies have been discussed by Leach (1961) and, more thoroughly, by Needham (1971, 1972). I have argued that these unprincipled and fuzzy typologies are based on interpretive rather than descriptive criteria; see Sperber (1985a, 1986).

such an interpretive usage is a heavy loss of faithfulness: the conception of a ritual, that of an appropriate precaution, what it means for a practice to be imposed on someone, who is considered a father, etc. varies from culture to culture. At the level of generality adopted by anthropologists in their 'theoretical' work, these local conceptions could be interpreted indefinitely in many ways. One interpretation is retained by the anthropological tradition; local variations and other interpretive possibilities are ignored.

Is the loss of faithfulness with respect to local representations compensated for by a gain in relevance? More specifically, are the types defined by means of such interpretive generalisations useful types for scientific work? I see no reason to believe that they are. Why should one expect all tokens of an interpretively defined type to fall under a common and specific functional explanation - or, for that matter, under any common and specific causal explanation? The point is not particular to the couvade; it holds for all cases of interpretively defined institutions, that is for all the types of institutions defined in anthropology: from a causal explanatory point of view, anthropological typologies, being based on interpretive considerations, are quite arbitrary.

Epidemiological models

We call 'cultural', I suggested, those representations that are widely and durably distributed in a social group. If so, then there is no boundary, no threshold between cultural representations and individual ones. Representations are more or less widely and durably distributed and hence more or less cultural. In such conditions, to explain the cultural character of some representations amounts to answering the following question: why are these representations more 'contagious' than others, more successful in a given human population? And in order to answer such a question, the distribution of all representations must be considered.

The causal explanation of cultural facts amounts, therefore, to a kind of *epidemiology of representations*. Comparing cultural transmission and contagion is hardly new. The comparison can be found, for instance, in the work of the French sociologist Gabriel Tarde, or in that of the diffusionists at the beginning of the twentieth century. It has recently been revived by biologists such as Cavalli-Sforza (Cavalli-Sforza and Feldman 1981) or

Dawkins (1976). The epidemiological metaphor has often been
grounded in rather superficial resemblances as, say, between
fast moving, short-lived epidemics on the one hand, and
rumours or fashions on the other, or between slow moving,
long-lasting endemics on the one hand, and traditions on the
other. An application of epidemiological models to the
transmission of cultural representations based on such
superficial similarities both misses essential differences and
deeper resemblances.

The transmission of infectious diseases is characterised by
processes of duplication of the infectious agent. Mutations are
relatively rare. In contrast, the transmission of representations is
characterised by processes of transformation. In verbal
communication, for instance, addressees construct their own,
more or less faithful interpretation of the speaker's meaning and
go on to correct or adjust the information received in light of
their previous beliefs.[6] Duplication of thought through
communication or imitation, if it ever occurs, is better seen as a
limiting case of zero-degree transformation. This makes an
epidemiology of representations, unlike that of infectious
diseases, first and foremost a study of the transformation of
representations in the process of transmission.

In spite of the differences between the transmission of
diseases and that of representations, the epidemiological
metaphor has other, appropriate and important implications.
Epidemiology is not an independent science or the studying of
an autonomous level of reality. Epidemiologists study the
distribution of diseases which themselves are studied by
pathologists. The distribution of diseases cannot be explained
without taking into consideration the way in which they affect
individual organisms, that is without having recourse to
pathology, and, more generally, to the biology of individual
organisms. Conversely, epidemiology is a major source of
assumptions and evidence for pathology.

What pathology is to the epidemiology of diseases, cognitive
psychology is to an epidemiology of representations. A causal
explanation of cultural representations in the form of an
epidemiological model should therefore stand in a relationship
of partial overlap and of mutual relevance with cognitive

6. As discussed in detail in Sperber and Wilson (1986).

psychology. This is no reduction of the cultural to the psychological: cultural facts properly so-called, the facts anthropologists should try to explain, are not individual representations, but distributions of representations. A distribution of psychological phenomena is itself not a psychological but an ecological phenomenon.

From an epidemiological perspective, a cultural phenomenon such as Little Red Riding Hood is not an abstract tale hovering about in the abstract context of European culture; it is a causal chaining of public narratives having given rise to the construction of mental stories, themselves having given rise to further public narratives, and this millions of times. To explain Little Red Riding Hood as a cultural phenomenon is to identify the factor that made possible this chaining of communications and the resilience of the communicated contents. One of the factors involved in this case (as in the case of all spontaneously transmitted oral narratives) is the fact, experimentally ascertainable, that this story is very easily memorised.

In this perspective, the couvade among the Txikao is not an immaterial institution; it is a causal chain of individual thoughts and behaviour. To explain the phenomenon is not to assign it some abstract meaning, but, again, to identify the mechanisms and factors maintaining this causal chain. No doubt, some of these factors are psychological, such as the Txikaos' views on life and its transmission discussed by Menget; other factors are ecological and include perinatal morbidity and mortality which, at every birth, reactualise the means of avoiding these risks that the Txikaos believe they have.

The epidemiological approach renders manageable the methodological problem raised by the fact that our access to the content of representations is unavoidably interpretive. In this approach, the methodological problem of ethnography is not to devise some special hermeneutics giving us access to representations belonging to a culture, yet uninstantiated in the individual heads or the physical environment of its members. The methodological problem is merely to render more reliable our ordinary ability to understand what people like you, Opote or me say and think. This is so because, in an epidemiological explanation, the explanatory mechanisms are individual mental mechanisms and inter-individual mechanisms of communication; the representations to be taken into account are those which are constructed and transformed at this low level by these micro-mechanisms. In other words, the relevant representations are at the same concrete level as those that daily social intercourse causes us to interpret.

Another methodological advantage of the epidemiological approach is that it provides a principled way to identify the types of cultural things for which a more general explanation is to be sought. The proper objects for anthropological theorising are types of causal chains of the kind I have described. These types of causal chains are to be individuated in terms of features that play a causal role in their emergence and maintenance. These features may be ecological or psychological: for instance, the lability of oral texts as opposed to the stability of written ones is a key ecological factor in explaining their respective distributions; the high memorability of narratives as opposed to the low memorability of descriptions is a key psychological factor. The two factors just mentioned interact in an obvious way and justify considering oral narratives as a proper anthropological type.

The psychological features pertinent to determining types of cultural things may well include content features. Of course, content features can be characterised only interpretively. To say that various representations share a content feature amounts to saying that they can all be interpreted, at a given level and from a given point of view, by means of a common interpretation. Still, that property of common interpretability, with all its vagueness, may suffice, if not to describe, then at least to pick out a class of phenomena all affected by some identical causal factors. For instance, the very notion of a genealogy, as a type of cultural representation, is interpretively defined and, as a result, quite vague: for what counts as a genealogical relationship in one society may not do so in another, and even the very idea of a genealogical relationship has many very different versions. Still, it is quite plausible that genealogies, in all their versions, are locally relevant, and hence culturally successful, for partly universal reasons.

In an epidemiological perspective, I suggest, the explanation of a cultural fact, that is, of a distribution of representations, is to be sought not in a global macro-mechanism, but in the combined effect of countless micro-mechanisms. What are the factors that lead an individual to express a mental representation in the form of a public representation? What mental representations are the addressees of the public representation likely to construct? What transformation of content is this process likely to bring about? What factors and what conditions render probable the repeated communication of some representations? What properties, either general or contextual, does a representation need in order to maintain a relatively stable content in spite of such repeated communications?

These and other questions raised by an epidemiological approach are difficult, but at least anthropologists share many of them with cognitive psychologists; a relationship of mutual relevance between the two disciplines may emerge and help. In order to answer these questions, as with all anthropological questions, interpretations must be used as evidence. But at least, the interpretations required in this approach are of a kind with those we use all the time in our daily interactions. This does not make these interpretations unproblematic, but we should recognise their value as evidence – actually we already do recognise the evidential value of such interpretations in matters much dearer to us than mere scientific theorising.

Chapter 9

Beyond the words: the power of resonance

Unni Wikan

I was completing the manuscript for my book on Bali (Wikan 1990) with a deep sense of puzzlement; something seemed wrong, and it was not that Balinese, as portrayed by me, were so different from those of major anthropological works – I was reconciled to that, and quite prepared to stand up for my own interpretation. What troubled me, however, was that the Balinese of my account should seem so plain and ordinary, so non-exotic. True, they did believe in black magic and that one could speak with the souls of the dead, etc. but that did not detract from the fact that they seemed basically like you and me, picking their way about the world much as we do, and living by the same sort of stratagems. The Balinese of Bateson, Belo, Mead and C. Geertz, by contrast, seemed to come out of an other world. And they were brilliantly exotic.

Think of Bateson's and Mead's notion of a lack of climax in Balinese affairs (Bateson and Mead 1942: 32f). Or, to take another example, note that Balinese are said to be entirely confused if they lose their sense of direction, knowing 'which way is North' (ibid.: 6). Or, to take Belo's observation: 'The babies do not cry. . . . The women accept without rancour the role of an inferior. . . . The system of stratification works smoothly as a rule, and all those individuals who conform to it seem happy' (1970: 106–9); or Geertz's observation that Balinese have no selves beyond what is encapsulated in their masks (1984: 128); or that they are not guided by morality, it is aestheticism which spurs them on: 'to please the gods, to please the other. . . but to please as beauty, not as virtue pleases' (Geertz 1973: 400).

What I, at least, gathered from such accounts was that Balinese were truly, as Geertz had said, impossible to meet. They even do not 'meet' one another (ibid.: 365). Those I met, by contrast, though puzzling in many ways, seemed to reach out to me in a very recognisable way.

Now there might be varying reasons for this discrepancy of our accounts, and I tried to speculate. I had focused on people's ordinary, everyday affairs, not their colourful rituals and ceremonies. But so, to some extent, had Bateson, Belo, Mead and C. Geertz. What is more, these various authors *converged* in their accounts; their Balinese resembled one another, though they had been studied by different persons, at different places, and different times. Had I then missed an important dimension? Or why was my study lacking – as I felt it was – in exotic features?

There was a second reason for my sense of puzzlement. I had written a book which claimed to convey the lived experience of Balinese, yet I had not told what they did for a living, or what their political concerns were. I had, paradoxically, preached the virtues of contextualising interpretations and positioning actors and anthropologist while leaving actors, in these respects, floating in the air. Again, what was wrong?

I am posing these questions as my entry into the problem of translation. In the end, and while there was still time to do something to remedy these faults or omissions, Balinese came to my rescue and convinced me that what I had done was all right. Of course, it did not happen just like that, by people reading my manuscript and passing a final judgement, but inadvertently this was the message they gave me, when, on my last visit, in March 1989, I engaged some men – or they engaged me – in a discussion on epistemology. They proposed a theory of translation which I shall delineate below, and which I believe to hold potential general relevance.

I shall link this theory up with a theory of language and communication as proposed by Donald Davidson and elaborated by Richard Rorty in his book *Contingency, Irony and Solidarity* (1989). I shall further use these theories to reflect upon my fieldwork in three other 'cultures' – in Egypt, Oman and Bhutan – trying thus to test out their more general applicability for fieldwork methodology and transcultural understanding. Lastly, I shall trace some of the implications of our taking in earnest what these theories purport for the concept of 'culture',

arguing in the end that it needs fundamentally to be reworked if
we are to be able to help build a world based on enhanced
understanding among peoples.

What the two theories of translation – the Balinese and
Davidson's – prove to have in common is that both advocate a
procedure of going beyond words, of looking past outer
trappings and semblances to that which counts more,
similarities in human experience.[1] Moreover, they converge in
each being anchored in 'practical reason' (Schutz 1970) – a
universe of moral discourse about how best to learn in order to
live, and vice versa. To put it in Rorty's words:

> The view I am offering says that there is such a thing as moral
> progress. . . in the direction of greater human solidarity. . . thought
> of as the ability to see more and more traditional differences (of tribe,
> religion, race, customs, and the like) as unimportant compared with
> similarities with respect to pain and humiliation – the ability to think
> of people wildly different from ourselves as included in the range of
> 'us'. (1989: 192)

His words echo those of a Balinese priest and healer who, upon
lecturing my husband on the stark differences between the
world religions, Hinduism, Buddhism and Islam, concluded
with a bright smile: 'You see, completely different, exactly the
same!'

It is this sameness in the face of diversity which is my starting
point and ultimate concern. It is born not from conviction but by
the recalcitrant realisation of a confirmed cultural relativist that
the stance I earlier had embraced was not substantiated by my
own experience cross-culturally. Robert Paul has warned that
we should take care as social scientists not to build theories that
contradict our own experience of what being alive is like.[2] This
essay is an exercise in that spirit. I begin with the Balinese theory

1. This may not be in line with Davidson's or Rorty's own intentions. I have read out of
Rorty not a theory of language and communication as such but some broader perspectives
that helped me identify a misplaced emphasis in much of the anthropology that I see. I am
encourgaged to find, after this was written, that Tambiah (1990) also finds in Davidson a
useful perspective on anthropological problems of translation, relativism, and the
commensurability of cultures. I have also been intrigued with Sperber and Wilson's theory
in *Relevance* (1986) and its convergence with my own perspective.

2. If this sounds overly self-referential it is because this does in fact represent my first
endeavour to bring aspects of my life as an anthropologist fully to bear on my ordinary life,
and vice versa. What is intended is self-critique, and reappraisal of certain aspects of
anthropological method and representation.

which first opened my eyes to these issues. To embed it in 'practical reason', let me start with a case.

Convergence of tongues

I once went with a Muslim friend to a Hindu *balian* or traditional healer. My friend was in great pain. Her family had long been afflicted with a series of misfortunes. She had tried to alleviate their suffering by seeking the help of healers – all Muslim, as she told me – from all over Bali. When her efforts had proved in vain, I persuaded her to come with me to this Hindu healer. He was a man I understood her to hold in high esteem for she had initially been the one to introduce me to him and quite enthusiastically.[3]

She had argued against it. It would be of no use. The balian would treat her as if she were a Hindu, and prescribe remedies consonant with his own religion. And she considered herself with pride to be a fanatical Muslim (*orang Islam fanatik*), and was also so highly respected by her community. When now she agreed to accompany me, she stressed that it was only as my friend, and to help me in my work. She would *not* bring up her own problems with the balian.

When the balian saw my friend, his face lit up. He was so glad she had come. Actually, he had been waiting for her. He knew all about her problem which had triple causation. And taking her in with his broad, infectious smile, he proceeded to explain. There was black magic involved, and supernatural spirits. But third, and most importantly, there was an *oath* which her husband's ancestors had sworn to the gods to present offerings in the Muslim holy place once they became prosperous enough to go there. But they had not kept their promise, and this constituted a grave sin in the eyes of the gods. *That* is why her family had been so afflicted.

My heart sank as I listened. I was distraught to think how she would now have her worst suspicions confirmed. This talk of oath and ancestors and offerings in the Muslim holy place reeked even to me of idolatry and ancestor worship. What must she - a 'fanatical Muslim' – not feel and think!

---

3.   Muslims and Hindus live interspersed in North Bali, with c. 8 per cent Muslims to the c. 85 per cent Hindus. They intermingle, and consult each other's healers in misfortune and illness, though the preference is to use one of one's own kind. Some deny that they ever consult one of the other religion (Wikan 1990, Chs 12 and 13).

On the way home my friend's face was luminous and her voice buoyed with hope. It was true all what he had said! The black magic, the supernatural spirits, but particularly the oath. She would take upon herself to remedy the faults of the ancestors. She would make a promise to God that very night. And she launched into a long, enthusiastic appraisal of the balian's wisdom and erudition, which perforce I must cut short. Her eulogy ended with the words: 'He says *karma pala*, I say *taqdir* – it's all the same!'

In terms of religious ideology they certainly are not the same, and she should know, she is reputed for her religious learning. *Karma pala* is the doctrine of reincarnation according to which one's fate in this life is determined by the actions (of oneself or the ancestors) in previous lives. But for Muslims, who refute the doctrine of reincarnation, there *is* only one life; and so *taqdir* – fate or destiny – refers merely to God's omnipotence in deciding how the course of *this* life will be. Nor, for them, should *oath* have any meaning, for the ancestors are powerless to afflict you by what they do or fail to to. Only God has such power.

So I brushed off my friend's facile reconciliation of major theological differences as the wishful thinking of an afflicted soul desperately in search of meaning and relief. I did not even ask: what could she mean to say by her words? What was at stake? To me, *karma pala* and *taqdir* are 'completely different', not at all 'all the same'. If words do not actually stand for themselves – to paraphrase Wagner (1986) – at least there must be limits to how one can circumvent them.

Resonance

A long time afterwards, I was sitting with a group of men pondering western views of knowledge compared to Balinese epistemology. They belonged to a *lontar* society, an association devoted to the study of sacred scriptures harbouring age-old wisdom, and were all very learned: one was a philosopher-priest, another a poet and professor, a third a medical doctor, etc. Now they were at pains to impart to me their visions of how I must write – and think – if I was to convey to the world an understanding of what Balinese are like. (They knew my book was nearing its completion.) Their number one message was: I must create 'resonance' (*ngelah keneh*) between the reader and my text.[4] Before that, I must create resonance in myself with the people and the problems I try to understand.

To explain what this concept of resonance meant, the poet cum university professor said: 'It is what fosters empathy or compassion. Without resonance, there can be no understanding, no appreciation. But resonance requires you (and here he looked entreatingly at me) to apply both feeling and thought. Indeed, feeling is the more essential, for without feeling we remain entangled in illusions.'

It bears mention that Balinese do not split feeling from thought but regard both as part of one process, *keneh*, which I translate as feeling-thought (Wikan 1989, 1990). While they recognise in themselves feelings as apart from thoughts, and have concepts to differentiate the two, the Indonesian *perasaan* and *pikiran*, they are emphatic that the two are linked: 'Can anyone think but with their heart?' they ask incredulously.[5] They know some people can – in a self-afflicting motion which severs one's comprehension and ability to live ethically. Feeling and thinking, equally rational, are both essential. And so, to thus separate the two, as some do, whether for wordly gain or in search for knowledge, is self-defeating.[6] One remains trapped 'in illusions'.

Perhaps he saw the deep furrows on my forehead, reflecting my endeavour to understand, once again, by the power of thoughts, for the philosopher-priest, Made Bidja, now spoke. What he had to say hit me in my heart with a resonance he could not have anticipated:

'Take as an example Muslims in Bali who have no concept of *karma pala*', said he, 'and yet they understand what it's all about. How do they come to appreciate? By the power of resonance! They use their

4. The closest Indonesian translation would be *timbang rasa* which the dictionary gives as 'a sense of rhythm; balance; reasonableness'.

5. Obeyesekare (personal communication) has pointed out that I seem to use 'heart' in its literal western sense, whereas the crucial idea is simply that feeling and thought are fused. Space prevents a closer scrutiny of the problem of 'heart'; and I regret that it has also not been tackled adequately in my book (Wikan 1990).

6. It is easier to be selfish and greedy if one deafens oneself to one's 'heart'. Balinese say of such people that they act 'as if thinking alone will do', or that they have 'a short string (*tali*)'. In the long run the price will have to be paid along with the principle of *karma pala*, though it need not be before the next generation.

feelings, and so they understand its basic idea as just returns, heaven and hell. But Westerners have no resonance with the idea of karma pala because they use their thoughts only, and so ideas and understandings do not spring alive. . .'

My thoughts leapt, as he spoke, to my Muslim friend with the Hindu balian. Now I saw why his talk of 'oaths' (*sumpah*) and 'ancestors' (*leluhur*) and offerings (*banten*) in the Muslim holy place – concepts that go against the grain of Muslim thinking – had yet resonated with her, a fanatic Muslim. She had listened to him with attention to what he was trying to say and do, going beyond the words. It was I who failed to understand, for I had attended too closely to the words and their precise conceptual entailments – and so the true thrust of his message did not spring alive to me.[7]

Made Bidja continued (we were on the point of how ideas and understanding do not spring alive):

> Take my friend, Dr. Soegianto, who now writes the story of Panci Sakti [Balinese culture hero and reputed founder of the Buleleng dynasty *c*. AD 1660–80; cf. Worsley 1972]. How do you think he can? Well, because of his earlier readings about Hannibal and Alexander the Great! He used his feelings then to understand about their lives, and so there was *resonance* between him and them. Now he uses this appreciation to understand [the texts] about Panci Sakti, and to communicate an understanding to others.

Resonance thus demands something of both parties to communication, or both reader and author: an effort at feeling-thought; a willingness to *engage* with another world, life or idea; to use one's experience with the example of the Muslim and the Hindu balian, to try to grasp, respectively convey, meanings that reside neither in words, 'facts' nor text, but are evoked in the meeting of one experiencing subject with another, or with a text;

---

7. To forestall a possible misinterpretation on the part of some readers, let me hasten to add: at issue is not semantics vs. pragmatics. I take it *both* processes are typically involved in verbal communication. As Sperber and Wilson point out: 'Verbal communication involves both code and inferential mechanisms. . . . Thus both models can contribute to our understanding. However, it is usually assumed that one or the other must provide the right overall framework. . . . These are reductionist views. . . . Hence upgrading either to the status of a general theory is a mistake' (1986: 3). I take it both the Muslim woman and I were engaged in a pragmatic effort to understand, and where I went wrong was not in searching for coded meaning, but in the assumptions I brought to bear, the context I imposed, and the critical (non-charitable) stance I employed, all of which meant I lost out on the relevance – to her and me – of what the speaker 'meant' to say.

in the next instance, then, to communicate such understandings to others.

Hannibal, Alexander the Great and Panci Sakti – they had something in common, as these Balinese scholars saw it. Separated by some 200 years, and great distances, yet they were men and warriors, heroes. They had friends and enemies, lovers, parents – they fought for what was dear to them, and in this they had some commonality of experience. So it is with Muslims and Hindus, or with Balinese and us. We can *use* this common experience – 'our shared space' (Tambiah 1990: 122) – to try to understand one another. Indeed, we must, for we have nothing else. The friends' advice to me was that I make this the very foundation of my writing and understanding.

Language as tool for task

But how could this be accomplished across cultures? And what of the role of language, and the pitfalls if we do not learn it – and learn it exceptionally well? Was it not inadequate knowledge of Balinese that misled Bateson, Belo, Mead and Geertz? Did not that also disable me? Moreover, I have argued for the need to ground interpretations in people's own forms of discourse, and the concepts *they* use in their daily lives. Does that not contradict the very notion that one should leapfrog words, so to speak, to try to grasp the meanings that lie somehow beyond them, and are evoked in the meeting of one experiencing subject with another? This takes me on to Donald Davidson.

Davidson, in Rorty's account, takes the ultimately radical stance of trying to break completely with the notion that there 'is' any such thing as language in the sense of a medium that could represent or express a relation between a core self, i.e. a self with an intrinsic nature, and the world (Rorty 1989: 10). Davidson faces up to the *contingency* of language, that truths are made rather than found, because all vocabularies are man-made, they do not 'fit' the world – indeed, as Rorty reminds us, 'most of reality is indifferent to our descriptions of it' (ibid.: 7). Language thus can neither express the intrinsic nature of an organism – for there is no such thing – nor can it represent facts

of the world to the self – for there are no such 'facts'. In Rorty's
words, 'The world does not speak. Only we do' (ibid.: 6).[8]

What we are offered, then, is a more adequate view of
language, adequate in the sense of fitting certain purposes
better; Davidson (1986) suggests we regard language not as a
medium, but more like a tool which works better or worse for
the tasks at hand. As Hobart (1985b) has observed, 'It is not a
question of what words mean, but what people do in using
them.'

To apply this to my experience in Bali: Part of the trouble I
had in fitting my perceptions of the world to the formulas I had
received by way of anthropological texts was not simply that the
vocabularies coined by Bateson, Belo, Mead and Geertz were
faulty or untrue but rather that they seemed unfit for the
purpose at hand, inadequate as tools, at least for me. By the use
of the language of theatricality, aestheticism and faceless social
personae I would not have been able ever to 'meet' Balinese.

Davidson suggests we think of words as ways of producing
effects rather than as having or conveying intrinsic meaning
(Rorty 1989: 15). Entailed is an advocacy of the pragmatics of
language and how we 'do things with words' (Austin 1975)
which could be frightening in its implications for anthropology.
There are at least two issues here: how we use language to
communicate with others 'out there', in the field; and how we
use words to communicate an understanding to readers and
colleagues. In Davidson's theory both are fraught with effects –
indeed, the pragmatic and the 'meaningful' cannot and should
not be separated.

This is a view that resonates with Balinese perceptions of the
world and of knowledge. People expressed astonishment that
'we', people of the West, could think of knowledge and
morality, or speech and action as separable – when these
converge. Why we end up confused seemed clear to the men
referred to above. The philosopher said: 'Westerners mistake
their feelings for thoughts, and so they misunderstand and
create disturbance. . .'. The others nodded their heads in
emphatic consent.

---

8. Cf. also Putnam: 'there are external facts, and we can *say what they are*. What we
cannot say – because it makes no sense – is what the facts are *independent of all conceptual
choices*' (1981: 33).

But if words are ways of producing effects, then searching the words for meaning may sink one deep into a quagmire. A pragmatic view of language taken in its full implication would entail – and here is where I think the most fundamental challenge to anthropological theory and representation lies – that anthropology's romance with words, concepts, symbols, text and discourse may be counterproductive. It may be necessary – compellingly necessary for our purposes – to go beyond; and to transcend the words, we need to attend to the speaker's intention, and the social position they emanate from, to judge correctly what they are doing.

As Sperber and Wilson point out, in speaking, people take all manner of risks. It is a miracle that speaker's 'meaning' is communicated at all, given that any utterance can convey an almost limitless number of meanings. And yet people are able to understand one another well much of the time (ibid.: 19ff, 23). Their path-breaking book seeks to explain how this is achieved in everyday life. My more limited objective is to draw implications for fieldwork method and representation. But what Tambiah – after Davidson – refers to as 'the maxim of interpretive charity' (1990: 122) and Sperber and Wilson as 'the co-operative principle' (1986: 32ff) is clearly of major relevance. Were it not for her practising such charity, what would a balian have achieved speaking *karma pala* to a Muslim woman?

Experience and sameness

But is there not a danger here for the anthropologist engaged in cross-cultural translation: namely that in trying to practise such interpretive charity with people of different cultures, we may come to impute to them a commonality with our own experience? That experience is nothing in and of itself, but culturally construed, is one of anthropology's most basic insights (Turner and Bruner 1986). How are we to harmonise this with an approach which says Hannibal, Alexander the Great and Panci Sakti are more or less the same? Is it at all worth heeding?

We have in anthropology a relevant and powerful testimony: Renato Rosaldo's (1984) account of his failure to come to grips with Ilongot saying they took heads to cleanse their hearts of anger. It was only when he let their words *resonate* with himself that he began to be in a position to understand. This might be taken to mean that he took 'their' anger and 'his' anger to be 'the same', but such an interpretation seems unjust (cf. Rosaldo 1989: 10). What the story teaches are the dangers of going to the opposite extreme. To me it stands as one of the most persuasive demonstrations ever of *method* in anthropology.

But what 'is' resonance? And how does one induce it? Rosaldo stresses the point of applying one's life experience with the realisation that this can be an asset, a resource, which will enable one to grasp certain phenomena better. This seems in harmony with a Balinese stance. Several aspects stand out from what my scholar friends said: Resonance is what fosters compassion and empathy; it enables appreciation; without resonance, ideas and understandings will not spring alive. There is an underlying appeal to shared experience here. Perhaps what Shweder says: 'psychic unity is . . . that which makes us imaginable to one another' (1991: 18), is in tune with Balinese views.

Resonance thus seems akin to an attitude we might label sympathy, empathy or understanding. Whether it is 'the same' or 'different', I cannot say. Balinese see as critical that it entails using one's feelings as well as and at once with one's thoughts. Only this enables *appreciation* – which is more than just understanding.[9] So saying, they are making an argument.

I believe not much is gained by trying to pin 'resonance' down further. Most of us intuitively know what it means. Words by the celebrated Tibetologist Tucci spring to mind: 'Words are symbols which can evoke living experiences which the word as such can only suggest but not define' (1988: viii). What Sperber and Wilson (1986) write of 'relevance' applies to 'resonance' as well, and I take the liberty to replace my term for theirs in the following text. Either term is:

> a fuzzy term, used differently by different people, or by the same people at different times. It does not have a translation in every human language. There is no reason to think that a proper semantic analysis of the English word ['resonance'] would also characterise a concept of scientific psychology. (1989: 119)

---

9. Shweder (1991: 9) gives 'appreciation' as understanding and experience. I think this would converge with Balinese views.

Nevertheless, there seems to be:

an important psychological property – a property of mental processes – which the ordinary notion of ['resonance'] roughly approximates, and which it is therefore appropriate to call ['resonance'] too, using the term now in a technical sense. What we are trying to do is describe this property: that is, to define ['resonance'] as a useful theoretical concept. (ibid.: 119)

At first, the lesson Rosaldo draws from his experience might seem to be the opposite of mine. He cautions, as does Keesing (1989), against going beyond words in the sense of reading them too deeply. Thus: 'Ilongot older men mean precisely what they say. . . . Taken at face value and granted its full weight, their statement reveals much. . .' (1989: 3). And yet I believe we converge. What is at issue is the need to *attend to* what people say, and to heed the *intent* they are trying to convey, rather than groping for some 'larger' answers in the particulars of their spoken words.

I call this 'going beyond the words' for two reasons. First, the term offered itself when I became apprised of my, and others', 'stuckness' in words like *karma pala*. It seems to point in the direction I want: *to* actors' intentions, somehow 'beyond' their manifest sayings.[10] It is consistent with this that one may have to take at face value what people say to get at their intentions. But my use of 'beyond the words' has another goal as well: I am concerned with the current preoccupation in anthropology with 'words' in the sense of text, discourse, meaning. My 'beyond' is a plea that the pendulum be swung. I have great respect for discourse analysis as such which has accomplished some excellent works (e.g. Brenneis and Myers 1984; Watson-Grego and White 1990). What I take exception to is the broader application of 'discourse' as a template to represent *all* aspects of life. I sense a danger here that persons – the living, human beings who act in the world – fade from view when the focus is on 'the said' of people's lives, however much this is situated in context and with a view to power and pragmatics.[11]

10. For an impressive discussion of intent which would seem to qualify my own point of view, see Strathern (1990b).
11. Excellent formulations of this perspective are found in Abu-Lughod and Lutz (1990), and Abu-Lughod (1990). While I am in sympathy with their endeavour, I am uneasy about their deployment of 'context' as well as 'discourse' which I see as *disimpersonating*. This would seem to me to shift the attention away from agents and persons grappling with their lives, to more abstract phenomena imbued with the power to act, not unlike 'culture' was once seen to do.

Contextualisation of the said, and of discourse, will not suffice to ensure an adequate rendering of what is being said or understood. As Hobart has observed, contextualising 'raises the delicate issue of whose criteria of relevance are at stake?' (1986: 8). Think of a contextualised interpretation of the Hindu balian's discourse with the Muslim woman. Would not 'the context' here have to be made up, in large part, of their discrepant religious positions leading us to presuppose, in fact, that here was a blatant confusion of tongues? Certainly, this was the context I brought to bear on the scene, as it was what the Muslim's deliberations beforehand suggested would be the appropriate one. Had I not been unusually close with her, I do not see how this context could have been invalidated, I might even have embedded my (mis)interpretation in thick description to make it emerge as highly plausible.

The reference to 'context' can lend a false sense of security, whereas invoking it explains nothing. I sense a tendency in our field, to call on context as if to underscore the authority of one's account. 'Context' parades like 'I was there' (Clifford 1988) to lend credibility to one's account. Also, for this reason, does Rosaldo's story stand out as exceptional. It exposes the arbitrariness of context. His reinterpretation called for a new context, but it was one which was there – in Ilongot's conceptual universe – all the time. Such reappraisals are sorely lacking in anthropology (but see Colson 1984).

Context is 'just an analytical convenience . . . but there is a danger of it being seen as somehow substantive' (Hobart 1985b: 34). Another problem, as Sperber and Wilson point out, is that 'context' tends to be invoked as if it were given beforehand, whereas in real life it is continually shifting and changing since 'each new utterance . . . requires a rather different context' (1986: 137, 16; see also Sperber, this volume). Their theory of relevance is a major step in helping us understand how context is selected in actual everyday communication.

I suggest what may be needed is not so much 'contextualisation' as finding ways of transcending what we conventionally have conceived of as 'the context'. Thick description is not an answer, for it leaves unexplained *what* is to be thickly described (cf. also Rosaldo 1989: 94ff). We need to find ways to tune in to what people are telling us and why they do, rather than *how* or *the* way they are telling it. Delaney (1988: 293) speaks of the need to refine one's sensibilities; to know how to listen. We need to listen in such a way that we heed the *effect* people are trying to make and the *relevance* of their worlds in terms of how they are positioned and where they want to go, rather than the message that their word might seem to create.[12]

Does this not come closer to what we all do in our daily lives when understanding is of the essence, and we can ill afford to go wrong? It would entail another kind of reading of anthropological texts: again a going beyond – in a manner I myself have failed to do in my readings, and critiques, of Bateson, Belo, Mead and Geertz – and for which my understanding, and eventual representation, of Bali may have suffered (Wikan 1987, 1990). I now propose to follow Davidson on an experimental tour which exoticises the anthropologist's familiar round. With his theory, what light might be shed on the fieldwork encounter?

Passing theories

Now think that our task was to meet another person, or other persons, from a different culture – how could we proceed? Davidson suggests we would need to try to develop a vocabulary which would fit the task at hand. Most probably we could use 'mumbles, stumbles, malapropisms, metaphors, tics', etc. (Rorty 1989: 14) to avoid being taken by surprise: and we would resort to a set of guesses about what the other person would do under the circumstances. Most probably, so would she in response to us. Davidson refers to such guesswork, not-to-be-taken-by-surprise, as a '"passing theory" about the noises and inscriptions presently being produced by a fellow human' (Davidson 1986, quoted in Rorty 1989: 14). This is part of a larger passing theory about this person's total behaviour. Such a theory is 'passing' in the sense that it must constantly be corrected to allow for mumbles, stumbles, occasional egregious stupidity, strokes of genius, and the like:

12. An implication of what I am saying is that I consider the use of tape recorder and often also notebook as problematic in the field, and best to be avoided except for certain clearly defined purposes. Reliance on such devices seems to reinforce, and express, our over-reliance on words and the *exact* utterance.

If we ever succeed in communicating easily and happily, it will be because her guesses about what I am going to do next, including what noises I am going to make next, and my own expectations about what I shall do or say under certain circumstances, come more or less to coincide, and because the converse is also true. . . To say that we come to speak the same language is to say, as Davidson puts it, that 'we tend to converge on passing theories'. Davidson's point is that all 'two people need, if they are to understand one another through speech, is the ability to *converge on passing theories* from utterance to utterance'. (Rorty 1989: 14, italics mine)

Let me invoke my own experience recently of being a language-less person in a foreign land – Bhutan – confronted with the task of striking up some accord with (as well as obtaining the practicalities of life from) villagers in remote valleys. I did precisely what Davidson suggests: form a passing theory about what kinds of humans they were so as not to be taken by surprise; and in order to get them to accept, and preferably to like, me. My passing theory was constantly in flux. So, no doubt, were the passing theories of my hosts and acquaintances. After three months I could not claim much: most aspects of Bhutanese 'culture' remained enigmas. But – and I think this is not to be bypassed as the banal insight it seems – a lot had been learned by the use of rudimentary speech, which, freed from the tyranny of attending to spoken words, took in a wealth of information on all manners of parameter within which life in Bhutan unfolds – all that given and the self–evidence within which any Bhutanese speech is cast. *And* – I had managed to get along quite well (see Barth and Wikan 1989).

In terms of field method, what does this mean? It means attending closely to people's daily lives, their fears and trials and tribulations as well as joys and jubilations, against a backdrop of where they are and what they must do (cf. Barth, in press). How much subtle analysis of words and discourse is not obviated when I have seen the remoteness of farms and walked the distances; noted the gross structure of power, class privilege, opulent monasteries and poverty; and discovered the absence of any kind of marriage rituals and contracts. Simple signs of insecurity and anxiety in the face of sickness and misfortune, or *vis-à-vis* men in power, will start to resonate in me. Childhood, love, pregnancy and old age are coloured by such circumstances. And as I slowly learn the language, I shall have a reference point, a 'context'. I can better understand something of what they mean (Wikan 1991). To link up with Davidson, his account of linguistic communication dispenses with the notion of

> *different languages as barriers between persons of cultures.* To say that . . . two communities have trouble getting along because the words they use are so hard to translate into each other is just to say that the linguistic behaviour of inhabitants of one community may, like the rest of their behaviour, be hard for inhabitants of the other community to predict. (Davidson 1986: 446, quoted in Rorty 1989: 15, italics mine)

Now if this seems a far cry from Bali, let us go back to the Muslim woman with the Hindu balian. She may be seen to have done just what Davidson suggests: evolve a passing theory – even before we set off to the balian – so as not to be taken by surprise. On this theory, she was able to tell me, more or less, what was going to happen. And experience proved her right – as far as the sheer 'facts' of the case go.

What she may have failed to consider was the divergence between thinking out a scenario and living it in practice. Faced with the balian's broad infectious smile, his expression of an earnest concern for her, and his compassion, what became of a fanatic Muslim's determination not to be taken in? Her passing theory, I take, started to change. She must have begun to feel that he truly willed her well, and that his efforts to reach her, using his Hindu ways, yet came with a pledge of relevance to her.[13] He, who is expert in handling 'surprises', probably uses communication to its fullest effect, and is skilled at fashioning and refashioning passing theories.

Whatever happened between them, I cannot say. But it could be considered a miracle of a kind, one of those daily miracles of achieving mutual understanding which we easily forgo as a matter of fact. Their theories converged. They were able to communicate quite well, though, in a sense, speaking different tongues: 'He says *karma pala*, I say *taqir*: it's all the same. . .'.

Enter the Hindu man: 'But Westerners do not understand because they do not use their feelings, and so they have no resonance with the word. . .' Indeed, for the longest time I did

---

13. Sperber and Wilson speak of 'a tacit guarantee of relevance. . . . Ostensive behaviour provides evidence of one's thoughts. It succeeds in doing so because it implies a guarantee of relevance' (1986: 49–50).

not. For I thought meaning resided in words: I had to grasp
them, or I would grasp nothing.

Beyond the words

Now let us move to Egypt and try out a theory of going beyond
words on the field experience I had. When I began work with
families in a poor quarter of Cairo, my language facility was
poor at the start (Wikan 1980, 1983). I had studied Arabic for a
year at a university in Cairo, but I could not speak much. Did
that deter people from speaking to me? Far from it! They poured
their hearts out, as if I could understand everything they said,
though it was quite clear to them I could not. When their
attempts to reach at me met with a blank expression, they would
produce *another* set of noises and mumbles, verbal and non-
verbal, to try to convey to me their points. In due course, thanks
to this extensive exposure, I learned to speak quite fluently.

Did I then communicate better? Of course I did. And the
materials I thereby obtained were essential to enable me to write
my ethnography and compose my analysis in a way that might
make it compelling to a reader. But what is striking to me now,
when I reflect back, is how much I understood without knowing
much Arabic, and how *they took it for granted that I could
understand a lot* without having much of a language. Recalling
that we should not develop theories that contradict our
experience of what being alive is like, I fear we have done just
that.

Let me move again: to Oman, where I worked in the mid-
1970s (Wikan 1982). I *had* language by then, I prided myself on
speaking quite fluent lower-class Egyptian-Arabic. Now the
Omanis spoke a very different dialect, but at least they could
understand me well from the start for Cairene is a kind of lingua
franca throughout the Middle East. The problem was, however,
that having or not having this kind of language availed me little.
For Omanis *did not speak much*. It is the one place I have been
where people treasure silence, it is truly golden. It is written that
even foreigners who stay in the country for some time come to
cherish silence.

As an anthropologist, what do you do then? Well, I despaired.
I got no 'material', thinking material must necessarily reflect

words, utterances, concepts, etc. Every evening when I came back to our house to write the day's 'notes', pages would stare back blankly at me, and I felt miserable. I yearned for words – that true fountain of insight.

I managed poorly for the first six months. Then, by the force of circumstance and not any superior insight on my part, I developed a passing theory which actually worked – the first clearly had not. I became receptive to the silence around, and suddenly I tuned in to a lot that was being 'said'. To experience silence not as a void or absence or emptiness but as full and pregnant with meaning is difficult for a word-mongering academic. In my case it took resonance of a kind I came to develop only by the force of circumstance. I sensed then that *they* came to think of me more as a decent human being. This is not to depreciate the good use of having a particular language, but it is to undermine – and undermine quite drastically – some of its importance.[14]

One implication of what I am saying is that no neophyte anthropologist should despair at having rudimentary language or even 'no' language at first. There is a time and place for everything, and perhaps even a time when one might bless oneself as lucky not to have words to get in the way of one's senses or vision. We all know what happens once we have those words – coupled with limited time on our hands.

Back to Egypt, and lessons to be learned in view of a theory of resonance. How did I learn my most fundamental insights? Today – and only after I began preparing this essay – I no longer believe it was by virtue of my good Arabic. Of course, in some respects it helped. It meant I had rich verbal data with which to falsify passing theories and refine my insights so that when people spoke – often many at a time, competing for the attention of one another and myself – I had the ballast of my knowledge of a rich vocabulary and its uses. And yet I had grasped many essentials of what life was all about, what was at stake for people, ('the sources of their pain and humiliation', to quote Rorty) already in the early stages, when I tried to see beyond the words, because I could not understand them.

14. Many of the problems alluded to here on silence and non-verbal communication are set out in a special methodological section of my book (1982). Relevant readings are also Tual (1986) and Basso (1990).

The sources of the pain and humiliation of poor people I met in Cairo were the ceaseless struggle for money, to make ends meet; the inability ever to make all one's children happy *all at once* because there was never enough to go around; the fear that one's sheer material deprivation would be exposed to the world with the *Schadenfreude* and gossip this would elicit; the continual bickering with husbands who could not be counted on to listen to one's pain. Yes, it is a woman's view I am giving, for sources of pain and humiliation are necessarily never the same for all.

If I had gone about it the way anthropology teaches us to do today, I would have gone for the words much more, for we live in an era where 'meaning' is focal, and 'cultural construction' is an essential part of our jargon. Take an example: Egyptians have this word *za'l*, which means sadness, anger, distress, disappointment, etc. Think what I could have done with it! As it were, I did nothing. It didn't strike me that here was anything to do. I listened to people's accounts in which *za'l* – along with many other things – featured. And I tried to grasp what they were trying to tell me about their lives. They, after all, were speaking for effect. They could not care less – I dare say – whether I grasped the meaning of *za'l* so long as I grasped what they were trying to tell me. I am reminded of Veena Das' rendering of a perspective from Wittgenstein: 'To say "I am in pain" is not a statement, it is a complaint' (n.d.).

Learning to attend

How can we build an anthropology which enables us to heed better people's complaints, along with their joys? What concerns me is much more than just field method: I am pleading for a broader and simpler theory for seeing communication within social relationships, putting what is unspoken and self-evident to speakers into place before focussing on concepts and discourse (Barth, in press). Thus my plea that we attend to the concepts by which people feel and think about and handle the tasks and tribulations of their individual existences, is meant not as an invocation to attend to concepts *per se*, but to the shifting aspects of being in the world and acting on those by which concepts uniquely spring alive.

How can it be that when in Cairo, with the poor, I 'forget' my anthropology and become absorbed in people's lives, whereas in Bali, with poor people, I tend to be all too well aware of something we call 'culture' which separates them and me? I have raised the issue elsewhere and tried to formulate an answer (Wikan, in press). Here I suggest it has something to do with my differential ability to listen and become engaged. I am reared in a tradition which makes it very clear Balinese are a truly exotic people. But no one makes such a claim on behalf of the Cairo poor. And so I meet them as one human to another.[15]

Balinese friends suggest the problem may be that I, as a Westerner, have no resonance with their words, *and not because I do not speak their language*. It is essential to hammer this point home. The problem, as they see it, is not lack of 'language' facility – but that we fail to use what means we have available to us, provided we let other people's concerns resonate with our selves.

They would side, I think, with Davidson's point that knowing one's way about the world and knowing a language amount to practically the same thing. Or with the Cairo poor who poured out their hearts to me, trusting I would understand, though for all practical purposes I was deaf and dumb. Who says deaf-mutes cannot understand (Sacks 1989)?

Ingold (this volume) notes that we share a world with others by 'learning to attend to' it in the same way. And how is that done, other than by resonance? We need not have the same experiences to be able to tune in. In the wellsprings of ourselves there is generally something we can use as a bridgehead to begin to attend. It does not come by an act of will, though will helps. 'Learning to attend' in the same way requires painstaking engagement on a day to day basis in events and routines which are theirs, so we come to share something of them too. But an act of will *is* required to shed the kind of stifling preconception which can be a stumbling-block along the way: that others are essentially different from us, to be understood only by means of the concept of 'culture'; and that their words bespeak different life-worlds.

---

15. Appadurai's (1988) discussion of 'natives' is relevant here. Though he seems to say that *native* is used for 'persons and groups who belong to those parts of the world that were, and are, distant from the metropolitan West' (pp. 36–7), I submit that Cairenes are not *natives*. Natives are found in villages, tribes – or in places like Bali.

They do, but only to an extent. And so *karma pala* can spring alive even to me – given that I am prepared to understand.[16] *That* is what is required in the face of the prospect ahead: we might have to shed our preconceptions of what understanding is. And that is the main challenge I see my Balinese scholar friends posing.

The concept of 'culture', of course, is crucial to our endeavour. But I argue, as have others before me, that we are at cross-purposes with ourselves in the concept of culture we promulgate if we allow it to freeze difference and magnify it beyond proportion (Keesing 1987a, in press; Abu-Lughod 1991; Lock 1990; Spencer 1990; Ingold, this volume). A greater awareness of the need for resonance can help us. I illustrate below with a painful failure of my own from fieldwork in Bali.

Truth vs. 'how we feel-think'

How did I work in Bali? It was rather different from in Egypt and Oman. Also here, from the start, I had little language in common with people. But whereas in Cairo I would forgo *za'l*, so as to listen rather than hear, in Bali *karma pala*, *atma*, *sakti*, etc., were exotic glosses to be probed for their meanings. Now, to be frank, this was more marked towards the end, when my concerns grew that my attempts to represent something of life and society in Bali might be dismissed if I disclosed that I did not know what such words 'meant'. The anthropological discourse intervened much more to decide my priorities than was the case in Egypt or Oman.

I have elsewhere (Wikan, in press) stressed problems of relevance and the need to attend to people's multiple, compelling concerns, and to follow them *as* they move – if we are to grasp what is at stake, and how they construe their own experience. I argue for the need to cross thresholds along with people, and to bridge domains, if we are to grasp what concerns

---

16. Spiro makes a striking observation about the universality of a concept like *karma*, arguing that it bears 'a striking family resemblance to concepts found in many other cultural traditions. . . such . . . as luck, fate, predestination, God's will, *kismet*, fortune, destiny. . . . Although formally and semiotically different from each other. . . all of those concepts, just like *karma*, provide an explanation for the vagaries of an actor's "life chances". . . without recourse to the agency. . . of the actor himself' (1986: 247–8). Tambiah's (1990: 124ff) discussion, after Putnam (1981), of 'concept' vs. 'conception' is also relevant here.

cannot be shed, but that impinge and require simultaneous handling. This methodological stance reflects my own best effort to get a hold on those trials and tribulations in terms of which people often feel 'trapped', and that Balinese bear testimony to when they complain 'there's so much to care about in life!' It comes across as an often exasperated sigh about how to manage, to cope, in a life of multiple, simultaneous concerns.

Here my concern is substantially the same, but analytically different. Responding to Davidson's challenge I explore hitherto unproblematised assumptions in my own work regarding how my most crucial field-insights were gained. I have had a nagging suspicion for long that things were not as I made them out to be. How is this borne out by my work? Let me provide one example for what it reveals of the power of words to illuminate and mislead.

Once, in what I have called 'an enlightened moment in fieldwork' (Wikan 1982: 282), a Balinese woman made the cataclysmic statement: 'It is very bad if you are sad and they laugh, that's why we hide our feelings.' I had taken these words to be crucial for my understanding, but they were only crucial, I now recognise, because they were taken together with a host of other clues of significance, most of them non-verbal; they helped me perceive the struggle. Her words were also misleading because I failed to perceive how they were spoken for effect. A full year later she brushed aside her 'confused' (*bingung*) reading of a year ago, and spoke other words to effect. Again, those were not to be taken literally. The first was a complaint, a cry of pain and pressure. The other was euphoric, testimony to her relief and joy. How would she express or give an account of the same events today? Doubtless, by the use of *other* words and *other* concepts, as she recalled it from another positioning. Balinese seem aware of this, and consistently interpret words in the knowledge that they are spoken for effect.[17] Why does it seem to be more difficult for anthropologists?

Partly because when we work as anthropologists we are not truly implicated in the world of other people. It does not really matter all that much if we understand them or not. Our misunderstandings are not likely to resonate with crucial effects for us. We are concerned to produce effects on the

---

17. Hobart observes, 'The agent's thoughts or feelings are seen as an active part of knowledge, speculation and speech' (1985b: 123); see also Wikan (1990: Ch. 7).

anthropological community, and only secondarily on the natives
whose language we are trying to grasp.

Meaning vs. what it's all about

Language is a quagmire into which one can sink deeply, and I
wonder how many of us have done so, 'wordstuck' as we tend
to be. One implication of what I am saying is that it is not given
that better language facility will necessarily improve the quality
of our accounts or our understanding. There is even a danger it
may have the opposite effect. I am concerned with the
unquestioned assumption that as regards language more is
necessarily better; and with the rather peculiar place to which
we have elevated it.

Whereas in our daily lives we use words mostly to get things
done and to 'work on' family and colleagues, the
anthropological enterprise construes language as a kind of
technical fix – not unlike biomedicine's hegemonic representation of its salutory solutions and laboratory tests. One reason
why we can do this is that we do not experience the
consequences of our own misinterpretations. As Bourdieu says,
we have this 'freedom from urgency, from necessity'; our
anthropological observation-point is 'founded upon the
neutralisation of practical interests and practical stakes' (1990b:
381, 383). We are in a protected situation where we build up our
own little secret – then carry it home, and busy ourselves 'with
problems that serious people ignore' (ibid.: 181). We are not
forced to be implicated in the other's world, hence our search for
'meaning' goes undisturbed.

But when we are part of a world that we and they take for
real we may be sanctioned, for failing to use words to the effect
for which they are 'supposed' to be used. Power and pragmatics
enter, whether we like it or not. The interpretive quest in which
many of us are wittingly or unwittingly entangled works to
segregate our lives from our works, and shield us from
confronting certain self-defeating aspects of our enterprise – it
blinds us to the predicaments of people and thereby also to our
own (Shankman 1984; Keesing 1987a; Nader 1988).

When the Cairo poor remain peripheral to the
anthropological scene, it is probably not because famous

anthropologists failed to go there, but because there is not much to fetch there that is exotic. They do not use big words, or cite poetry, nor do they perform elaborate rituals. So also with the Neapolitans whom Belmonte (1979) so beautifully lent voice to. Were I to formulate *our* predicament in the simplest possible way, it would be that *the quest for meaning blinds us to what life is all about*. It entices us to get lost in words, and lose sight of the larger issues: That *karma pala* is really, as my Balinese friends said, about 'just returns, heaven and hell'. When we engage in an interpretive quest we may indeed come to discover esoteric meanings in *karma pala* - but to what purpose?

Implicit in the preceding pages has been a deep concern with 'culture', and our ways of using it. Crucial is what my Balinese and Bhutanese experiences have been. Also of relevance are the uses to which I see the concept of 'culture' being put by various parties to the struggle that is underway in Norway.[18]

With 'culture' having entered common parlance, have 'others', perhaps, become inhuman exotic breeds – perceived by 'us' as propelled by a force – culture?[19] I think it is essential that we show the utmost caution in how we deploy the term, and that an ingrained disposition to represent 'difference' is joined by a no less an urgent need to acknowledge the limits to 'alterity' (Spiro 1986; Delaney 1988; McHugh 1989; Carrithers 1990; Shweder 1991).

'Resonance' and 'culture' seem to point in different directions: the one evokes sameness, the other extols the exotic and strange. As concepts they are not on a par: 'Resonance' connotes a faculty, a feeling-thinking engagement; 'culture' is an abstraction, a gloss on experience; or a model of and for life: what we see with, rather than what we see (Quinn and Holland 1987: 11). And yet the two can be compared – if we take a Davidsonian approach. Then both emerge as words which can produce effects, and as embedded in languages better- or ill-suited for the relevant task. These languages can be hailed as

18. The situation with 'culture' in the discourse and strategic plays between immigrant workers and refugees and Norwegian authorities is worth a separate article. Power enters disturbingly when spokesmen of ethnic groups, or families, define *what the culture is*, and government officials, committed to respecting 'their culture' *act on* their definition, with dire effects for those who are not lent a voice, or dare not speak: children, youth and women. An honest commitment to respect 'their culture' can serve under such circumstances as a collusion with those already in power.

19. A incisive statement on this problem is found in Said (1981).

flags to signal the benefit or detriment of deploying one or the other – depending on one's task.

I read Balinese friends' plea for resonance as in tune with a growing call in anthropology for de-exoticisation. Resonance evokes shared human experience, what people across place and time can have in common. Where culture separates, resonance bridges – from a lived realisation that this is the only practicable way. It does not deny difference: Hinduism, Buddhism and Islam *are*, as the balian said, completely different. But it renders difference relatively insignificant in the face of that which counts more for certain purposes: shared human potential.

Let me close with a personal vignette which set me on these paths. But for one morning's unexpected encounter with a person of 'my own culture' I might not have come to reconsider – as I now do – my own position in configuring the lives of others. To put the incident into perspective, some comparative perspective is needed: In Bali I was confronted with the puzzle that Balinese did seem to express a profound ability to empathise (*kelangen*) even in respect of people whose suffering they hardly knew. It was a puzzle because other anthropologists had maintained that they could not (Mead 1942: 23; Geertz 1973); and also because I could not see how they could see beyond the people's facades when those were always 'bright and clear'.

After long pondering, I hit upon an answer. Balinese had another way of situating emotion away from us. Rather than seeing it as an idiosyncratic response, arising *in* the individual, they perceived emotion as embedded in social situations, and thus to be probed by the assessment of sheer social facts (Wikan 1990: 161). When I came across an article proposing a Chinese theory of emotion similar to the one I had hit upon (Kleinman and Kleinman 1989), I was intrigued. But then I had long suspected there were similarities between Balinese and Chinese.

Months later, reading the morning paper, I came across an interview with the poet Kolbjörn Falkeid (Bistrup 1990). He was in pain, his daughter had recently died. And the portrait could not avoid touching also on his sorrow. How did he cope? Did he and his family, and the neighbours, talk much about the tragic event? He answered:

> To survive, it may be necessary to barricade oneself behind tons of indifferent thoughts, behind a shield of everyday concerns, behind

conversations about the weather, and the exhausting trivia of life. 'How are you?' people ask. It can be a gentle way of approaching, a light brush across the cheek, words that wish to remove bandages gently so the wound will not start bleeding again.

And I could have answered with long explanations, I could have told of all the rents in the fabric we call life, I could have told everything. But I answer: 'Fine, thank you'. *Each in our own way we know it so well.* And it is good to have everyday trivialities to cover it with. (italics mine)

To think I had invoked a particular emotion theory to make sense of Balinese, when I could have dipped into my own culture and self and applied resonance. To me the incident stands as an 'enlightened moment' in life and work – a poignant reminder of the dangers of a cultural constructionist analysis. It entails that expressions as well as words need to be gone beyond, not in the literal sense of reading deeper meanings into surface behaviour, but to attend to the concerns and intentions they emanate from. If we are not to be allured by the spectacle of *karma pala* or bright face (*mue cedang*), resonance is a technique which will help us appreciate their pan-human relevance.

Chapter 10

The art of translation in a continuous world

Tim Ingold

Tradition and civilisation

The concept of culture is something of an obsession with anthropologists. It has been hailed as their supreme contribution to human understanding, as though its mere recognition had, in one stroke, resolved the greatest riddle of human life, namely the extraordinary diversity and complexity of ways of living it. Claims of this kind should not be taken too seriously. For one thing, if culture is the name for human difference, then to attribute such difference to culture gets us nowhere (cf. Hannerz, this volume). For another, anthropology did not invent the concept of culture, rather its establishment was a product of the same general movement of European thought during the late eighteenth and nineteenth centuries, which, among other things, gave rise to the discipline of anthropology. Despite recurrent attempts to pin down the concept, and to give it some definitive meaning, which would henceforth authorise its use as a technical term for the discipline, 'culture' has continued to swim with the tide of intellectual fashion, leaving behind it an accumulating trail of discarded significances not unlike a pile of old clothes. From time to time anthropologists have tried to sort them all out: the most celebrated of these attempts was made almost forty years ago by A. L. Kroeber and Clyde Kluckhohn, who compiled a catalogue of no fewer than 161 different definitions of culture (Kroeber and Kluckhohn 1952). Since then, their number has continued to multiply apace.

One definition, however, has always stood out among all the others. It was proposed in 1871 by the Englishman, Edward Tylor, and formed the opening sentence of his massive, two-volume *Primitive Culture* – a work that effectively launched the comparative study of cultural forms. To this day, textbooks in anthropology continue to credit Tylor with the original, authoritative and as yet unsurpassed definition of the subject matter of the discipline (e.g. Beattie 1964: 20). Many other definitions have been implicitly or explicitly modelled on it: one such was presented by the distinguished American anthropologist, Robert Lowie, in his *History of Ethnological Theory* (1937). Here, then, are Tylor's and Lowie's definitions, side by side:

Tylor (1871)	Lowie (1937)
Culture or Civilization, taken in its widest ethnographic sense, is that complex whole which includes knowledge, belief, art, law, morals, custom, and any other capabilities and habits acquired by man as a member of society.	By culture we understand the sum total of what an individual acquires from his society – those beliefs, customs, artistic norms, food-habits and crafts which come to him not by his own creative efforts but as a legacy from the past.

At first glance, these certainly look very similar. There is the same inclusive listing, in both, of belief and custom, art and craft, and anything else that could be regarded as having been 'acquired' in the course of social life. But in the similarity there lies a puzzle. Like most of his Victorian contemporaries, Tylor was convinced of the inevitability of social progress, of man's rise from savagery to civilisation, an ascent attributed to the cultivation of uniquely human faculties of reason and intellect. His *Primitive Culture*, documenting the stages of this intellectual progress in its various fields of endeavour, could be described as establishing a kind of core curriculum for humanity. Lowie, however, was a prominent representative of the American cultural anthropology of the mid-twentieth century, an anthropology that had repudiated Victorian ideals of progress and reform, and that saw in culture an almost haphazard diversity of habitual ways of living and thinking, each with its own internal criteria of judgement. For the entirety of human culture, the 'complex whole' of Tylor's definition, Lowie

famously substituted a 'planless hodgepodge' (1921: 428). Could
Tylor and Lowie, then, really have been talking about the same
thing, under the rubric of 'culture', when their premisses were
so entirely opposed? The answer is that they could not, and
closer inspection reveals that in adapting Tylor's definition to
his own purposes, Lowie was reading it in a way that Tylor
never intended.

Notice that Tylor begins by introducing Culture (which, in his
writing, appears frequently with a Capital C and invariably in
the singular form) as a synonym for *civilisation*, meaning by that
not so much an achieved state or condition as a process by which
human populations are propelled from childlike ignorance
towards rational enlightenment (Stocking 1968: 69–90; Ingold
1986a: 31–47). But this notion of civilisation nowhere appears in
Lowie's definition; instead he treats culture as a 'legacy from the
past', a *tradition* passively acquired, there being as many such
traditions as there are populations to carry them. The
contradiction between these two senses of culture, as civilisation
and as tradition, is apparent to this day in the way the term is
used in what has come to be known, in academic circles, as
'western discourse' (of which more below). A 'cultured' person is
supposed to be one well-versed in science, literature and the arts,
one in whom reason and knowledge have been cultivated to a
high degree. To 'live in a culture', on the other hand, is to be
condemned to a life of traditional monotony, to be imprisoned in
one's thoughts by belief and superstition, and in one's actions by
customary routine. The man in a culture thus appears as the very
opposite of the cultured man, for the latter, in reaching for
enlightenment, claims to have liberated himself from the shackles
of tradition that hold the former in suspended animation.

In this opposition lies the connection between the two
contradictory usages: we are cultured and they are not *because*
they live in a culture and we do not. Like works of art, their
ways of life become objects of contemplation for us, but not *vice
versa*, since we are the spectators in the gallery of human
variety, whereas they are the figures in the pictures. In effect,
the concept of culture operates as a distancing device, setting up
a radical disjunction between *ourselves*, rational observers of the
human condition, and those *other people*, enmeshed in their
traditional patterns of belief and practice, whom we profess to
observe and study.

Now Tylor thought that all human beings were engaged in an ascent, however while some nations had made rapid progress and had already reached commanding heights, others were still struggling up the lower slopes. But suppose that, having reached the summit, we turn to look back, to see the whole panorama of human life spread out like a tapestry beneath our feet. This is the change of perspective implied when anthropologists turned from talking about Culture (in the singular) to talking about cultures (in the plural): the former refers to the ascent, the latter to the view from the top (Ingold 1986a: 46). In the first case, where Culture is equated with the process of civilisation, we consider *ourselves* to be relatively cultured and *them* (that is, traditional folk) to be relatively cultureless. But in the second case, following Lowie's identification of culture with tradition, *they* appear as its bearers and custodians, whereas *we* are the cultureless ones. Notice, however, that the implied superiority of us over them, of observers over observed, remained unquestioned. Indeed it was further exaggerated, for what Tylor had viewed in terms of greater or lesser *degrees* of culture became, in the hands of Lowie and others, an *absolute* distinction. According to ourselves the equivalent of an aerial view, we claim to be able to see into the many worlds of culture even though their inhabitants, locked into their limited visions of humanity, are unable to see out. For anthropologists, as I shall now show, this creates an awkward dilemma.

The culture of Culture

If it is a condition of being human that we should belong to one culture or another, it surely follows that – short of placing ourselves beyond humanity – our own vision must also be culture-bound. Thus it is said that we study *other* cultures rather than our own. What, then, is *our* culture? And why should not the people of other cultures study ours as we study theirs? If in the very act of identifying a form of life as a culture we dissociate ourselves from it, taking up the position of outsider spectators rather than insider participants, then the very notion of 'our culture' must be a contradiction in terms. This accounts, in part, for the great difficulty we have in expressing what it is.

One conventional response is to say that it is 'western'. But whereas non-western cultures are always somewhere, the West is apparently nowhere, or everywhere. Following the direction of the setting sun, one might traverse the globe and still not find it. In relation to any particular local community, however remote or close to home, the West figures as the 'outside world', the 'wider society' or the 'majority'. It is a world negatively characterised by the experience of non-belonging or alienation, a world where mass uniformity has overtaken the diversity of tradition, and in which everyman exists not for others but for himself alone. More positively, perhaps, the idea of the West conjures up an image of autonomous, bounded selfhood and the spirit of individual freedom, twin cornerstones of the political philosophy of liberal democracy with which the western world is of course popularly identified. The 'western individual', like his sibling 'economic man', is a being constituted independently and in advance of his entry into any kinds of relationships. It follows that there can be no such creature as a 'westerner', in so far as the suffix '-er' connotes belonging to place or people as an ingredient of personal identity (as the Londoner, for example, is someone whose biographical roots in the city, and continual attachment to the place, are felt to contribute in some essential way to making him the particular person that he is). For to be committed to the West is to deny that belonging, in this sense, can form any part of personal identity at all.

Alternatively, we might claim 'our culture' to be 'modern'. But a moment's reflection on the values associated with modernity shows that they add up to the very ideal of rational enlightenment classically epitomised by the concept of civilisation. Indeed the conventional dichotomy between the modern and the traditional does no more than substitute for another which most anthropologists are nowadays ashamed to use, between the civilised and the primitive. Devoted to the relentless pursuit of civilised values, and to repudiating at every turn the 'irrational' constraints of custom, the 'modern West' has set itself up as a culture of Culture. The predicament of the individual situated within such a culture might be compared to that of a man enclosed within a hall of mirrors, who sees in others only endless reflections of himself.

One recent pathology that stems directly from such hermetic self-regard is the intellectual tendency known ironically as post-modernism, ironically because it is of course symptomatic of the project of modernity that practitioners should forever seek to define themselves as beyond, or 'post', whatever might be construed as the prevalent orthodoxy (cf. Ardener 1985: 57). There is nothing more modern than speculation in the intellectual futures market. Nor is there, in fact, anything remotely novel about the conception of culture as 'fluid, interconnected, diffusing, interpenetrating...', words which Sanjek (1991: 622) uses to describe the allegedly post-modernist vision. It has been there from the very beginning of the 'era of cultures', when anthropology first turned its sights from the singularity of the civilisational process to the plurality of sedimented traditions. Seventy years have passed since Lowie reduced Tylor's 'complex whole' of Culture to a 'planless hodgepodge', yet self-styled post-modernists continue to engage in much the same exercise as though it heralded a new epoch.

But if western culture is a culture of Culture, it is not at all on a par with the 'other cultures' that anthropologists purport to study. The latter, each historically unique, are seen to differ one from another in the constituents of tradition, as do animal species in their hereditary attributes. To be western, however, is not to be the bearer of yet another tradition, but to disclose a condition that is utterly opposed to the traditional – the condition of modernity. Hence to compare any other culture with what is called 'our own' is to instantiate the general opposition between traditionalism and modernity. I should like at this point to draw attention to the remarkable parallel between the argument for the uniqueness of western culture and the argument for the uniqueness of humankind. As regards the latter, it is said that although every animal species is unique, humans are unique in their uniqueness (Ingold 1990: 210). Thus beavers may be compared with elephants, and both may be compared with humans, but whereas the former comparison attests to a particular contrast within animality, the latter instantiates a general contrast between the contrary conditions of animality and humanity, the one allegedly governed by instinct, the other by reason. Analogously, Eskimos might be compared with Australian Aborigines, and both might be compared with 'Westerners'; but whereas Eskimos differ from

Aborigines in their tradition, 'Westerners' are said to differ from both in being modern *rather than* traditional. In Figure 10.1 I have illustrated these arguments schematically.

In short, just as humanity – in this discourse – marks the triumph of reason over animal instinct, so does modernity mark its triumph over learned tradition. The two arguments are of course related, the link between them being the old evolutionary premiss that the modern West represents the culmination of the development of intellectual potentials common to the species. If humans are distinguished by the capacity to reason, it is in the

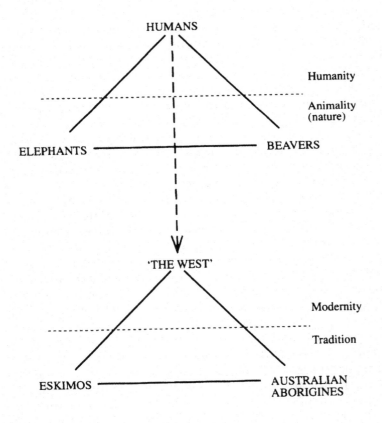

Figure 10.1

West that reason has taken the upper hand in the direction of human affairs. We would be advised to treat both these arguments with equal caution. In particular, we should guard against the temptation to insert a temporal distance between ourselves and others, as though in the confrontation between the two, past meets present. Humans, least of all so-called 'modern' humans, are not the only inhabitants of the contemporary world, as they are sometimes inclined to think, nor do supposedly traditional folk afford a window into the earlier conditions of human life (cf. Fabian 1983: 25–35). Anthropological fieldwork is not, as many of our predecessors believed, a form of time travel.

Such warnings have been issued often enough. But they have been phrased in terms of a concern to avoid the twin evils of anthropocentrism and ethnocentrism. This is singularly contradictory. For the project of overcoming these 'centrisms', of using observation and reason to transcend the limited horizons of species and culture, is none other than the project of modernity. With regard specifically to the avoidance of ethnocentrism, this invokes the ideas both that ordinary folk – that is 'ethno-people', whether our own 'folks at home' or the people we study – are locked into a particular ethos and worldview, and that our scientific objective should be to produce an account that recognises these understandings for what they are, namely specific cultural constructions of reality. And both these ideas, as we have seen, are central to the western discourse on tradition and civilisation. To sign up for the project of avoiding ethnocentrism is therefore to make an unequivocal assertion of superiority over the run of ordinary humans, patronisingly known as 'cultural members' or 'informants', and to do so in a strikingly western idiom. It is the characteristically anthropological expression of the West's symbolic appropriation of the rest. This brings me, at length, to the subject of translation.

Translation and inversion

Just as literary translation involves taking ideas expressed in one language and 'carrying them across' into the terms of another, so – it is said – anthropology involves the translation of the ideas and concepts of other cultures into terms comprehensible to a western readership. Yet a glance at Figure 10.1 shows that the analogy is fundamentally misleading. I aim to show that what is involved is not a 'lateral' process of translation but a 'vertical' process of inversion. In this, the experience of everyday life for the people among whom the anthropologist has lived is represented in an analytic discourse that seeks at every juncture to deny the reality and constitutive force of the relationships that those people have with one another and with their environments, and that underwrite their sense of belonging to locality and community. This is evident, for example, in the dichotomy that western thought draws between individual and society, which effectively removes social relations from the field of direct experience of particular persons in their mutual involvement and assigns them to an alien presence, 'society', which is imposed upon or wedged between them (Ingold 1986a: 289; cf. Strathern 1990a). Society, here, represents an external discipline, a set of walls within which individuals lead a private and solitary existence, and outside of which – in the public domain – they surrender their autonomy to the impersonal forces of the machine, the market and the state.

I submit that it is in the attempt to render the common understandings that make everyday life possible, within the terms of an alienating and universalising discourse, which anthropology has been led to divide and enwrap the world of humanity into discrete cultures. In other words, the anthropological fabrication of cultural systems is a *product* of the representation of difference in the discourse of homogeneity. What happens is that the total field of relationships within which persons are situated, and from which they derive their sense of identity and belonging, is supposed to be generated by an inner cognitive or representational schema which *belongs to them*. That is to say, people's *engagement* with the world, far from constituting them as the particular persons they are, is treated as the consequence of a particular mode of *construction* of it, such that particularity and difference are attributed not to the specific positions occupied within a relational field, but to the inner contents of the mind. This replacement of the person as a node within a nexus of relationships with the person as a bearer of a set of cognitive rules for constructing them is what I call *inversion* (see Figure 10.2).

To explain how this inversion works I have to introduce a digression on the subject of theories of perception. Orthodox culture theory in anthropology rests on the premiss that the perception of the environment – whether of other humans or of non-human agencies and entities – is *indirect*. According to this theory, the perceiver cannot access the world directly but has to figure it out, or 'construct' it, from the raw material registered through the senses. Such data, resulting from the continual bombardment of the body's sensory receptors by external stimuli, are inherently chaotic, so that any order or patterning that the perceiver claims to behold in the environment must be contributed by his or her own mind, through the organization of the raw sensory input into higher order structures or

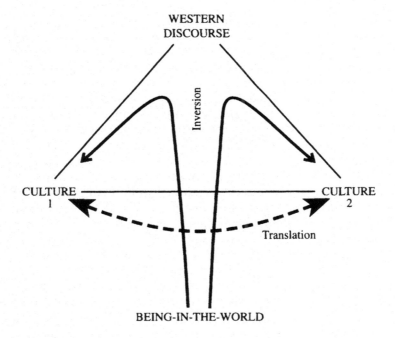

Figure 10.2

representations. Notice how this theory is underpinned by the classic Cartesian dualism of mind and body. The senses, for example of vision, hearing and touch, along with their associated neural pathways, are said to belong to the human organism, given in advance as parts of its biological nature. They are what we are 'born with'. But to organise the sensory input into meaningful patterns requires an activity of mind, and the schemata that direct this construction of meaning, that add the form to the content of sensation, are supposed to be *acquired* through a process of enculturation. As culture is added to the organism, so meaning is added to the data of experience.

There is, at the heart of this theory of perception, one major and unresolved – indeed irresolvable – dilemma. On the one hand, the acquisition of cognitive schemata must involve an engagement with others, yet a precondition for meaningful engagement must be that these schemata are already 'in place'. How can culture, as a system of meanings, be acquired by experience if experience only acquires meaning by way of culture? The unenculturated infant, initially locked into a private world of meaningless sensation, could never even get started on the road to cultural knowledge. To resolve this dilemma, we need an alternative theory of *direct* perception, and along with this, a different view of learning. Such a theory, which I have drawn from the so-called 'ecological psychology' of Gibson (1979), regards perception not as an activity of mind on the bodily deliverances of sense but as the ongoing activity of the *whole person*, moving around in – and exploring – an environment, and seeking out what it affords in the context of current projects. Thus, seeing, hearing and touching are not passive reactions of the body to external stimuli but processes of actively and intentionally *attending* to the world, of continually adjusting the receptor organs so as pick up, from the resulting modulations of the sensory array, information specifying significant features of the environment (Ingold 1992).

That we *learn* to see, hear and touch must be obvious to any artisan, musician or lover. Such learning, according to the theory of direct perception, involves a kind of sensitisation or fine-tuning of the entire perceptual system (comprising the brain, receptor organs and associated neural and muscular linkages functioning in an environmental context) to the pickup of certain kinds of information. For the artisan, it is vital to detect flaws in the material that might jeopardise the completion of his work: if experienced practitioners perceive imperfections that are invisible to the novice, it is not because the former have imposed a more elaborate or finely discriminating construction on the same body of sensual data, but because they are attuned to picking up critical information, which the novice simply fails to notice. It is the same in social life, which is much akin to the practice of a craft. We get to know others in our social world in the particular ways that we do, as the artisan gets to know his material, not by categorising them as persons of certain kinds within some encompassing schema (such as a system of kinship classification), but by becoming attentive and responsive to those subtle cues that reveal the nuances of our relationships towards them. In short, learning to perceive depends less on the acquisition of schemata for *constructing* the environment, as on the acquisition of skills for direct perceptual *engagement* with its various constituents, both human and non-human. In Gibson's words, learning is an 'education of attention' (1979: 254), a matter not of enculturation but of enskilment. The perceptual system of the skilled practitioner may be said to *resonate* with significant features of the environmental context of action (1979: 249; cf. Wikan, this volume).

Far from providing the individual, initially closed to the world, with a set of schemata that make it possible for him subsequently to deal with it, perceptual learning is, in this view, concurrent with life itself. 'One can keep on learning to perceive as long as life goes on' (Gibson 1979: 245). The process begins with the novice's immersion, right from birth (if not before) in a relational field that includes other humans, animals, plants, landscape features and so on – all of which add up to an environment. Every normal human infant comes into being already situated within such a field, and as it grows older, developing its own structures of awareness and patterns of response, so it emerges as an autonomous agent with the capacity to initiate further relationships (Ingold 1990: 221). Thus in the course of development the configuration of a person's relationships becomes enfolded into the very organisation of his or her perceptual system: ways of perceiving are the sedimentation of past histories of direct, mutual involvement between persons and their environments. And it is in the context of such involvement that constituents of the

environment have meaning. We do not superimpose meaning
on a world ('nature' or 'physical reality') that pre-exists apart
from ourselves, for to live we must dwell *in* the world, and to
dwell we must already relate to its constituents. Meaning
inheres in these relationships.

We can now return from this detour into theories of
perception to my initial point, that the anthropological
representation of 'other cultures' involves a process not of
translation but of inversion. Philosophers have long speculated
on the predicament of the anthropological fieldworker, set
down in the midst of an alien culture whose members speak a
quite different language, and who organise their world
according to a conceptual scheme as yet unknown. How is the
fieldworker even to begin the job of getting to understand the
culture of his hosts? It is supposed that if members of the
culture understand one another, and can share their perceptions
of the world, it is only because – thanks to language – they
organise their sensations (whose registration by each individual
is a strictly private affair) according to an agreed set of
categories publicly validated by verbal convention. To tap into
local perceptions the fieldworker must become privy to this
convention, yet how can he do so – how can he learn to translate
between the local convention and his own – if a condition for
meaningful social interaction is that conventions are already
shared? Indeed, the fieldworker's predicament seems analogous
to that of the child, except that the child does not come on the
scene with a convention already in place, so that to acquire one
convention is not to translate from the terms of another. Yet
children the world over have confounded the philosophers in
achieving with ease what the logic of orthodox culture theory
would deem impossible. They have grown to become
knowledgeable members of their communities. And if children
can do it, why cannot fieldworkers?

Children can do it, as we have seen, because learning to
perceive is a matter not of acquiring conventional schemata for
ordering sensory data, but of learning to *attend* to the world in
certain ways through involvement with others in everyday
contexts of practical action. This, too, is how the anthropologist
learns to perceive in the field. I, for example, have learned (up to
a point) to see the world in the way a reindeer herdsman does. I
have done so, as any other fieldworker, through becoming

immersed in joint action with my fellow practitioners in a *shared* environment. I experience the components of this environment as they do, not because I have learned to construct them in my mind according to the same categorical conventions, but because I have learned to attend to them in the same way, according to what they afford in the situational context of herding activities. Such communion of experience, the awareness of living in a common world, establishes a foundational level of sociality that exists – in Bourdieu's (1977: 2) phrase – 'on the hither side of words or concepts', and that constitutes the relational baseline on which all attempts at verbal communication must subsequently build. It is, of course, what makes fieldwork possible.

From this experiential baseline, then, the anthropologist sets out to construct an ethnographic account. But in framing the account within the concept of culture, that very position of engagement in the world which was a precondition for learning through fieldwork is immediately relinquished for a superior (and imagined) point of observation, uniquely constituted in western discourse: that of universal reason. It is from this point alone that the world is disclosed as a single, independently given domain of reality, indifferent to the various cultural schemata that may be placed upon it. And only an observer located at such a point would be able to make the claim of perceptual relativism, namely that each cultural schema '*organizes* or *fits* nature or the world of reality' (Hollis and Lukes 1982: 7). In fact, the perspective of universal reason is the product of a double disengagement, generated by compounding the two dichotomies of Figure 10.1: between humanity and nature and, within humanity, between reason and tradition. The effect is not unlike that produced by perspective painting, in which the picture specifies a point of observation that is itself detached from the subjective point of view of the spectator. Likewise, universal reason can treat, as objects of contemplation, diverse worldviews each of which is a specific construction of an external reality. In both cases, there is a 'viewing of views'. Perhaps it is no accident that both are the products of the same trajectory of western thought.

The double disengagement entailed in the representation of difference from the vantage point of universal reason is indicated schematically in Figure 10.3. Let me briefly restate the argument. For real people, dwelling in a real world, that world is revealed to them through their active engagement with it. It is an historical world, which is forever coming into being in the process of this engagement, just as they themselves come into being in the process of their dwelling. To reason, however, reality is revealed through an opposite process of disengagement, rupturing the unity of mind and nature and stretching the distance between them to the point of absolute separation. Rational science, as von Bertalanffy puts it (1955: 258–9), approaches reality through a 'progressive de-anthropomorphization', which ultimately dissolves the world into its minimal constituents of matter and energy. If this is 'real' reality, then it follows that whatever form and meaning perceivers claim to find in their own experience must be added on by their own minds. And if different people see different things, it cannot be because they have taken up different positions in the real world (since, as perceivers, they are already excluded from it); it must rather be because they are equipped with different cognitive models for representing or reconstructing the one given world inside their multiple heads.

Thus views *in* the world are replaced by views *of* the world, modes of engagement by modes of construction. Yet only to universal reason are worldviews disclosed *as* worldviews, as alternative ('emic') modellings of an independent ('etic') reality.

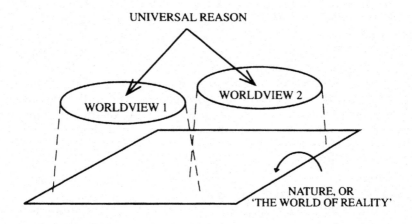

Figure 10.3

For the people themselves what reason calls a worldview appears as the only reality they know. So it is that by abdicating, for the high point of reason, the specific relational context of being-in-the-world that makes it possible to share in the experience of local people, anthropology contrives to turn that context, as it were, 'outside in' to constitute an ideal 'building plan' for the cultural construction of reality. Thus do people appear to be the inhabitants of their separate cultures; and thus, too, do cultures appear to have 'members', united by their adherence to a common scheme of mental representations – a scheme that, in Shweder's words (strikingly reminiscent of Lowie's formulation of 1937), 'is inherited or received from the past' (1990: 26).

Uniformity and difference

It is the logic of inversion, described above, that has set the terms for the never-ending and singularly futile epistemological debate, between the advocates of rationality and relativism. For example, in their defence of relativism, Barnes and Bloor can invite the reader to 'consider the members of two tribes, T1 and T2, whose cultures are both primitive but otherwise very different from one another' (1982: 26), while remaining seemingly oblivious to the fact that universal reason is already implicated in the very constitution of 'primitive tribes' as objects for consideration. It is, as I have shown, the view from the summit that wraps people up into their several cultures, each with its stock of 'beliefs' about an external 'reality' that stands apart from, and impartial to, diverse human attempts to represent it.

This, in turn, establishes the dichotomy, which anthropology has long taken for granted, between the universal and the particular, between the one world of nature and the many worlds of culture. Humans, possessed of both body and mind, are regarded as half in nature, half out, organising through culture the formless and undifferentiated substratum of sensory experience derived from their bodily immersion in a physical world. 'That is what the "diversity of human culture" really amounts to,' writes Edmund Leach; 'the variety of different ways which human beings choose to cut up the continuities of

their animal experience' (1982: 98). From time to time we are
warned that an excessive emphasis on cultural diversity may
obscure the capacity that humans (like many other animals)
have to respond to one another, on the level of basic emotions
and feelings, simply by virtue of their common nature. But why
should experiential continuity imply uniformity? And why,
conversely, should an emphasis on difference imply
discontinuity? Must we conclude that people can inhabit one
world only to the extent that they are all alike, and therefore
that, insofar as they differ, they must inhabit separate worlds?

To demonstrate why such a conclusion is unwarranted, I find
it helpful to imagine the world in which people dwell as a
continuous and unbounded landscape, endlessly varied in its
features and contours, yet without seams or breaks. As we
travel across the landscape we move from place to place. Each
place is different from the last, each is surrounded by its own
horizons, yet these horizons dissolve on approach as new ones
loom up ahead – they are never crossed. So how do we describe
the particular character of a place? I answer: 'By the way the
world looks from that place, by the vista it affords to someone
standing there' (Ingold 1986b: 155). Move to some other place,
some way away, and the prospect will be very different, yet
what it reveals is not another world but the same world viewed
from another vantage point within it. It is a panorama available
to anyone who chooses to stand at that spot, so that if you and I
stand together there, we can share the same view.

The logic of inversion, however, leads me to re-present that
view as a construction of your own, superimposed upon a
homogeneous substrate, just as in the making of a map, a
pattern of symbols is impressed upon a blank sheet of paper (cf.
Bourdieu 1977: 2). And so it seems that two individuals, even
though they stand at the same spot and look all around, may see
quite *different* prospects, because they carry in their heads
different maps. Thus the character of a place will depend no
longer on the way the world looks from there, but on the way it
is represented in one or another map (regardless of where one
stands). As all difference is drawn out from the landscape onto
the plane of its representation, so the landscape itself is
rendered uniform: it is reduced to 'space', a vacuum to the
plenum of culture. In short, the opposition between culture and
space, like that between the particular and the universal, is a

product of the logic of inversion, working on the experience of dwelling in a landscape.

Long ago, the philosopher G. H. Mead made the same argument for the perception of the social world that I have made for the perception of the landscape. Just as a place arises in a landscape and is constituted as the place it is by its position within the whole, so, Mead argued, selves are constituted with their specific identities by their respective positions in the total social process. This involvement in the whole, Mead insisted, is not in the least destructive of individual difference: quite the contrary, it is because they are participants in one social world, and caught up in a continuous field of ongoing relationships, that people differentiate themselves one from another:

> Each individual self within that [social] process, while it reflects in its organized structure the behaviour pattern of that process as a whole, *does so from its own particular and unique standpoint within that process*, and thus reflects in its organized structure a different aspect or perspective of this whole social behaviour pattern from that which is reflected in the organized structure of any other individual self within that process. (Mead 1934: 201, my emphases)

But if difference is a function of involvement *with* others in a continuous social process, why does anthropology persist in depicting it as a function of discontinuity and contrast?

Examples abound. One is Leach's celebrated remark that '*I* identify myself with a collective we which is then contrasted with some *other*' (1967: 34). For Anthony Cohen, the sense of self, at the levels both of individuality and of collectivity, is 'informed by implicit or explicit contrast' (1985: 115). More ostentatiously, Boon writes that 'like languages, cultures are fundamentally beside themselves. . . . Analytically, cultures are constituted contrastively' (1982: 230–1). And he goes on to draw the inevitable conclusion that the problematic of translation, established by the way each culture defines itself as a '*vis-à-vis*' to the other, is an inherent feature of the human condition.

Once more, it is the logic of inversion that establishes this sense of identity-by-contrast. Consider, for example, the meaning of 'community'. In its German form, *Gemeinschaft*, the term was classically used by Ferdinand Tönnies (1955[1887]) to denote a particular quality of relatedness, one marked by intimacy and close mutual involvement. In this sense it was opposed to *Gesellschaft*, the impersonal association of discrete interests. Now as a form of intimate sociality, community can inhere in a network of interpersonal relationships that, just like the landscape of my earlier example, is continuous and unbounded. This is reportedly affirmed among many groups of hunters and gatherers, who define themselves collectively by terms that translate as 'people', and among whom – as Woodburn states – 'there is simply no basis for exclusion' (1982: 448). The category *we*, then, expands indefinitely outwards from the centre where *I* stand to embrace others, along the lines of social relationships, rather than rebounding inwards on myself from an exterior opposition with *them*. So what leads us to slip, so easily and so imperceptibly, from thinking of community to thinking of communities, and hence to thinking of *this* community rather than *that*? Why does the invocation of community immediately intimate the presence of boundaries?

The answer is that from the perspective I have identified as 'western', the experiential centre from which a person lives his life in the world (and from which lines of relationship radiate *outwards* to incorporate others) is converted into a boundary *within* which his life-world, and hence the domain of his relationships, is contained. *We*, far from expanding to embrace the other, can include only those who share this life-world, as opposed to *they* who do not. Notice how, by pushing all difference onto the boundary between us and them, an artificial uniformity is created within each category. *We* are all the same, by virtue of our contrast with *them*. Once again, difference is rendered in the discourse of homogeneity, with the result that it comes to be seen as a property of boundaries, of discontinuity and contrast, as opposed to the uniformity that is supposed to prevail within them. To return to the language of Tönnies, it would be fair to say that the switch from community as a quality of sociality to communities as bounded units is a consequence of rendering *Gemeinschaft* in the terms of *Gesellschaft*.

This conclusion has an immediate bearing on theories of ethnicity. For my argument would suggest that ethnic consciousness does not lie in the discovery and articulation, in the course of people's dealings with outsiders, of boundaries that are *already there* on account of a primordial division of humanity into cultures or communities. I believe that ethnicity should

rather be regarded as tantamount to the very process in which
people's sense of belonging, to place and people, comes to be
reframed in terms of cultural affiliation. It is, in other words, a
process of inversion, by which one form of identity, which I call
relational, is converted into another, which I call *attributional*.
Relational identity is given by one's position in a continuous
network or field; attributional identity is given by characteristic
patterns of inner mental representation. In the former case,
belonging is expressed through difference, in the latter it is
expressed through similarity. Ethnicity arises when people seek
to recapture a lost or threatened sense of relational identity by
expressing it in attributional terms. As such, it is a response to the
condition of alienation induced by modernity – a response,
however, that is couched in a peculiarly modern idiom. The very
rhetoric of culture, whether used by anthropologists or by the
ideologues of ethno-political movements, is of First World (i.e.
western) provenance. That is why the politics of culture, carried
on in recent decades under the banner of the 'Fourth World', is
invariably confined to what Paine (1985: 50) calls 'Fourth-in-First'
situations. Once again, it involves the codification of difference in
the discourse of homogeneity.

Conclusion

Let me conclude by returning to the question of translation. To
construe the anthropological project in general as one of
translation is to assume a world of humanity already parcelled
up into discrete cultures, each having a distinctive essence and
credited with the power to 'construct' the experience of the
people living under its sway. To construe this project more
specifically as one of translation from 'other cultural' to 'western
cultural' understandings is to assume that 'western culture'
exists as an entity of a similar kind that can be ranged alongside
the others. Both assumptions have been shown to be false. On
the one hand, the idea that humans inhabit culturally
constructed worlds is part of a specifically western discourse; on
the other hand, that discourse places its practitioners –
including anthropologists – above culture.

This has led to strangely paradoxical results. Catherine Lutz,
for example, informs us that understanding the emotional lives of

people in other cultures is 'first and foremost a problem of translation' (1988: 8), and warns against the dangers of importing such western dichotomies as mind versus body and reason versus emotion into our interpretations of the lives of people – such as the Ifaluk whom she studied – who do not make these distinctions, and who see the whole person as an undivided centre of experience and agency. And yet the very same distinctions are themselves implicated in attributing the Ifaluk view to a mode of cognitive apprehension of sensory experience specific to their culture. In its relativisation, the challenge that this view presents to western discourse is conveniently neutralised, and the dichotomies between cognition and sensation, and between mind and body, are further reproduced. It is 'just another' cultural construction of reality.

To take the challenge seriously is to assert that real people are indeed whole, rather than composites of body and mind, and that the world in which they – we – dwell is not divided into blocs but is *continuous*. This continuity is a precondition for our engagement with others and for the mutual understanding without which the entire anthropological enterprise would be impossible. I have shown that the division of the world into discrete cultures is not an initial condition but the *end product* of a process which is best described as one of inversion, the representation of people's varying senses of belonging within the continuous world as a series of distinct and incommensurable ways of constructing it. Thus in its application, the concept of culture fragments the experiential continuity of being-in-the-world, isolating people both from the non-human environment (now conceived as 'nature') and from one another. It is this fragmentation, then, that sets the stage for the *artificial* reconstitution of the continuity of the world in the act of translation. Hence my title: 'The art of translation in a continuous world'. It could be said, I suppose, that through the deployment of the concept of culture, anthropology has created the problem of translation rather than solved it. Having divided the world, through an operation of inversion, we are now left with pieces that have to be connected together again through translation. Would it not be preferable to move in the opposite direction, to recover that foundational continuity, and from that basis to challenge the hegemony of an alienating discourse? If so, then the concept of culture, as a key term of that discourse, will have to go.

References

Abraham, S. Y. 1983. 'The development and transformation of the Palestine national movement', in *Occupation: Israel over Palestine*, ed. N. Aruri, Belmont, MA: AAUG Press, 391–425

Abrahamian, Levon H. 1983. *Primitive Festival and Mythology*, Yerevan: Izdatel'stvo Akademii nauk ArmSSR, (in Russian)

———— 1990a. 'Ritual, proto-theatre, and Theatre Square', *Bem* 1, 7–19 (in Armenian)

———— 1990b. 'Perestroika as carnival: notes by a culturologist', *XX Century and Peace* 6, 45–8

Abrahamian, L. H. and H. T. Maroutian n.d. 'History in pictures: the Karabagh movement through the prism of transparencies and posters' (ms. in Russian)

Abu-Lughod, Lila 1990. 'Shifting politics in Beduin love poetry', in *Language and the Politics of Emotion*, eds C. Lutz and L. Abu-Lughod, Cambridge: Cambridge University Press, 24–45

———— 1991. 'Writing against culture', in *Recapturing Anthropology: working in the present*, ed. R. G. Fox, Santa Fé: School of American Research Press, 137–62

Abu-Lughod, Lila and Catherine Lutz 1990. 'Introduction: emotion, discourse, and the politics of everyday life', in *Language and the Politics of Emotion*, eds C. Lutz and L. Abu-Lughod, Cambridge: Cambridge University Press, 1–23

Akhtar, Shabbir 1989. *Be Careful with Muhammad!* London: Bellew

Alexander, Paul 1977. 'Sea tenure in southern Sri Lanka', *Ethnology* 16 (3), 231–51

Appadurai, Arjun 1988. 'Putting hierarchy in its place', *Cultural Anthropology* 3(1), 36–49

Ardener, E. 1985. 'Social anthropology and the decline of modernism', in *Reason and Morality*, ed. J. Overing (ASA Monograph 24), London: Tavistock

Arendt, Hannah 1958. *The Human Condition*. New York: Doubleday

Asad, Talal ed. 1973. *Anthropology and the Colonial Encounter*, London: Ithaca Press

———— 1986. 'The concept of cultural translation in British social anthropology', in *Writing Culture: the poetics and politics of ethnography*, eds James Clifford and George E. Marcus, Berkeley, CA: University of California Press, 141–64

_____ 1987. 'Are there histories of peoples without Europe? A review article', *Comparative Studies in Society and History 29* (3), 594–607

The Asian Wall Street Journal, 20 March 1980

Atkinson, Paul 1990. *The Ethnographic Imagination: textual constructions of reality*, London: Routledge

Austin, J. L. 1975[1962]. *How to do Things with Words*, Cambridge, MA: Harvard University Press

Azumi, Ryo 1984. *Senshi no utage*, Tokyo: Sakuga Group shirizu, SG-Kiga

_____ 1986–8. *Akai Tsurugi*, Vols 1–4, Tokyo: Sakuga Group shirizu, SG-Kiga

Bakhtin, Michael 1965. *The Works of François Rabelais and the People's Culture of the Middle Ages and Renaissance*, Moscow: Khudozhestvennaya Literatura (in Russian)

Barnes, B. and D. Bloor 1982. 'Relativism, rationalism and the sociology of knowledge', in *Rationality and Relativism*, eds M. Hollis and S. Lukes, Oxford: Basil Blackwell

Barth, Fredrik 1969. Introduction, in *Ethnic Groups and Boundaries: the social organization of cultural difference*, ed. F. Barth, Bergen: Universitets Forlaget, 9–38

_____ (In press). 'Assessing anthropology: past perspectives, future directions', in *Assessing Developments in Anthropology*, ed. Robert Borofsky

Barth, Fredrik and Unni Wikan 1989. *Bhutan report: results of a fact-finding mission 1989*, New Delhi: UNICEF

Basso, Keith H. 1990. '"To give up on words": silence in western Apache culture', in *Western Apache Language and Culture*, Tucson: The University of Arizona Press

Bateson, Gregory and Margaret Mead 1942. *Balinese Character: a photographic analysis*, New York: Academy of Sciences

Beattie, John 1964. *Other Cultures: aims, methods and achievements in social anthropology*, London: Routledge and Kegan Paul

Beidelman, T. O. 1971. *The Translation of Culture: essays to E. E. Evans-Pritchard*, London: Tavistock Publications

Belmonte, Thomas 1979. *The Broken Fountain*, New York: Columbia University Press

Belo, Jane 1970[1935]. 'The Balinese temper', in *Traditional Balinese Culture*, New York: Columbia University Press, 85–110

Ben-Ari, E. and Y. Bilu 1987. '"Saints'" sanctuaries in Israeli development towns: on a mechanism of urban transformation', *Urban Anthropology 16*, 243–73

Ben-Rafael, E. 1982. *The Emergence of Ethnicity: cultural groups and social conflict in Israel*, Westport, CT: Greenwood

Bertalanffy, L. von 1955. 'An essay on the relativity of categories', *Philosophy of Science 22*, 243–63

Bird-David, Nurit 1988. 'Hunter-gatherers and other people: a re-examination', in *Hunters and Gatherers 1: history, evolution and sociall change*, eds T. Ingold, D. Riches and J. Woodburn, Oxford: Berg, 17–30

———1990. 'The giving environment: another perspective on the economic system of gatherer-hunters', *Current Anthropology 31* (2), 189–96

Bistrup, Rie 1990. 'Risser sorgen i runer. Interview with Kolbjörn Falkeid', *Aftenposten*, 11 April

Bitterli, Urs 1986. *Cultures in Conflict: encounters between European and non-European cultures 1492–1800*, Stanford, CA: Stanford University Press

Bloch, Maurice 1983. *Marxism and Anthropology*, Oxford: Oxford University Press

———1991. 'Language, anthropology and cognitive science', *Man 26* (2), 183–98

Bohannan, Laura 1966. 'Shakespeare in the bush', *Natural History Magazine*, August/September

Bongie, Chris 1991. *Exotic Memories: literature, colonialism, and the Fin de Siécle*. Stanford, CA: Stanford University Press

Boon, J. A. 1982. *Other Tribes, Other Scribes*, Cambridge: Cambridge University Press

Bourdieu, Pierre 1977. *Outline of a Theory of Practice*. Cambridge: Cambridge University Press

——— 1984. *Distinction: a social critique of the judgement of taste*, trans. Richard Nice, Chicago: University of Chicago Press

———1990a. *The Logic of Practice*, trans. Richard Nice, Cambridge: Polity Press

———1990b. 'The scholastic point of view', *Cultural Anthropology 5* (4), 380–91

Brenneis, Donald L. 1990. 'Shared and solitary sentiments: the discourse of friendship, play, and anger in Bhatagon', in *Language and the Politics of Emotion*, eds C. Lutz and L. Abu-Lughod, Cambridge: Cambridge University Press, 114–25

Brenneis, Donald L. and Fred Myers (eds) 1984. *Dangerous Worlds: language and politics in the Pacific*, New York: New York University Press

Burch, Ernest S. 1988. 'Modes of exchange in north-west Alaska', in *Hunters and Gatherers 2: property, power and ideology*, eds T. Ingold, D. Riches, and J. Woodburn, Oxford: Berg, 95–109

Carrithers, Michael 1990. 'Is anthropology art or science?' *Current Anthropology 31* (3), 263–72

Carroll, Raymonde 1987. *Cultural Misunderstandings: the French-*

American experience, Chicago: University of Chicago Press

Cavalli-Sforza, L. L. and M. W. Feldman 1981. *Cultural Transmission and Evolution: a quantitative approach*, Princeton, NJ: Princeton University Press

Chamberlain, Lori 1988. 'Gender and the metaphorics of translation', *Signs* 13 (3), 454–72

Chang, Yvonne 1990. 'Move over Batman – here comes Akira', *The Japan Times*, 4 February

Chomsky, Noam 1980. *Rules and Representations*, Oxford: Basil Blackwell

Clifford, James 1986. 'On ethnographic allegory', in *Writing Culture: the poetics and politics of ethnography*, eds J. Clifford and G. E. Marcus, Berkeley, CA: University of California Press, 98–121

_____ 1988. *The Predicament of Culture: twentieth-century ethnography, literature, and art*, Cambridge, MA: Harvard University Press

Clifford, James and George E. Marcus (eds) 1986. *Writing Culture: the poetics and politics of ethnography*, Berkeley, CA: University of California Press

Cohen, A. P. 1985. *The Symbolic Construction of Community*, London: Tavistock

Cole, Sally 1988. 'The sexual division of labor and social change in a Portuguese fishery', in *To Work and to Weep: women in fishing economies*, eds J. Nadel-Klein and D. Lee Davis, St. John's: Institute of Social and Economic Research, Memorial University of Newfoundland, 169–89

Colson, Elizabeth 1984. 'The reordering of experience: anthropological involvement in time', *Journal of Anthropological Research* 40 (1), 1–13

Cottrell, W. F. 1939. 'Of time and the railroader', *American Sociological Review* 4 (2), 190–8

Crapanzano, Vincent 1989. 'Preliminary notes on the glossing of emotions', *Kroeber Anthropological Society Papers* 69–70, 78–85

Crick, Malcolm 1976. *Explorations in Language and Meaning: towards a semantic anthropology*, London: Malaby Press

Crumrine, N. Ross 1970. 'Ritual drama and cultural change', *Comparative Studies in Society and History* 12 (4), 361–72

Damon, William 1981. 'Exploring children's social cognition on two fronts', in *Social Cognitive Development: frontiers and possible futures*, eds J. H. Flavell and L. Ross, Cambridge: Cambridge University Press, 154–75

Das, Veena n.d. 'What do we mean by health?' Deptartment of Sociology, New Delhi University (ms.)

Davidson, Donald 1984. *Inquiries into Truth and Interpretation*, Oxford: Oxford University Press

_____ 1986. 'A nice derangement of epitaphs', in *Truth and Interpretation: perspectives on the philosophy of Donald Davidson*, ed. Ernest LePore,

Oxford: Basil Blackwell, 433–46

Dawkins, R. 1976. *The Selfish Gene*, Oxford: Oxford University Press

Delaney, Carol 1988. 'Participant observation: the razor's edge', *Dialectical Anthropology* 13, 291–300

Derrida, Jacques 1985. 'Des tours de Babel', in *Difference in Translation*, ed. Joseph F. Graham, Ithaca, NY: Cornell University Press

Deshen, Shlomo 1982. 'Israeli Judaism: introduction to the major patterns', in *Religion and Society in Asia and the Middle East*, ed. C. Caldorola, Berlin: Mouton, 85–118

1989. 'The religiosity of Israeli Middle-Easterners and the 1988 elections', *Politiqa* (Tel-Aviv) 24, 40–3 (in Hebrew)

Deshen, S. and M. Shokeid 1974. *The Predicament of Homecoming: cultural and social life of North African immigrants in Israel*, Ithaca, NY: Cornell University Press

Douglas, Mary 1973. *Natural Symbols*, New York: Vintage Books

1975. *Implicit Meanings*, London: Routledge & Kegan Paul

1986. *Risk Acceptability According to the Social Sciences*, London: Routledge & Kegan Paul

Douglas, M. and A. Wildavsky 1982. *Risk and Culture: an essay on the selection of technical and environmental dangers*, Berkeley and London: University of California Press

Drummond, Lee 1987. 'Are there cultures to communicate across?: an appraisal of the "culture" concept from the perspective of anthropological semiotics', in *Developments in Linguistics and Semiotics: language teaching and learning communication across cultures*, ed. Simon P. X. Battestini, Washington: Georgetown University Press, 215–25

Dumézil, Georges 1968. *Mythe et Epopée: l'idéologie des trois fonctions dans les epopées des peuples Indo-Européens*, Paris: Gallimard

Dunn, Judy 1988. *The Beginnings of Social Understanding*, Cambridge, MA: Harvard University Press

Durkheim, E. and M. Mauss 1963. *Primitive Classifications*, London: Cohen & West

Durrenberger, E. Paul 1975. 'Understanding a misunderstanding: Thai-Lisu relations in northern Thailand', *Anthropological Quarterly* 48, 106–20

Durrenberger, E. Paul and Gísli Pálsson 1986. 'Finding fish: the tactics of Icelandic skippers', *American Ethnologist* 13 (2), 213–29

Eco, Umberto 1976. 'Le mythe de Superman', *Communications* 24, 24–5

Ellen, Roy (ed.) 1984. *Ethnographic Research: a guide to general conduct*, London: Academic Press

Endicott, K. and K. L. Endicott 1986. 'The question of hunter-gatherer territoriality: the case of the Batek of Malaysia', in *The Past and Future of !Kung Ethnography: critical reflections and symbolic perspectives. Essays in honour of Lorna Marshall*, eds M. Biesele, R.

Gordon and R. Lee, Hamburg: Helmut Buske Verlag, 137–62

Evans-Pritchard, E. E. 1951. *Social Anthropology*, London: Cohen & West

Fabian, J. 1983. *Time and the Other*, New York: Columbia University Press

Fagan, Brian M. 1984. *Clash of Cultures*, New York: W. H. Freeman

Featherstone, Mike (ed.) 1990. *Global Culture: nationalism, globalization and modernity*, London: Sage

Feleppa, Robert 1988. *Convention, Translation, and Understanding: philosophical problems in the comparative study of culture*, Albany, NY: State University of New York Press

Ferguson, Brian R. with Leslie E. Farragher 1988. *The Anthropology of War: a bibliography*, New York: The Harry Frank Guggenheim Foundation, Occasional Paper No. 1

Figueira, Dorothy Matilda 1991. *Translating the Orient: the reception of Sakūntala in nineteenth century Europe*, Albany, NY: State University of New York Press

Fischer, Michael M. J. and Mehdi Abedi 1990. 'Bombay talkies, the word and the world: Salman Rushdie's *Satanic Verses*', *Cultural Anthropology* 5, 107–59

Flavell, John H. and Lee Ross 1981. 'Concluding remarks', in *Social Cognitive Development: frontiers and possible futures*, eds J. H. Flavell and L. Ross, Cambridge: Cambridge University Press, 306–16

Foucault, Michel 1972. *The Archaeology of Knowledge and the Discourse on Language*, New York: Pantheon

1980. *Power/knowledge*, ed. C. Gordon, Brighton: Harvester Press

Friedman, Jonathan 1987. 'Beyond otherness or: the spectacularization of anthropology', *Telos* 71, 161–70

Friedman, M. 1990. 'The Haredim and the Holocaust', *Jerusalem Quarterly* 53, 86–114

Gamst, F. C. 1986. 'Women as operating and clerical railroaders; some considerations of enculturation and intrinsic and external barriers', *Urban Anthropology* 15 (3–4), 245–320

Gardner, Howard 1983. *Frames of Mind*, New York: Basic Books

1984. 'The development of competence in culturally defined domains: a preliminary framework', in *Culture Theory: essays on mind, self, and emotion*, eds R. A. Shweder and R. A. LeVine, Cambridge: Cambridge University Press

Geertz, Clifford 1960. 'The Javanese Kijaji: the changing role of a cultural broker', *Comparative Studies in Society and History* 2, 228–49

1973. *The Interpretation of Cultures*, New York: Basic Books

1977. 'Found in translation: on the social history of the moral imagination', *Georgia Review* 31, 788–810

1984[1974]. 'From the native's point of view: on the nature of anthropological understanding', in *Culture Theory: essays on mind, self, and emotion*, eds R. A. Shweder and R. A. LeVine, Cambridge: Cambridge University Press, 123–36

1988. *Works and Lives: the anthropologist as author*, Stanford, CA: Stanford University Press

Gellner, Ernest 1988a. *Plough, Sword and Book: the structure of human history*, Chicago: University of Chicago Press

1988b. *State and Society in Soviet Thought*. New York: Basil Blackwell

Gewertz, Deborah and Frederick K. Errington 1991. *Twisted Histories, Altered Contexts: representing the Chambri in a world system*, Cambridge: Cambridge University Press

Gibson, J. J. 1979. *The Ecological Approach to Visual Perception*, Boston: Houghton Mifflin

Godelier, Maurice 1986. *The Mental and the Material*, London: Verso

Goldberg, H. (ed.) 1987. *Judaism Viewed from Within and from Without: anthropological studies*, Albany, NY: State University of New York Press

Goody, Jack 1977. *The Domestication of the Savage Mind*, Cambridge: Cambridge University Press

Gross, Larry P. 1973. 'Modes of communication and the acquisition of symbolic competence', in *Communications Technology and Social Policy*, eds G. Gerbner, L. P. Gross and W. H. Melody, New York: Wiley

Gudeman, Stephen and Alberto Rivera 1990. *Conversations in Colombia: the domestic economy in life and text*, Cambridge: Cambridge University Press

Gurevich, Aron 1988. *Medieval Popular Culture: problems of belief and perception*, trans. János M. Mak and Paul. A. Hollingsworth, Cambridge: Cambridge University Press

Gutt, Ernst-August 1991. *Translation and Relevance: cognition and context*, Oxford: Basil Blackwell

Habermas, Jürgen 1989. *The New Conservatism: cultural criticism and the historians' debate*, ed. and trans. S. W. Nicholsen, Cambridge, MA: The MIT Press

Hairapetian, V. 1991. 'Interpretation of the word: a brief introduction into hermeneutics for scholars in Russian philology', in *The Noosphere and Creative Arts*, Moscow: Nauka, 119–38 (in Russian)

Hall, Edward T. and William F. White 1960. *Intercultural Communication: a guide to men of action*, Indianapolis: Bobbs-Merrill (reprint series in the social sciences)

Hanks, W. F. 1989. 'Text and textuality', *Annual Review of Anthropology* 18, 95–127

Hannerz, Ulf 1985. 'Structures for strangers: ethnicity and institutions in a colonial Nigerian town', in *City and Society*, eds Aidan Southall, Peter J. M. Nas and Ghaus Ansari, Leiden: Institute of Cultural and Social Studies, University of Leiden

1987. 'The world in creolisation', *Africa* 57: 546–59

1988. 'American culture: creolized, creolizing', in *American Culture: creolized, creolizing and other lectures from the NAAS Biennial Conference in Uppsala, 28–31 May 1987*, ed. Erik Åsard, Uppsala: Swedish Institute for North American Studies

1989a. 'Notes on the global ecumene', *Public Culture* 1 (2), 66–75

1989b. 'Culture between center and periphery: toward a macroanthropology', *Ethnos* 54, 200–16

1990. 'Cosmopolitans and locals in world culture', *Theory, Culture and Society* 7, 237–51

Hanson, F. Allan 1979. 'Does God have a body? Truth, reality and cultural relativism', *Man* 14: 515–29

Harkabi, Y. 1988. *Israel's Fateful Hour*, New York: Harper & Row

Harris, Philip R. and Robert T. Moran 1987. *Managing Cultural Differences* (2nd edition), Houston, TX: Gulf Publishing

Harris, Roy 1988. *Language, Saussure and Wittgenstein: how to play games with words*, London: Routledge

Hart, Keith 1990. 'Swimming into the human current', *The Times Higher Education Supplement* 18 May, 13–14

Haskell, Thomas L. 1985. 'Capitalism and the origin of humanitarian sensibility, part 1', *American Historical Review* 90 (2), 339–61

Hatch, Elvin 1989. 'Theories of social honor', *American Anthropologist* 91 (2), 341–52

Hatim, Basil and Ian Mason 1990. *Discourse and the Translator*, London: Longman

Heilman, S. C. and S. M. Cohen 1989. *Cosmopolitans and Parochials: modern orthodox Jews in America*, Chicago: University of Chicago Press

Hirschfeld, Lawrence A. 1988. 'On aquiring social categories: cognitive development and anthropological wisdom', *Man* 23: 611–38

Hirschman, Albert O. 1982. 'Rival interpretations of market society: civilizing, destructive, or feeble?', *Journal of Economic Literature* 20, 1463–84

Hirschkop, Ken and David Shepherd, (eds) 1989. *Bakhtin and Cultural Theory*, Manchester and New York: Manchester University Press

Hobart, Mark 1985a. 'Anthropos through the looking-glass, or how to teach the Balinese to bark', in *Reason and Morality*, ed. Joanna Overing, London: Tavistock, 104–34

1985b. 'Texte est un con', in *Context and Levels: anthropological essays on hierarchy*, eds R. N. Barnes, D. de Coppet, and R. J. Parkin, Oxford: Jaso Occasional Papers 4, 33–53

1986. 'Introduction: context, meaning and power', in *Context, Meaning and Power in Southeast Asia*, eds M. Hobart and R. H. Taylor. Ithaca: Cornell Southeast Asia Program, 7–19

Hollis, M. 1970. 'Reason and ritual', in *Rationality*, ed. B. Wilson,

Oxford: Basil Blackwell, 221–30

Hollis, M. and S. Lukes 1982. 'Introduction', in *Rationality and Relativism*, eds M. Hollis and S. Lukes, Oxford: Basil Blackwell

Holy, Ladislav (ed.) 1987. *Comparative Anthropology*, Oxford: Basil Blackwell

Horton, R. 1982. 'Tradition and modernity revisited', in *Rationality and Relativism*, eds M. Hollis and S. Lukes, Oxford: Basil Blackwell, 201–60

Hvalkof, Sören and Peter Aaby (eds) 1981. *Is God an American? An anthropological perspective on the missionary work of the Summer Institute of Linguistics*. Copenhagen and London: IWGIA and Survival International

Ingold, Tim 1986a. *Evolution and Social Life*, Cambridge: Cambridge University Press

—— 1986b. *The Appropriation of Nature: essays on human ecology and social relations*, Manchester: Manchester University Press

—— 1990. 'An anthropologist looks at biology', *Man* (NS) 25, 208–29

—— 1992. 'Culture and the perception of the environment', in *Bush Base: forest farm*, eds E. Croll and D. Parkin, London: Routledge

Ishiko, Jun 1979. *Nihon Mangashi*, Vols 1 and 2, Tokyo: Otsuki Shoten

Ishinomori, Shotaro 1960. *Cyborg 009*, Tokyo: Shinwa-Densetsu Hen

Jackson, Michael 1989. *Paths toward a Clearing: radical empiricism and ethnographic inquiry*, Bloomington: Indiana University Press

Jussawalla, Feroza 1989. 'Resurrecting the prophet: the case of Salman, the Otherwise', *Public Culture* 2 (1), 106–17

Katz, J. 1989. *The Shabbes Goy: a study in Halakhic flexibility*, Philadelphia: Jewish Publication Society

Keesing, Roger M. 1987a. 'Anthropology as interpretive quest', *Current Anthropology* 28 (2), 161–9

—— 1987b. 'Models, "folk" and "cultural": paradigms regained?' in *Cultural Models in Language and Thought*, eds D. Holland and N. Quinn, Cambridge: Cambridge University Press, 369–93

—— 1989. 'Exotic readings of cultural texts', *Current Anthropology* 30 (4), 459–79

—— (In press). 'Theories of culture revisited', in *Assessing Developments in Anthropology*, ed. Robert Borofsky

Kemnitzer, L. S. 1977. 'Another view of time and the railroader', *Anthropological Quarterly* 15 (3–4), 25–9

Kimmerling, B. (ed.) 1989. *The Israeli State and Society: boundaries and frontiers*, Albany, NY: State University of New York Press

Kleinman, Arthur and Joan Kleinman 1989. 'Suffering and its professional transformation: toward an ethnography of experience', Paper presented to the First Conference on the Society for Psychological Anthropology, San Diego, 6–8 October

Kopytoff, Igor 1987. 'The internal African frontier: the making of

African political culture', in *The African Frontier*, ed. Igor Kopytoff, Bloomington: Indiana University Press

Krausz, E. (ed.) 1985. *Politics and Society in Israel*, New Brunswick: Transaction Books

Kristof, Ladis K. D. 1959. 'The nature of frontiers and boundaries', *Association of American Geographers Annals* 49, 269–82

Kroeber, A. L. 1945. 'The ancient *Oikoumené* as an historic culture aggregate', *Journal of the Royal Anthropological Institute* 75, 9–20
_____ 1952. 'Culture', in *Papers of the Peabody Museum in American Archaeology and Ethnology*, eds A. L. Kroeber and C. H. Kluckhohn, Cambridge, MA: Harvard University Press

Kroeber, A. L. and C. H. Kluckhohn 1952. *Culture: a critical review of concepts and definitions*, Papers of the Peabody Museum of American Archaeology and Ethnology, Harvard University, Vol. XLVII, no. 1, Cambridge, MA

Kuper, Adam 1988. *The Invention of Primitive Society: transformations of an illusion*, London: Routledge

Lakoff, George 1972. 'Linguistics and natural logic', in *Semantics of Natural Language*, eds D. Davidson and G. Hartman, Dordrecht: D. Reidel

Lakoff, George and Mark Johnson 1980. *Metaphors we Live by*, Chicago: University of Chicago Press

Larsen, Tord 1987. 'Action, morality, and cultural translation', *Journal of Anthropological Research* 43 (1), 1–28

Leach, Edmund R. 1954. *Political Systems of Highland Burma: a study of Kachin social structure*, Boston: Beacon Press
_____ 1961. *Rethinking Anthropology*, London: Athlone Press
_____ 1967. *A Runaway World?* London: Oxford University Press
_____ 1973. 'Ourselves and the others', *Times Literary Supplement*, no. 3, 722, 6 July, 771–2
_____ 1982. *Social Anthropology*, Glasgow: Fontana

Lee, Richard 1988. 'Reflections on primitive communism', in *Hunters and Gatherers: history, evolution and social change*, eds T. Ingold, D. Riches and J. Woodburn, Oxford: Berg, 252–68

Lefevere, André and Susan Bassnett 1990. 'Introduction: Proust's grandmother and the Thousand and One Nights: the "cultural" turn in translation studies', in *Translation, History and Culture*, eds S. Bassnett and A. Lefevere, London: Pinter Publishers, 1–13

Lévi-Strauss, Claude 1962a. *La Pensée Sauvage*, Paris: Libraire Plon
_____ 1962b. *Le Totémisme aujourd'hui*, Paris: Presses Universitaires de France
_____ 1963. *Structural Anthropology*, Middlesex: Penguin Books
_____ 1966. *The Savage Mind*, Chicago: The University of Chicago Press
_____ 1972. *The Savage Mind*, London: Weidenfeld & Nicolson
_____ 1973. *Anthropologie Structurale Deux*, Paris: Plon

Liebman, C. and E. Don-Yehiya, 1984. *Religion and Politics in Israel,* Bloomington: Indiana University Press

Lienhardt, Godfrey 1954. 'Modes of thought', in *The Institutions of Primitive Society,* Oxford: Basil Blackwell

Limón, J. E. and M. J. Young 1986. 'Frontiers, settlements, and development in folklore studies, 1972–1985', *Annual Review of Anthropology 15,* 437–60

Lock, Margaret 1990. 'On being ethnic: the politics of identity breaking or making, or: *Nevra* on Sunday', *Culture, Medicine, and Psychyatry* 14 (2), 237–54

Long, Norman (ed.) 1989. *Encounters at the Interface: a perspective on social discontinuities in rural development,* Wageningen: Agricultural University Wageningen

Lowie, Robert H. 1921. *Primitive Society,* London: Routledge & Kegan Paul

_____ 1924. *Primitive Religion,* New York: Boni & Liveright

_____ 1937. *The History of Ethnological Theory,* London: Harrap

Lustick, I. (ed.) 1988. *Books on Israel,* Albany, NY: State University of New York Press

Lutz, C. 1988. *Unnatural Emotions,* Chicago: University of Chicago Press

Mackintosh, Maureen M. 1988. 'Domestic labour and the household', in *On Work: historical, comparative and theoretical approaches,* ed. R. E. Pahl, Oxford: Basil Blackwell, 392–406

MacNeil, Robert 1989. *Wordstruck: a memoir,* New York: Penguin Books

Maine, Henry 1861. *Ancient Law,* London: John Murray

Malinowski, B. 1923. 'The problem of meaning in primitive languages', in *The Meaning of Meaning,* eds C. K. Ogden and I. A. Richards, London: Kegan Paul, Trench, Trubner, 451–510

_____ 1929. *The Sexual Life of Savages in North-Western Melanesia,* New York: Eugenics Publishing Company

Mandelbaum, JoannaLynn K. 1989. *The Missionary as a Cultural Interpreter,* New York: Peter Lang

Marcus, George E. and Michael M. J. Fischer 1986. *Anthropology as Cultural Critique: an experimental moment in the human sciences,* Chicago: University of Chicago Press

Matsumoto, Reiji and Hidaka Satoshi (eds) 1980. *Manga Rekishi Daihakubutsukan,* Tokyo: Buronzusha

Mbabuike, Michael C. 1989. 'Ethnicity and ethnoconsciousness in the N.Y. Metropolitan Area: the case of the Ibos', *Dialectical Anthropology 14,* 301–5

McCarthy, Thomas 1978. *The Critical Theory of Jürgen Habermas,* Cambridge, MA: MIT Press

McCay, B. J. and J. M. Acheson (eds) 1987. *The Question of the Commons: the culture and ecology of communal resources,* Tucson: The University of Arizona Press

McCloskey, Donald N. 1985. *The Rhetoric of Economics*, Madison, WI: University of Wisconsin Press

McEvoy, Arthur F. 1986. *The Fisherman's Problem: ecology and law in the California fisheries, 1850–1980*, Cambridge: Cambridge University Press

―――― 1988. 'Toward an interactive theory of nature and culture: ecology, production, and cognition in the California fishing industry', in *The Ends of the Earth: perspectives on modern environmental history*, ed. D. Worster, Cambridge: Cambridge University Press

McHugh, Ernestine 1989. 'Concepts of the person among the Gurungs of Nepal', *American Ethnologist* 16 (1), 75–87

McKenna, F. 1980. *The Railway Workers 1840–1970*, London and Boston: Faber and Faber

Mead, G. H. 1934. *Mind, Self and Society*, Chicago: University of Chicago Press

Mead, Margaret 1942. 'Introduction', in *Balinese Character*, eds G. Bateson and M. Mead, New York: Academy of Sciences, 1–54

Melville, Herman 1846. *Typee*, London and Glasgow: Collins Clear-Type Press

Menget, Patrick 1982. 'Time of birth, time of being: the couvade', in *Between Belief and Transgression: structuralists essays in religion, history, and myth*, eds Ichel Izard and Pierre Smith, Chicago: The University of Chicago Press

The Mighty THOR, 1–400 serialised issues, New York: Marvel comics

Miller, M. L. and J. van Maanen 1979. '"Boats don't fish, people do": some ethnographic notes on the federal management of fisheries in Gloucester', *Human Organization* 38 (4), 377–85

Molund, Stefan 1988. *Transnational Cultural Flows and National Cultures: report on a workshop*, Stockholm: Svenska Unescorådet

Nader, Laura 1988. 'Post-interpretive anthropology', *Anthropological Quarterly* 61 (4), 149–59

Needham, Rodney (ed.) 1971. *Rethinking Kinship and Marriage*, London: Tavistock

―――― 1972. *Belief, Language and Experience*, Oxford: Basil Blackwell

Neild, Elizabeth 1989. 'Translation is a two-way street: a response to Steiner', *Meta* 34 (2), 238–41

Ortner, Sherry B. 1974. 'Is female to male as nature is to culture?' In *Woman, Culture and Society*, eds M. Z. Rosaldo and L. Lampere, Stanford: Stanford University Press, 67–87

―――― 1984. 'Theory in anthropology since the sixties', *Comparative Studies in Society and History* 1, 126–66

Paine, R. B. 1985. 'The claim of the Fourth World', in *Native Power*, eds J. Brosted et al., Oslo: Universitetsforlaget

Pálsson, Gísli 1990. 'The idea of fish: land and sea in the Icelandic world-view', in *Signifying Animals: human meaning in the natural world*, ed. Roy Willis, London: Unwin Hyman, 119–33

—— 1991. *Coastal Economies, Cultural Accounts: human ecology and Icelandic discourse*, Manchester: Manchester University Press

Pálsson, Gísli and E. Paul Durrenberger 1983. 'Icelandic foremen and skippers: the structure and evolution of a folk model', *American Ethnologist* 10 (3), 511–28

—— 1990. 'Systems of production and social discourse: the skipper effect revisited', *American Anthropologist* 92 (1), 130–41

Pletsch, Carl E. 1981. 'The three worlds, or the division of social scientific labor, circa 1950–1975', *Comparative Studies in Society and History* 23 (4), 565–90

Pollack, David 1986. *The Fracture of Meaning: Japan's synthesis of China from the English through the Eighteenth Century*, Princeton, NJ: Princeton University Press

Pons, Philippe 1988. *D'Edo à Tokyo*, Paris: Edition Gallimard

Postmodernism, 1988. Special issue of *Theory, Culture and Society* 5 (2–3)

Prakash, Gyan 1990. 'Writing post-Orientalist histories of the third world: perspectives from Indian historiography', *Comparative Studies in Society and History* 32 (2), 383–408

Putnam, Hilary 1981. *Reason, Truth, and History*, Cambridge: Cambridge University Press

Quine, W. 1960. *Word and Object*, Cambridge, MA: MIT Press

Quinn, Naomi and Dorothy Holland (eds) 1987. *Cultural Models in Language and Thought*, Cambridge: Cambridge University Press

Redfield, Robert 1956. *Peasant Society and Culture*, Chicago: University of Chicago Press

Redfield, Robert, Ralph Linton and Melville J. Herskovits 1936. 'A memorandum for the study of acculturation', *American Anthropologist* 38, 149–52

Ricoeur, Paul 1965. 'Universal civilization and national cultures', in *History and Truth*, Evanston, IL: Northwestern University Press, 271–84

Rivière, Peter 1974. 'The couvade: a problem reborn', *Man* (n.s.) 9 (3): 423–35

Robinson, Douglas 1991. *The Translator's Turn*, Baltimore, MD: Johns Hopkins University Press

Rorty, Richard 1989. *Contingency, Irony, and Solidarity*, Cambridge: Cambridge University Press

Rosaldo, Renato 1984. 'Grief and a headhunter's rage: on the cultural forces of emotion', in *Text, Play, and Story: the construction and reconstruction of social self and society*, eds E. M. Bruner and S. Plattner, Washington, DC: American Ethnological Society, 178–95

—— 1989. *Culture and Truth: the remaking of social analysis*, Boston: Beacon Press

Rosenberg, Daniel V. 1990. 'Language in the discourse of emotions', in *Language and the Politics of Emotion*, eds C. Lutz and L. Abu-Lughod, Cambridge: Cambridge University Press, 186–206

Ruthven, Malise 1990. *A Satanic Affair*, London: Chatto & Windus

Sacks, Oliver 1989. *Seeing Voices: a journey into the world of the deaf*, Berkeley, CA: University of California Press

Sahlins, Marshall 1972. *Stone Age Economics*, London: Tavistock Publications
    1976. *Culture and Practical Reason*, Chicago: The University of Chicago Press

Said, Edward 1978. *Orientalism*, New York: Vintage Books
    1981. *Covering Islam: how the media and the experts determine how we see the rest of the world*, London: Routledge & Kegan Paul
    1989. 'Representing the colonized: anthropology's interlocutors', *Critical Inquiry* 15 (Winter), 205–25

Sangren, P. Steven 1988. 'Rhetoric and the authority of ethnography: "postmodernism" and the social reproduction of texts', *Current Anthropology* 29 (3), 405–24

Sanjek, Roger (ed.) 1990. *Fieldnotes: the makings of anthropology*, Ithaca, NY: Cornell University Press
    1991. 'The ethnographic present'. *Man* (n.s.) 26, 609–28

Sartre, Jean-Paul 1938. *La Nausée*, Paris: Gallimard

Saussure, F. de 1959 [1916]. *Course in General Linguistics*, New York: McGraw-Hill

Schutz, Alfred 1970. *On Phenomenology and Social Relations: selected writings*, Chicago: University of Chicago Press

Scott, James C. 1990. *Domination and the Arts of Resistance: hidden transcripts*, New Haven and London: Yale University Press

Shankman, Paul 1984. 'The thick and the thin: on the interpretive theoretical program of Clifford Geertz', *Current Anthropology* 25 (3), 261–70

Sharabi, Hisham (ed.) 1990. *Theory, Politics and the Arab World*, New York: Routledge

Sharp, Henry S. 1988. 'Dry meat and gender: the absence of Chipewyan ritual for the regulation of hunting and animal numbers', in *Hunters and Gatherers: property, power and ideology*, eds T. Ingold, D. Riches and J. Woodburn, Oxford: Berg, 183–91

Sherzer, Joel 1987. 'A discourse-centered approach to language and culture', *American Anthropologist* 89 (2), 295–309

Shweder, Richard A. 1990. 'Cultural psychology – what is it?', in *Cultural Psychology: essays on comparative human development*, eds J. W. Stigler, R. A. Shweder and G. Herdt, Cambridge: Cambridge University Press
    1991. *Thinking through Cultures: expeditions in cultural psychology*, Cambridge, MA: Harvard University Press

Smith, Courtland L. 1974. 'Fishing success in a regulated commons', *Ocean Development and International Law Journal* 1, 369–81

Smith, M. G. 1965. *The Plural Society in the British West Indies*, Berkeley, CA: University of California Press

Smith, Pierre and Dan Sperber 1971. 'Mythologiques de Georges Dumézil', *Annales, XXVI*, 559–86

Smooha, S. 1978. *Israel: pluralism and conflict*, London: Routledge & Kegan Paul

Spencer, B. and F. Gillen 1904. *The Northern Tribes of Central Australia*, London: Macmillan

Spencer, Jonathan 1989. 'Anthropology as a kind of writing', *Man* 24 (1), 145–64

_____ 1990. 'Writing within: anthropology, nationalism and culture in Sri Lanka', *Current Anthropology* 31 (3), 283–91

Sperber, Dan 1985a. *On Anthropological Knowledge*, Cambridge: Cambridge University Press

_____ 1985b. 'Anthropology and psychology: towards an epidemiology of representations (The Malinowski Memorial Lecture 1984)', *Man* (n.s.) 20, 73–89

_____ 1986. 'Issues in the ontology of culture', in *Logic, Methodology and Philosophy of Science VII*, eds R. Barcan Marcus, P. Weingartner and G. Dorn, Elsevier Science Publishers B.V.

_____ 1989. 'L'étude anthropologique des representations: problèmes et perspectives', in Denise Jodelet (ed.), *Les Représentations sociales*. Paris: Presses Universitaires de France

_____ 1990. 'The epidemiology of beliefs', in Colin Fraser and George Gaskell (eds), *The Social Psychology of Widespread Beliefs*. Oxford: Clarendon Press

Sperber, Dan and Deirdre Wilson 1986. *Relevance: communication and cognition*, Oxford: Basil Blackwell; Cambridge, MA: Harvard University Press

Spiro, Melford E. 1986. 'Cultural relativism and the future of anthropology', *Cultural Anthropology* 1 (3), 259–86

_____ 1990. 'On the strange and the familiar in recent anthropological thought', in *Cultural Psychology: essays on comparative human development*, eds J. W. Stigler, R. A. Shweder and G. Herdt, Cambridge: Cambridge University Press, 47–61

Stearn, Gerald E. (ed.) 1967. *McLuhan: hot and cool*, New York: Dial Press

Steinberg, M. 1988. *Trends in Palestinian National Thought*, Jerusalem: Hebrew University Davis Institute (in Hebrew)

_____ 1989. 'The demographic dimension of the struggle with Israel as seen by the PLO', *Jerusalem Journal of International Relations* 11, 27–51

Steiner, George 1976. *After Babel*, London: Oxford University Press

_____ 1979. *Language and Silence*, Harmondsworth: Penguin Books

Stocking, G. W. 1968. *Race, Culture and Evolution*, New York: Free Press (ed.) 1983. *Observers Observed: essays on ethnographic fieldwork*, Madison, WI: University of Wisconsin Press

Strathern, Marilyn 1988. *The Gender and the Gift: problems with women and problems with society in Melanesia*, Berkeley, CA: University of California Press

—— 1990a. 'For the motion', in *The Concept of Society is Theoretically Obsolete*, ed. T. Ingold, Manchester: Group for Debates in Anthropological Theory

—— 1990b. 'Disembodied choice', in *The Cultural Analysis of Intentionality: explorations in the understanding of other minds*, Santa Fé: School of American Research

Sugawara, Kunishiro 1974. 'Aisurando kotenbungakuhonyakyjo no ichimondai – Koy-meishi no honyakuho nitsuite' ('On a problem relating to the translations of classical Iclandic literature – concerning methods for translating proper names'), *Hokuo 8*, December

—— 1976. 'A report on Japanese translations of Old Icelandic literature', *Scripta Islandica – Islandska sellskapets årsbok 27*, Uppsala: Lundequistska Bokhandlen, 24–37

Tambiah, Stanley J. 1990. *Magic, Science, Religion, and the Scope of Rationality*. Cambridge: Cambridge University Press

Taniguchi, Yukio 1976. *Edda to Saga*, Tokyo: Shinchosha

—— 1984. 'Jojishi no honyaku' ('On translations of epic poetry'). *Gengo*, June, 64–8

Tannen, Deborah 1990. *You Just Don't Understand: women and men in conversation*, New York: Ballantine Books

Tanner, Adrian 1979. *Bringing Home Animals: religious ideology and mode of production of the Mistassini Cree hunters*, London: C. Hurst & Company

Thomas, Nicholas 1991. 'Anthropology and *Orientalism*', *Anthropology Today* 7(2), 4–7

Thompson, S. 1966. *Tales of the North American Indians*, Bloomington: Indiana University

Tisseron, Serge 1990. *La Bande dessinée au pied du mot*, Paris: Aubier

Todorov, Tzvetan 1984. *The Conquest of America*, New York: Harper & Row

—— 1988. 'Knowledge in social anthropology', *Anthropology Today* 4 (2), 2–5

Torgovnick, Marianna 1990. *Gone Primitive: savage intellects, modern lives*. Chicago: University of Chicago Press

Tönnies, F. 1955[1887]. *Community and Association*, trans. C. P. Loomis, London: Routledge

Tual, Anny 1986. 'Speech and silence: women in Iran', in *Visibility and Power: essays on women in society and development*, eds L. Dube, E. Leacock and S. Ardener, Delhi: Oxford University Press, 54–73

Tucci, Giuseppe 1988[1970]. *The Religion of Tibet*, Berkeley: University of California Press

Turner, V. W. and E. M. Bruner (eds) 1986. *The Anthropology of Experience*, Urbana, IL: University of Illinois Press

Turton, David 1988. 'Anthropology and development', in *Perspectives on Development*, eds P. F. Leeson and M. M. Minogue, Manchester: Manchester University Press, 126–59

Tyler, S. A. 1986. 'Post-modern ethnography: from document of the occult to occult document', in *Writing Culture*, eds J. Clifford and G. E. Marcus, Berkeley, CA: University of California Press, 122–40

Tylor, E. B. 1871. *Primitive Culture*, London: John Murray

Ulin, Robert C. 1991. 'Critical anthropology twenty years later: modernism and postmodernism in anthropology', *Critique of Anthropology 11* (1), 63–89

van der Veer, Peter 1989. 'Satanic or angelic? The politics of religious and literary inspiration', *Public Culture 2* (1), 100–5

Volosinov, V. N. 1973[1929]. *Marxism and the Philosophy of Language*, trans. L. Matejka and I. R. Titunik. Cambridge, MA: Harvard University Press

Växlingsarbete 1986. *Arbetarskyddsstyrelsens författningssamling, 11*

Wagner, Roy 1986. *Symbols that Stand for Themselves*, Chicago: University of Chicago Press

Watson, Graham 1984. 'The social construction of boundaries between social and cultural anthropology in Britain and North America', *Journal of Anthropological Research 40* (3), 351–66

Watson-Grego, Karen A. and Geoffrey M. White (eds) 1990. *Disentangling: conflict discourse in Pacific societies*, Stanford, CA: Stanford University Press

Weingrod, A. (ed.) 1985. *Studies in Israeli Ethnicity: after the ingathering*, New York: Gordon & Breach
    1990. *The Saint of Beersheba*, Albany, NY: State University of New York Press

Wikan, Unni 1980[1976]. *Life among the Poor in Cairo*, London: Tavistock
    1982. *Behind the Veil in Arabia: women in Oman*, Baltimore: Johns Hopkins University Press
    1983. *Tomorrow, God Willing: lives in the back streets of Cairo*, Oslo: Universitetsforlaget (in Norwegian)
    1987. 'Public grace and private fears: gaiety, offense, and sorcery in North Bali' *Ethos* 15, 337–65
    1989. 'Illness from fright or soulloss: a North Balinese culture-bound syndrome?' *Culture, Medicine, and Psyciatry 13*, 25–50
    1990. *Managing Turbulent Hearts: a Balinese formula for living*, Chicago, IL: University of Chicago Press
    1991. 'The situation of the child in Bhutan'. Report submitted to UNICEF and NWAB (National Women's Association of Bhutan), Thimphu, Bhutan
    (In press). 'Challenges to the concept of culture: towards an

experience–near anthropology', *Cultural Anthropology*

Wilson, Bryan R. (ed.) 1970. *Rationality*, Oxford: Basil Blackwell

Wilson, M. 1957. *Rituals of Kinship among the Nyakyusa*, London, New York and Toronto: Oxford University Press

Winch, Peter 1958. *The Idea of a Social Science*, London: Routledge & Kegan Paul

Wolf, Eric R. 1956. 'Aspects of group relations in a complex society', *American Anthropologist* 58, 1065–78

—— 1982. *Europe and the People Without History*, Berkeley, CA: University of California Press

Woodburn, James 1982. 'Egalitarian societies', *Man* (NS) *17*, 431–51

—— 1988. 'African hunter-gatherer social organization: is it best understood as a product of encapsulation?' in *Hunters and Gatherers 1: history, evolution and social change*, eds T. Ingold, D. Riches and J. Woodburn, Oxford: Berg, 31–64

Worsley, P. J. 1972. *Babad Buleleng: A Balinese dynastic genealogy*, The Hague: Nijhoff

Worth, Sol 1981. *Studying Visual Communication*, Philadelphia: University of Pennsylvania Press

Young, Oran R. 1986. 'International regimes: toward a new theory of institutions', *World Politics 39* (1), 105–22

Index

Notes on the Contributors

Levon H. Abrahamian (PhD Moscow Institute of Ethnography, 1978) is Researcher in the Institute of Archaeology and Ethnography, Academy of Sciences of Armenia. His writings include *Primitive Festival and Mythology* (1983, in Russian) and several articles, in Armenian, Russian and English, on primitive culture, mythology and modern national processes in Armenia and the former USSR.

Shlomo Deshen (PhD Manchester University, 1968) is Professor of Social Anthropology at Tel-Aviv University. A past president of the Israel Anthropological Association, he has worked in Middle Eastern anthropology. His most recent books are *The Mellah Society: Jewish community life in Sherifian Morocco* (University of Chicago Press) and *Blind People: The private and public life of sightless Israelis* (State University of New York Press).

Birgitta Edelman received her first degree in comparative religion and sociology from Abo Akademi, Finland. Later, she received a diploma in social anthropology from University College, London. After a spell in North Africa she worked as a shunter on the railways in Stockholm. She is now a doctorate candidate in social anthropology at Stockholm University.

Ulf Hannerz (PhD Stockholm University, 1969) is Professor of Social Anthropology at Stockholm University. He has carried out fieldwork in the United States, the West Indies and Nigeria. His writings include *Soulside* (1969), *Exploring the City* (1981) and *Cultural Complexity* (1992) (both Columbia University Press) and numerous articles published in international journals.

Tim Ingold (PhD University of Cambridge, 1975) is Professor of Social Anthropology at the University of Manchester and currently the editor of *Man*. His books include *Hunters, Pastoralists and Ranchers* and *Evolution and Social Life* (both Cambridge University Press) and *The Appropriation of Nature* (Manchester University Press). He is the editor of *What is an Animal?* (Unwin Hyman) and co-editor of *Hunters and Gatherers* (Berg Publishers).

Gísli Pálsson (PhD Manchester University, 1982) is Professor of Social Anthropology at the University of Iceland. His writings include *Coastal Economies, Cultural Accounts: Human ecology and Icelandic discourse* (Manchester University Press) and several articles published in anthropological journals. He is the editor of *From Sagas to Society: Comparative approaches to early Iceland* (Hisarlik Press) and co-editor of *The Anthropology of Iceland* (University of Iowa Press).

Dan Sperber is a Research Scholar at the Centre National de Recherche Scientifique (CNRS) and at the École Polytechnique in Paris. His writings include *Rethinking Symbolism* (1975), *On Anthropological Knowledge* (1985) and, with Deirdre Wilson, *Relevance: Communication and cognition* (1986), as well as numerous articles in anthropology, linguistics, psychology and philosophy.

Halldór Stefánsson received his training in anthropology at Université Paris VII and Osaka University. He has carried out extensive fieldwork in Japan and is presently Professor of Anthropology at Osaka Gakuin University in Japan. His writings include several articles on ancestor worship and death rites in rural Japan.

Unni Wikan is Professor of Social Anthropology at the University of Oslo. Her writings include *Life Among the Poor in Cairo* (Tavistock), *Behind the Veil in Arabia: Women in Oman* (University of Chicago Press), *Managing Turbulent Hearts: A Balinese formula for living* (University of Chicago Press) and numerous articles published in anthropological journals.